Cultures of Development

The North Atlantic development establishment has had a blemished track record over the past 65 years. In addition to a sizeable portfolio of failure, the few economic success stories in the developing world, such as South Korea and China, have been achieved by rejecting the advice of Western experts. Despite these realities, debates within mainstream development studies have stagnated around a narrow, acultural emphasis on institutions or the size and role of government.

Cultures of Development uses a contrapuntal comparison of Vietnam and Brazil to show why it is important for development scholars and practitioners to broaden their conceptualization of economies to include the socio-cultural. This smartly written book based on original, ethnographic research breathes new life into development studies by bringing cultural studies into conversation with development studies, with an emphasis on improving—rather than merely critiquing—market economies. The applied deployment of critical development studies, i.e., interpretive economics, results in a number of theoretical advances in both development and areas studies, demonstrating the economic importance of certain kinds of cultural work carried out by religious leaders, artists, activists, and educators. Most importantly, the reader comes to fully appreciate how economies are embedded within the subjectivities, discourses, symbols, rituals, norms, and values of a given society.

This pioneering book revives development practice and policy by offering fresh insights and ideas about how development can be advanced. It will be of special interest to scholars and students of Development Studies, Sociology, Economics, Anthropology, and Area Studies.

Jonathan Warren is Associate Professor of International Studies and Co-Director of the Center for Brazilian Studies at the University of Washington.

Routledge Studies in Development and Society

For a full list of titles in this series, please visit www.routledge.com/Routledge-Studies-in-Development-and-Society/book-series/SE0317

35 The Paradigm of International Social Development
Ideologies, Development Systems and Policy Approaches
Murli Desai

36 Governance, Development, and Social Work
Edited by Chathapuram S. Ramanathan and Subhabrata Dutta

37 Mining and Social Transformation in Africa
Mineralizing and Democratizing Trends in Artisanal Production
Deborah Bryceson, Eleanor Fisher, Jesper Bosse Jønsson and Rosemarie Mwaipopo

38 The End of the Developmental State?
Edited by Michelle Williams

39 The Language of Global Development
A Misleading Geography
Marcin Wojciech Solarz

40 Informal Urban Street Markets
International Perspectives
Edited by Clifton Evers and Kirsten Seale

41 Cultures of Development
Vietnam, Brazil and the Unsung Vanguard of Prosperity
Jonathan Warren

Cultures of Development

Vietnam, Brazil and the Unsung Vanguard of Prosperity

Jonathan Warren

Routledge
Taylor & Francis Group
NEW YORK AND LONDON

First published 2017
by Routledge
711 Third Avenue, New York, NY 10017

and by Routledge
2 Park Square, Milton Park, Abingdon, Oxon OX14 4RN

First issued in paperback 2018

Routledge is an imprint of the Taylor & Francis Group, an informa business

Library of Congress Cataloging in Publication Data
Names: Warren, Jonathan W., author.
Title: Cultures of development : Vietnam, Brazil and the unsung vanguard of prosperity / Jonathan Warren.
Description: Abingdon, Oxon ; New York, NY : Routledge, 2017. |
Series: Routledge studies in development and society |
Includes bibliographical references and index.
Identifiers: LCCN 2016026141| ISBN 9781138672475 (hardback) |
ISBN 9781315543338 (ebook)
Subjects: LCSH: Economic development—Cross-cultural studies. |
Economic development—Vietnam. | Economic development—Brazil. |
Economics—Sociological aspects.
Classification: LCC HD75 .W357 2017 | DDC 338.9597—dc23
LC record available at https://lccn.loc.gov/2016026141

ISBN 13: 978-1-138-59750-1 (pbk)
ISBN 13: 978-1-138-67247-5 (hbk)

Typeset in Times New Roman
by Florence Production Ltd, Stoodleigh, Devon, UK

For Chelle Chelle

Contents

Illustrations

Figures

Maps

Tables

Acknowledgments

It is impossible to thank the numerous people who have helped me with a project that spans three countries and over a decade of work. So I apologize in advance to the many individuals who deserve to be mentioned here but due largely to my poor memory are not credited below.

This project would never have happened were it not for the Asia Foundation in Hanoi and the Luce Fellowship that I received to kick start the research for this book. The various people there—Jonathan Stromseth, Dinh Thi Kieu Nhung, Pham Thu Thuy, and Kim Ninh—were remarkably professional, hospitable, and supportive of me and my family. Other Hanoians who have been deeply caring as well as inspirational include Pho Duc Long, Mai Thi Thanh, Pham An Hai, Dang Xuan Hoa, Hoang Thuc Hao, Luong Vuong, and Nguyen Cong Cu (special thanks for letting me use reprints of your amazing artwork!).

In Rio de Janeiro, I am heavily indebted to my dear friends who took care of me when I was penniless in Brazil some twenty-five years ago: Carla Simone Barbosa de Brito and Nando Neves (whose photos feature in this book) along with their children Matheus, Elizabeth, and Bia (who had to sacrifice her bedroom for me from time to time). I also wish to thank Eduardo Caio Torres dos Santos, Maria Isabel Sampaio, Ricardo Sheidemantel, and most especially Tania Torres dos Santos Scheidemantel for always keeping my wife and me in tears with her humor. I also much appreciate the camaraderie and academic guidance of the following scholars in Rio: Helena Galiza, Pedro de Novais Lima Junior, Carlos Vanier, and Ana Invanicki.

In Aracuai I have had the incredibly good fortune (actually it feels more like divine intervention) to have had the support, friendship, and guidance of the following sages for well over two decades: Geralda Chaves Soares, Franciscus Henricus van der Poel, Maria do Carmo Ferreira da Silva, Maria Lira Marques, and Cleonice Pankararu. I hope I have done some justice to your incredible lives and accomplishments.

In more recent years, I have been extremely lucky to have met and worked with the following activists and academics who have visited the University of Washington (UW) for extended periods of time and have offered me invaluable feedback on this project: Adailton de Oliveira Gomes, Kercia Figueiredo, Nivia Luz, Sylvana Marques, Marynize Prates de Oliveira, and Rodrigo Peixoto.

At Seattle, a number of colleagues and students read and weighed in on various drafts of chapters and provided much needed encouragement: Robert Andolina, Andrea Arai, Charles Bergquist, Patrick Christie, Jay Freistadt, Christoph Giebel, Gary Hamilton, Joe Hannah, Don Hellman, Judith Henchey, Brice Henson, Victoria Lawson, Jose Antonio Lucero, Angelica and Scott Macklin, Joel Migdal, Ngo Hoang, Nguyen Diu Huong, Christian Novetske, Vincent Raphael, Ileana Rodriguez-Silva, Matthew Sparke, and Jim Wellman. Special thanks, too, to the UW Center for Brazilian Studies faculty: Margaret Griesse, Orlando Baiocchi, and the Honorary Counsel General of Brazil, Pedro Leite Augusto Costa. The UW-Frankfurt HI-NORM faculty cluster also deserves praise for their contributions to my thinking: Jose Casanova, Jurgen Habermas, Mathias Lutz-Bachmann, Gregg Miller, Amos Nascimento, Andres Niederberger, Mike Shapiro, and Bill Talbott.

I would also like to say "*cam on nhieu*" to a range of Vietnamese scholars who have offered feedback at various conferences and in conversations over the years: Hsin-Chieh Chang, Peter Chaundry, Liam Kelley, Lam Minh Chau, David Marr, Phan Le Ha, Oscar Salemink, Phillip Taylor, and Peter Zinoman.

There are also some of my dearest friends spread out throughout the world who have been instrumental in so many invaluable ways: Luis Abusaid Garcia, John Foran, Sanjeev Khagram, Zeus Leonardo, Jelani Mahiri, Isabella Medici, Nhan Nguyen, Nikhil Singh, Meg Stalcup, and Christi Sue. *Obrigadao*!

In terms of editing, I owe a huge thanks to Tracy Stober (a fellow gardener and activist) and my dear friend and former classmate, Brian Cameron Folk, whose knowledge of the development literature humbled and helped me immeasurably.

I would be remiss to not mention the unconditional love and support of my father (Win Warren), mother (Janice Wilbur), grandparents (Pauline Warren and the late Wava Roberts and Mel Warren, who I miss everyday), and siblings (Chris Walker, Cathy Warren, Jessica Akaah, and Mitch Warren) and their families.

Finally, I am most thankful to my immediate family. My beautiful and inspirational children, Kien and Nghia, had to suffer through too many absences and hear me agonize over this project for far too long. My mother-in-law, Dung Padgett, kept evil spirits away with her constant prayers and was always ready to fill in with parental duty (along with her ever supportive cousin Di Di Huynh Canh) when I had to travel for research or stay at work late writing. Finally, my wife Michelle, to whom this book is dedicated, held our household together when I had to be away, never lost faith in this project, and kept me going with a bone-deep love that everyone deserves but only a lucky few like me ever get to experience—I am truly blessed.

1 Interpretive Economics

> To deny the importance of subjectivity in the process of transforming the world and history is naïve and simplistic. It is to admit the impossible: a world without people.
>
> Paulo Freire (1921–1997)[1]

"I believe that culture isn't separated from anything," a teacher in rural Brazil, Dostoevsky, once insisted, "Just the opposite—it's interwoven with everything." Remarkably the vast majority of development scholars and practitioners, many of who have studied at some of the most coveted universities in the world, have yet to learn this truth. They are beholden to the myth that economies transcend culture.

The presumed immateriality of the cultural results, among other things, in precious energies and resources being diverted away from those aspects of society most in need of change if poverty is to be reduced and economic growth to occur. Few question the relevance of taxation, tariff and monetary policies, government transparency, accounting practices, dam and sewage construction, or streamlining the processes for opening a business and securing credit. However, the artists, activists, and educators who are attempting to challenge colonial epistemologies, build racial literacy, transform the identities and perceptions of the poor, or realign honor codes, are rarely legitimated as development catalysts, let alone given a fraction of the resources devoted to various megaprojects and institutional reforms that are often of questionable economic benefit. They are, one is often told, social workers, human rights activists, anti-racists, or, as Joao, a university provost in Sao Paulo derisively joked with me, "Mother Teresa types," but they are rarely, if ever, seen as agents of development.

Before I begin disassembling the acultural fallacy of North Atlantic development thought and policy, let me offer a few points of clarification about some of my key concepts and goals. First, *Cultures of Development*'s call for interpretive economics is not meant to suggest that the conventional stuff of development is bunk. Instead one of my central arguments is that economic theories and development initiatives are incomplete, absent a consideration of culture. Therefore to continue to forward policies and institutional reforms as if they were crafted and articulated in an acultural vacuum would be, as the legendary Brazilian educator Paulo Freire observed, naïve and simplistic. This does not mean that culture is all that matters or that it is more significant. The point is simply that a society cannot expect to prosper without a sustained reckoning with the subjectivities, discourses, symbols, rituals, norms, and values that make up their economies. And, at least in the particular case of Vietnam and Brazil, the reader will find, perhaps unexpectedly, that taking culture into account does not so much overturn accepted economic wisdom as indicate more effective and cheaper methods for accomplishing such orthodox objectives as building human and social capital.

Second, interpretive economics is a term I use to distinguish *Cultures of Development* from both the neo-modernizationists and the radical critics of development. As I detail later in this chapter, there is a growing subset of development scholars and practitioners who have begun to take culture seriously. Unfortunately the neo-modernizationists hold assumptions about culture that hark back to the modernizationists of the mid-twentieth century, and the radical critics avoid reform efforts in favor of a more profound critique, if not rejection, of market-based development projects.[2] Forgotten or at best left in the background by the radical critics has been the question that most people in the world expect development experts to help them answer: "How do we become more prosperous?" Thus, interpretive economics is meant to signal my attempt to steer the nascent cultural turn in development studies in a direction that melds the theoretical sophistication of the radical critics with the neo-modernizationists' more pragmatic emphasis on improving economic practice. Such an analytical and methodological approach, which is both culturally astute and more directed at problem solving than problem naming, is a project that I associate with the Verstehen or interpretive tradition that Max Weber and George Simmel introduced into the social sciences.

Finally, the reader should note that I rely on the customary benchmarks of economic progress, such as gross domestic product (GDP) or purchasing power parity (PPP). The intent is not to infer that this is the only or necessarily the best way to gauge prosperity. Indeed, my own thinking has been profoundly shaped by those who have questioned such metrics of economic progress, raised broader criticisms of capitalism, and proposed alternative economic formations to market economies. However, as noted above, these are not the debates or projects that I attempt to further with this book. My focus is elsewhere. I aim to illustrate how culture shapes economic development, conventionally defined and measured, and in the process generate a great deal more analytical and applied interest in culture as well as bolster support for the economically relevant cultural work that is too often ignored or dismissed.

Contrapuntal Insights

Until I journeyed to Vietnam in 2001 I did not have the language or expertise to be able to clearly identify let alone offer a remedy for this inattention to culture.

Just as I never imagined that I would research and write about economic development, I did not anticipate conducting research in Vietnam. Indeed I first went there intent on slaying very different dragons.

Having grown up in rural Michigan in the 1960s and 70s, Vietnam played a formative role in my childhood. The war appeared nightly on TV, took away neighbors to die, and infused the symbols, politics, and popular culture of the era. It also funded an expansion of the university that I would eventually attend. As the US institution responsible for the training of the South Vietnamese police, Michigan State University nearly doubled in size.[3] Perversely the war afforded me an opportunity that I may otherwise not have had, given my barely above average grades from a mediocre high school. As an adult, Vietnam became iconic. It represented the dark side of US militarism as well as the capacity of humanity to defeat such a force against great odds. No doubt the epic meaning that I projected onto Vietnam was heightened by the fact that I was traveling there just two weeks after September 11th. The US public's response to this atrocity seemed so devoid of any knowledge of its country's iniquitous past that it drew my thoughts back to that war and the lessons not learned. The half empty plane was an ominous foreshadowing of how unexceptional the United States would likely continue to be. And so my trip was more than a vacation. It was a pilgrimage to a country that had shaped me; a journey to a historical touchstone oversaturated with meaning.

Map 1.1 Primary Research Sites in Brazil

Unexpectedly, then, what caught my attention in Vietnam had little to do with my war-inspired reflections. It was Brazil that shadowed me. Since 1992 I had spent more than three years living and conducting ethnographic research in the states of Minas Gerais and Rio de Janeiro. This experience had left its mark. Various dimensions of Vietnam were fascinating or noteworthy to me because of how they differed from the Brazil I knew. Top among the distinctions was the economy.

During the 1980s and 90s Brazil, like much of the world, warmly and sometimes enthusiastically embraced neoliberal macro-economic reforms, which returned to a classical faith in the ability of unregulated (or at least minimally regulated) markets. The Keynesian framework that posited governments as the allies of markets was replaced by a conviction that they were foes. The central idea that

Map 1.2 Primary Research Sites in Vietnam

lesser government combined with trade and currency liberalization facilitated economic growth took on the status of common sense. Policy was largely driven by the notion that if states could be reined in and curtailed, then the power of these putatively freer markets would be unleashed, resulting in greater economic prosperity. This new-found faith in laissez-faire capitalism led to a pat repertoire of specific policy recommendations aimed at limiting government: reduction of tariffs, lower taxes, privatization of public enterprises and services, the minimization of government regulation, and the lessening, if not the elimination, of the welfare state.

Initially my position toward neoliberalism in Brazil was agnostic. Public investment in the majority lower classes was already non-existent. Federal monies spent on education, social security, infrastructure, and so forth were simply subsidies to the well-heeled. For example, education spending was heavily skewed away from primary and secondary education in favor of universities—institutions that only the children of the elite could attend.[4] Tariffs had seemingly been in place to protect the profit margins of national manufacturers with little benefit to Brazilian consumers or the broader economy. And because of rampant tax evasion, the middle and lower classes shouldered most of the tax burden. It was not that I imagined that neoliberalism would be the silver bullet that many of its proponents promised, but it did seem that it could not make matters worse and might even bring some modest improvements.

I was wrong. Laissez-faire policies did not deliver. In the wake of neoliberal reforms, the average growth rate hovered at 2 percent in Brazil and throughout Latin America. This did not prove sufficient enough to tread water given that population increases were higher. Poverty, crime, and unemployment only worsened. Understandably most Brazilians were deeply pessimistic about their future.

Against this Brazilian backdrop of consistently weak economic performance, high levels of endemic poverty, and ubiquitous cynicism, Vietnam stood out. Since the 1980s Vietnam had registered an average growth rate of 6 percent and had already lowered poverty below that of Brazil. All indications were that it was to follow in the footsteps of Taiwan, South Korea, Japan, China, and Singapore, the so-called Asian Tigers. Here was a society with seemingly everything against it when compared to Brazil. It had endured more than three decades of intensive warfare, suffered an economic embargo from the United States, had relatively few natural resources, and struggled under an authoritarian government with many of the trappings of a Leninist state. And yet, unlike Brazil, the Vietnamese economy was humming and everyone with whom I spoke was upbeat about the future. My curiosity had been piqued.

State-Led Development

Upon returning to the United States I began brushing up on the development literature, especially the subfield comparing East Asia and Latin America. Given that I had spent a great deal of time researching identity formations, semiotics, and discursive regimes in Brazil, I was most keen to learn what development theorists would have to say about culture and its relationship to economic development. In reviewing the analyses and conclusions reached for the different economic trajectories in East Asia and Latin America, I encountered a near-complete silence on the question of culture. Most of the literature focused, instead, on the state and in particular the central role it played in East Asia in successfully incentivizing and orchestrating economic growth. It subsidized upstream resources, invested heavily in human capital and infrastructure projects, nurtured and protected manufacturers through tariffs, subsidies and investments in research and development, and manipulated consumer's options via luxury taxes and restrictions on travel. Moreover, in Vietnam, Taiwan, and China, state-owned enterprises (SOEs) were major bulwarks of the economy.

The results were stunning. After being devastated by WWII, Japan rose to become the second largest economy in the world until being surpassed by China, which has grown 10 percent per year for the past thirty years. South Korea went from being one of the poorest countries in the world after the Korean War to being one of the wealthiest. Its per capita annual income rose from $100 in 1963 to $35,300 in 2014. Another poor, relatively small country lacking in natural resources, Taiwan, averaged 8.7 percent annual growth rates between 1952 and 1982 and since then has continued to grow at 6 percent per year. And Vietnam, a country that was one of the five poorest in the world and where over 70 percent of the population lived in poverty in the mid-1980s, was already on the verge of becoming a middle-income economy and could stake out, with some credibility, the goal of becoming a developed economy by 2030.

The fact that this remarkable economic growth in East Asia was achieved through state-guided capitalism was noteworthy for at least two reasons. First, the narrative surrounding East Asia's robust growth, at least the one that circulated in the media and travel literature in the Atlantic in the early naughts, was that liberalization, largely understood as a reduction in the size and role of the government, had been responsible for the impressive economic development.[5] The reality, however, was and continues to be much the opposite. In Vietnam the transition from a planned to a market economy has corresponded with "a growth—not decline—in the size of state bureaucracy."[6] Marketization has been coupled with the commercialization rather than the privatization of SOEs as well as an expansion of the gate-keeping role of the state. Consequently, state bureaucrats have become state entrepreneurs. They have profiteered from their ability to issue permits, provide social services, and sell land and government positions. State and party officials also manage the state-held businesses that dominate the economy, sit on the boards of directors in various privately-owned businesses, and are often major shareholders in joint ventures that foreign investors are required to form when doing business in Vietnam.[7]

Second, with tremendous success East Asian countries have done precisely the opposite of what was advised and often implemented in Latin America. As noted above, in the 1980s neoliberalism came to enjoy broad acceptance amongst policymakers, experts, and the general public. Its acceptance eventually ran so deep in the common sense of the region that even economic catastrophe failed to prompt a reassessment. In *Managing Mexico*, to take one example, Sarah Babb observed that in the wake of the collapse of the Mexican economy in 1994 and the discrediting of neoliberalism's primary backers—such as president Carlos Salinas—there was "no reevaluation of either neoliberal principles or the US-trained technocrats who promoted them. Rather, a Yale-trained finance minister was replaced by a Stanford-trained finance minister, an International Monetary Fund structural adjustment package was signed, and economic policy continued essentially as before."[8]

Such an attachment to laissez-faire macro-economic formulas is striking given that the previous Latin American generation had decisively rejected it. Among other things, the devastation wreaked by the Great Depression in the 1930s prompted a reevaluation of classical economics throughout the world including Latin America. By the end of WWII, liberalism had been largely eclipsed by state-led development policies inspired in part by the ideas of the British economist Maynard Keynes (1883–1946). Keynes was most concerned with unemployment in developed economies during economic downturns and advocated that governments intervene to correct these downturns of the market, primarily through monetary policies such as short-term deficit spending. These seemingly innocuous ideas were in fact anything but. Mixed economies, in which the private sector predominated but the government and public sector collaborated to manage and correct market imperfections, were suddenly preferred and promoted by experts, publics, and policymakers throughout the Atlantic. This represented a departure from classical calls for a minimalist state. It also meant that monoeconomics, the belief that markets function according to the same logics and laws across time and place, was rejected. The assumption that there was one ideal type of capitalism was thus effectively replaced by the supposition that there were capitalisms in the plural.

Dependency theorists, such as Hans Singer, Raul Prebisch, and Celso Furtado, were some of the principal intellectual architects behind the brand of state-led development that emerged in Latin America. They observed that the terms of trade for developing countries, especially those that relied on the export of primary commodities, such as natural resources and agricultural products, deteriorated over time because they ultimately imported fewer manufactured goods relative to exports. Inspired by the German economist, Friedrich List (1789–1846), who had detailed how infant industrial protection in the form of tariffs was deployed by Britain and the United States to build up their manufacturing base, the *dependistas* argued that developing countries should strive to diversify their economies and lessen dependence on primary commodity exports by developing manufacturing via various forms of government intervention. These ideas helped to inspire and legitimate the import substitution industrialization policies that came to be adopted throughout much of Latin America. Increasingly governments in the region cultivated domestic industries by, for example, imposing tariffs on imported goods. In the name of economic growth, the state also took on a much larger role in research and development, the construction of infrastructure, and, to a

Table 1.1 Annual GDP Growth (%)

Year	*Brazil*	*Vietnam*
1985–1999	2.6	6.5
2000–2009	3.3	6.6
2010	7.5	6.8
2011	2.7	6.2
2012	.90	5.2
2013	2.2	5.3
2014	2.4	5.4

Source: The World Bank. Accessed March 27, 2014. www.data.worldbank.org.

Table 1.2 Exports of Goods and Services (% of GDP)

Year	*Brazil*	*Vietnam*
2009	11	63
2010	11	72
2011	12	79
2012	13	80

Source: The World Bank. Accessed March 27, 2014. www.data.worldbank.org.

smaller degree, the provision of social security, health care, and education to the general public.

Latin American developmentalism proved extremely successful in building a manufacturing base, especially in Mexico and Brazil. Moreover, it produced economic outcomes in Latin America that many hailed as miraculous. Like Asian state-led development, growth rates were robust. For several decades many of the Latin American economies grew at 6.5 percent annually. Optimism ran high. Reminiscent of the hype generated by the recent commodity boom and Brazil's inclusion in the group of emerging national economies known as BRICS,[9] Brazil became known both at home and abroad as "the country of the future." Unfortunately such a future has not, as of yet, materialized. For reasons to be discussed below, state-led development in Latin America, unlike in East Asia, began to stumble in the 1970s.

The Pragmatists

As fate would have it, the failures of developmentalism in Latin America coincided with a paradigmatic shift unfolding throughout the Atlantic. After the Great Depression, liberalism underwent a near-death experience throughout most of the world, only to be revived in the late 1970s and early 1980s. This anti-Keynesian zeitgeist was perhaps most on display with the elections of Ronald Reagan and Margaret Thatcher in the United States and the United Kingdom. With the

Cold War as the backdrop, these leaders skillfully reduced complex policy debates about the role of government to a simplistic, binary framework of laissez-faire capitalism versus socialism in order to undermine many of the gains labor had made in those countries in the previous decades. À la the Austrian economist Friedrich Hayek (1899–1992), any policies that deviated from classical economics were dubbed anti-capitalist. Mixed economies in which the government played a complementary role to the market were crudely equated with the socialist, planned economies of the communist bloc. Increasingly, political parties, editorialists, social scientists, and public intellectuals echoed and legitimized this perspective. Previously marginal economic thinkers, such as Milton Friedman, were suddenly propelled into the political mainstream. Liberal economics was now referred to as neo or the new liberalism.

It is widely recognized that one consequence of neoliberalism was that proponents of classical rather than Keynesian economics came to dominate leadership in the World Bank and International Monetary Fund (IMF). In Latin America, as elsewhere in the global South, this meant that countries dependent on these institutions were heavily encouraged, if not forced, by these lending institutions to adopt structural adjustment policies.[10] This repertoire of reforms usually included the reduction of tariffs, liberalization of monetary policies, state downsizing, and privatization of publically owned or operated industries. The rise of neoliberalism in Latin America, however, is far from a classic tale of imperialism. The shift in expert opinion combined with the shortcomings of state-led development—a bloated and inefficient government bureaucracy, gross levels of cronyism between the political and economic elite, excessive deficit spending that resulted in the Mexican default in 1982, and weak economic growth—spurred a new consensus in Latin America. Experts, publics, and policymakers came to hold that a smaller government and less fettered market, rather than a developmental state that regulated and managed capitalism, would lead to economic growth and modernity. Consequently neoliberal policies were not simply imposed by North Atlantic superpowers or cleverly enabled through crisis fabrication and management as argued by Naomi Klein in *The Shock Doctrine*. These macroeconomic initiatives were equally, if not principally, the outgrowth of a burgeoning neoliberal common sense that led publics and politicians to respond to economic shocks in very distinct ways.

Only in the past decade has neoliberalism begun to encounter a crisis of legitimacy in Latin America due primarily to its dismal economic performance. And yet, the region seems just as far as ever from a paradigm shift in that no alternative set of ideas appears poised to become broadly accepted.[11] The more strident repudiations of neoliberalism by heads of state such as Evo Morales in Bolivia, Nestor Kirchner in Argentina, and Hugo Chavez in Venezuela, have not been built around a political consensus or a fresh economic formula. Instead, an amped up anti-imperialism and populist rhetoric combined with an economic model that hinges largely on natural gas and oil revenues has proven politically divisive, economically unsustainable, and regionally unattractive as an alternative to neoliberalism. In other countries, notably Brazil, Peru, and Chile, there have been more politically centric efforts at reform both in tone and substance. This has entailed maintaining most of the neoliberal monetary, industrial, and trade policies while modestly expanding social welfare policies in an effort to reduce poverty and social inequalities. However, even these relatively minor attempts to modify neoliberalism in the direction of what Celia Kerstenetzky calls "a developmental state of the Sen type"[12] have been hugely controversial, in part because the center-left leaders in these societies have shied away from articulating an alternative macro-economic vision. Instead, they have attempted to skirt such a debate by positioning themselves as pragmatic managers rather than advocates of a different economic paradigm along the lines of, say, East Asian, Scandinavian, or German capitalism.

In an era of rapid Asian economic growth combined with a political economy long dominated by agro-business, mineral and timber extraction, and oil exports, what has appeared to be most "pragmatic" (as well as the most politically expedient) has been a set of macro-economic policies that are best described as commodity-led development. In *Dragon in the Room*, Kevin Gallagher and Roberto Porzecanski note, "between 2000 and 2006, 70 percent of export growth in Latin America was explained by the growth in the export of commodities."[13] Not coincidently macro-economic policies in Brazil, as throughout the region, have focused on nurturing agro-business and natural resource extraction to feed the adolescent appetites of the Asian economies. These policies help to explain why the administrations of Luiz Inacio Lula da Silva (2003–2011) and Dilma Rousseff (2011–), the first democratically elected left-of-center presidents in Brazilian history, have often clashed with the landless workers' movement

Figure 1.1 Sugar Cane Cutters in Sao Paulo. Photograph by Nando Neves, 2008

(*Movimento dos Trabalhadores Rurais Sem Terra* or MST), indigenous communities, and environmentalists. These factions threaten or are in direct conflict with the interests of a political-economic project anchored in primary commodities.

Ironically, then, most of Latin America has come full circle. It has returned to its traditional economic strategy, dating back to the colonial era, of relying on commodity exports. An often-noted downside of commodity-anchored economies is anemic industrialization because currencies tend to be overinflated (the notorious Dutch Disease), and energies and resources are often diverted away from the investments required to enhance manufacturing. Not surprisingly, then, this so-called resource curse has been plaguing Latin America yet again. There has been inadequate spending on transportation, education, and scientific research, among other things. As a result, the manufacturing sector has lagged. In Brazil, for example, just 1.5 percent of GDP is spent on research and development. This compares to 4 to 5 percent spent in the developed countries.[14] Investments in public infrastructure have been equally disappointing. Even at the height of the last commodity boom between 2001 and 2010, investments averaged just 2.15 percent of GDP. The Brazilian economist Samuel Pessoa pointed out that "It would be necessary to invest in the order of three percent of GDP just to maintain the existing infrastructure", let alone "improve the infrastructure such as building metros in the large metropolitan areas or improving rail and roadways."[15] Predictably these lackluster investments have hampered productivity and the development of value-added, export oriented manufacturing. As of 2010, Vietnam controlled the same share of the world's manufactured goods as Brazil—both at around 0.8 percent.[16] Chinese manufacturing, which now represents 12 percent of world manufacturing, second only to Germany, is quickly usurping or threatening to take over most of the Latin American manufactured exports. In fact, Gallagher and Porzecanski found that "over 94 percent of Latin American countries' manufacture exports were under threat from China" and most especially in high-tech products—those sectors that are regarded as key to economic growth.[17]

These trends have left many observers pessimistic about the economic future of Brazil and the rest of Latin America. It seems doubtful that the economic formula of commodity-led growth—during which time productivity has failed to increase, the manufacturing sector has stalled, and there have been insufficient investments in communication networks, research and development, education, and social services—will propel Latin American economies into a developed future. Many have warned that a more likely outcome will be the "re-primarization of Latin American economies," which will leave the region vulnerable to underdevelopment, or what Mario Cimoli and Jorge Katz have called the "low development trap."[18]

Homo Economicus

This fairly standard overview of macro-economic policies and outcomes in Latin America and East Asia offers a window into the aculturalism that prevails in the development literature. The emphasis in the above discussion was almost exclusively on degrees of investment in infrastructure, productivity levels, types of goods exported, the size and role of government, and the relative independence of markets from state oversight. The inference, as is common in development studies, was that identities, symbols, interpretive frameworks, values, and aesthetics are largely immaterial.

Undoubtedly one reason for this aculturalism is the vogue in the North Atlantic social sciences for explanations that reduce social action to a simple calculus of "a desire for greater wealth or power, or the means of survival or control over others."[19] This penchant is strongest within economics and political science,[20] the disciplines that dominate development economics, and manifests in the assumption that markets are the outgrowth of individuals who are instrumentally seeking to maximize their interests. This so-called rational choice theory deems economically irrelevant such factors as ethics, worldviews, and subjectivities.

A small subset of economists has pushed back against the interest-maximizing-individual thesis by drawing on insights from behavioral and cognitive psychology.[21] These psycho-economists have questioned the degree to which people have accurate information, expectations match reality, or whether individuals are at their core instrumentalists. To date their research and findings have had little impact on conventional economic wisdom. Most economists tend to ignore or brush these ideas off by arguing that, even if individuals are operating on faulty information, erroneous expectations, or are not by nature profit-maximizers, the realities of the market place require one to eventually behave as a cost-benefit player. And so the scholarship of the psycho-economists has not prompted a reevaluation, let alone a rejection, of rational choice suppositions. The vast majority of economists, at least in the North Atlantic, continue to hold fast to the belief that to survive in capitalist arenas one must, at least in the medium to long run, conform to the law of profit maximization, even if one is not innately an instrumentalist.

As a student of race, one of my first encounters with this economistic thinking was the writings of Richard Epstein, who argued in the early 1990s that in "a world of free access to open markets, systematic discrimination, even by a large majority, offers little peril to the isolated minority." The reason minorities should not worry about racism, he counseled, was that "(i)n competitive economic markets, discrimination is short-lived because ruthlessly competitive entrepreneurs will take advantage of the opportunities racial exclusion provides."[22] Epstein concluded that there was no sustainable space in open markets for racial bias because he presumed, like most development economists, that capitalism was unimpeded by the socio-cultural. That is, he postulated that individuals, who deviated from rational choice logics—such as hiring less meritocratic employees or not marketing to certain sectors because of race—would not only sacrifice profits but also risk survival by diminishing their competitiveness.

This is, of course, an idealized and grossly inaccurate conceptualization of capitalism. Markets are not and can never be isolated spheres that transcend socio-cultural dynamics such as race. It is no secret that, contrary to Epstein's prediction, competitive markets have not snuffed out racial discrimination. Instead, race continues to affect a wide range of economic practices in the United States and elsewhere: underwriting and lending, hiring, promotions, philanthropy, taxation, union membership, consumers' desires and expectations, investors' decision making, and so forth.[23]

Clearly, then, market actors are far more complex than most economists and various other social scientists, such as Epstein, would have us believe. Moreover markets themselves are situated within a socio-cultural context, which defines the rules, parameters, and possibilities of economic activities. For instance, if it was deemed more cost effective to employ children, prostitute men, ban religion, smoke opium, end sexism, or kill the elderly, most societies, even those with advanced market economies, are not likely to permit most, if any, of these practices.[24] This tongue-in-cheek list of examples underscores how no society is driven exclusively, or even primarily, by instrumentalism. Despite the fears of many that somehow the logic of profit maximization will overwhelm all other values and logics, a society's understandings of children, sex, the metaphysical, the elderly, gender, and so forth will always shape and put limits on acceptable capitalist pursuits.

A number of economics students at Harvard, Cambridge, and Ecole Normale Superieure, have formed the Post-Autistic Economics movement and labeled this acultural view of markets narrow-minded. "[L]ike suffers of autism," they assert, "the field of economics [is] intelligent but obsessive, narrowly focused, and cut off from the outside world."[25] Their critique, like mine, maintains that a sophisticated body of economic theory is constructed upon foundational assumptions about markets and market actors, which are myopic if not make-believe. At best, it is a one-dimensional distortion of markets and market agents. As the heterodox economists George Akerlof and Rachael Kranton note in *Identity Economics*, consumers, employers, employees, manufacturers, and investors are motivated by a complex web of values, symbols, identities, as well as material interests, which cannot be disaggregated from the socio-cultural.[26]

And yet, development economists have constructed their models and policy prescriptions on the idea that humans, or at least market actors, are acultural rational beings. To them markets are similar to the fictive Vulcan planet featured in the television series Star Trek. Mr. Spock, a Vulcan, embodied this ideal type rational actor. Loyalties, love, faith, hate, belief in the metaphysical, and so on were never legitimate grounds for conduct. Mr. Spock considered behaviors based on such motives as "illogical." The vast majority of economists assume that markets are peopled with Spock-like individuals, ever instrumentally focused on advancing their expected monetary advantages. Astonishingly, then, their theories and policies rest upon ideas of agency that do not apply to Earthlings.

The Dark Matter of Development

Perhaps one can blame neoclassical economists and their rational choice converts in the social sciences for the general state of development economics, but it is unfair to hold them solely or even primarily responsible for the cultural oversight in development studies and practice. Indeed the so-called institutionalists have been equally if not more influential than the neo-utilitarians in the past few decades. These development scholars, who span the ideological spectrum in terms of macro-economic philosophies, have found common ground in the premise that development will be advanced if the proper laws, policies, and organizations are forged. Consequently, they have focused a great deal of attention on identifying and delineating the contours of the institutions that are believed to be key to economic well-being. This has, in turn, been reflected in a range of policy interventions aimed at promoting "good institutions" throughout the developing world.[27]

The more Keynesian wing of the institutionalist movement has come primarily out of the influential group of development scholars studying East Asian capitalism. In Japan, South Korea, Taiwan, and more recently China, Peter Evans, Alice Amsden, Robert Wade, Ha-Joon Chang, among others, have documented how state-led capitalism is the modus operandi in the region and has produced "different production and investment outcomes than would have occurred with either free market or simulated free market policies."[28] The findings of these different, read superior, outcomes have put these scholars directly at odds with proponents of laissez-faire macro-economic policies. Impressed by the remarkable success of state-led capitalism in East Asia, they have concluded that "forms of state guidance that were first demonstrated to be effective by Japan . . . are a better model for the second and third worlds than Anglo-American capitalism."[29]

I refer to these researchers and advocates of an East Asian development model as institutionalists, however, not because of their support for Keynesian-like macro-economic policies but rather because of their analytical formalism. To their credit, these scholars have identified and detailed a number of the particularities and virtues of the East Asian institutional landscape such as monetary policies that tolerate higher levels of inflation, strict controls on capital flows, and infant industrial policies geared toward exports. Where matters go awry is with their failure to consider how policies, regulatory regimes, and organizations are nestled within a socio-cultural context. For example, a number of these scholars have shown how East Asian governments, especially when compared to Latin America, have a more meritocratic process of hiring and promoting government officials, a larger percentage of career civil servants (rather than political appointees), higher levels of pay and training, and better insulation of regulators from the pressures and influences of the industrial and landed elite.[30] The problem occurs when this valuable description of state bureaucracies is turned into a causal explanation. That is, the institutionalists imply or explicitly conclude that these sorts of organizational features are the principal reasons why East Asian bureaucracies have been less susceptible to rent seeking, corporatism, and other forms of corruption. Thus, as formalists, they abstract these features of East Asian states from East Asian societies and then presume that these variables account for why state-led capitalism in the region has been more successful in partnering, guiding, nurturing, and prodding the private sector to venture into more challenging and efficient kinds of production—rather than avoiding performance standards and becoming uncompetitive internationally as occurred with state-led capitalism in Latin

America. The policy implications being that the primary focus of development practices in Latin America and elsewhere should be on replicating similar kinds of institutions or organizational features.

One need only consider implementing such reforms in a society like the Philippines to be able to see the shortcomings of their reasoning. Here, according to Vincent Rafael (2000) in *White Love,* the official nationalism that emerged under US rule in the early twentieth century favored

> [a] cadre of mostly mestizo elites . . . [who] managed to monopolize the symbolic resources for imagining nationhood. Indeed they came to regard themselves not only as a ruling class with common interests to defend but as the exclusive spokespeople for the rest of the nation. . . . And since they believed that their class interests were coterminous with the national interests, they thought that their political lives determined the very existence of the Philippines itself.[31]

In such a context a well-paid, non-appointed, highly meritocratic bureaucracy that has corporate coherence and is relatively autonomous—the ingredients of a proficient developmental state according to the institutionalists—is still apt to behave in ways that mimic inept bureaucracies because of how national interests and elite subjectivities have been articulated. A predatory state is probable because interpretations of societal interests are heavily biased toward the elite. As a result administrative reforms of the kind inspired by the developmental state in East Asia are likely to be ineffective unless or until the cultural terrain is transformed.

What I find so perplexing about many of these institutionalists is that they are not completely oblivious to these kinds of socio-cultural factors. Indeed they sometimes openly acknowledge their importance, but then fail to follow through with a detailed explanation. For instance, in a comparative analysis of government bureaucracies in East Asia and Latin America, Ben Schneider argues that "the crucial factor that differentiates developmental from desarrollista states"[32] is the method of hiring and promoting government bureaucrats. In East Asia they tend to be career civil servants whereas in Latin America a much higher percentage are political appointees whose tenure is limited by how long a particular political party remains in power. In the conclusion of his article, Schneider attempts to broaden and complicate this thesis. He writes, "Officials in successful developmental states often have strong ethical, ideological (discourse), career or legal grounds for resisting the temptation [for illicit gain]."[33] Building on this line of thought, he adds that rent-seeking has been less pronounced in East Asia, as compared to Latin America, because "[i]n Asia, nationalism appears to have both stronger and deeper roots." Thus, Schneider ultimately identifies culture as critical to the success of state-led capitalism in East Asia, but offers no analytical substance. He does not explain what he means by stronger and deeper ethics, ideological grounds or nationalism. Moreover, Schneider never clarifies precisely how these cultural variables may affect bureaucrats' behaviors or address how a similar kind of ideological dynamic or its functional equivalent could be generated in Latin America.

One of Ha-Joon Chang's writings offers another good illustration of this cultural tease. In the context of a lengthy discussion of the contours of East Asian macro-economic policies and institutions, he inserts that the East Asian states have been successful in disciplining the recipients of rents because of "its brand of developmentalist ideology."[34] Inexplicably this tantalizing notion that development ideology is an important ingredient of a successful development state is left unexplored. There is no further discussion of what this ideology looks like and how in particular it has worked against rent-seeking. Once again, culture is deemed significant but then treated as a kind of dark matter of development—something that is believed to be important but ultimately left unexamined as if it were too difficult to understand or immeasurable.

Modernizationists

It is encouraging that since beginning this project a cultural approach to development has gained some traction. In the introduction to *Culture and Development in a Globalizing World*, Sarah Radcliffe writes, "there is no doubt that culture has arrived in development."[35] A number of observers have even described this arrival as a cultural turn. In 2001, for instance, Jan Nederveen Pieterse announced in headline fashion, "After the cultural turn upset most social sciences, it finally comes to economics and to the bundle of practices called development."[36]

One faction of this turn is best characterized as a return. In the mid-twentieth century, at the height of the US century, Talcott Parsons took Max Weber's insights about the cultural nature of economies and reduced it to a mechanistic theory about how value orientations—namely instrumental rationality, individualism, and meritocracy—drive development and modernity. The United States, as the presumed model of modernity, was believed to most closely approximate these value orientations, which were theorized as explaining its greater degree of economic development. Other societies were studied and evaluated by some of Parsons' disciples, such as the East Asian specialists John Fairbank, Edwin Reischauer, and Albert Craig,[37] to determine how and to what degree its value orientations deviated from those of the West and thus hindered economic growth.

Modernizationists, like development scholars in general, assumed that culture could be abstracted from the material. That is, they did not appreciate how values, discourses, identities, and symbols were intertwined with social orders, institutions, wealth, and political power. By theorizing culture as a disaggregated, free-floating, autonomous arena (rather than a co-articulated and materially tethered one), they made the unfortunate misstep of assuming that culture was *either* a dependent *or* an independent variable—but not both. Given the modernizationists' interest in culture, it is not surprising that they settled on the latter and thus succumbed to culturalism whereby the realm of ideas was hypothesized as *the* motor driving economic formations. Modernizationists further erred by conceptualizing culture in rudimentary, binary oppositional terms. This led them to selectively focus on cultural practices—such as obligations to kin—that they believed signified a lack of modernity in a developing society. Further, sociological complexities in the

United States were discounted or bracketed in order to sustain not only this dualism but also their ideal of the United States as the benchmark of modernity. The saliency of race, sexuality, and gender—just to name the most obvious oversights—were minimized or completely ignored because they did not fit with the ideal of the United States qua rational society where merit trumped custom. The outcome of these analytical mistakes—culturalism, equation of the metropole with modernity, and operationalization of societies within binary frameworks—was a rudimentary colonial-like formula that called for replacing parts or all of traditional (read "backward Third World") cultures with a modern (read "civilized Western") one.

Given the modernizationists' various shortcomings, it is indeed troubling that many scholars and practitioners involved in development studies' cultural turn are harking back to this tradition. One example is the writings of Lawrence Harrison, the director of the Cultural Change Institute at the Fletcher School of International Affairs at Tufts University who headed USAID in Haiti between 1977 and 1979. In a 2010 opinion piece in the *Wall Street Journal* and the edited volume, *The Hidden Form of Capital*, Harrison argued:

> I find compelling evidence that some religions do better than others in promoting the goals the UN Universal Declaration of Human Rights: democratic politics, social justice, and prosperity. [. . .] As an example of a religion that is highly resistant to progress, consider [Haitian] Voodoo [. . .], a religion of sorcery in which hundreds of spirits, very human and capricious, control human destinies. [. . .] Not only does Voodoo involve sorcery and nurture irrationality; it also nurtures a sense of impotence and fatalism and discourages entrepreneurial vocation. It focuses on the present, not the future. Voodoo is without ethical content and, consequently, a major contributor to the high levels of mistrust, paranoia, sense of helplessness, and despair noted in the anthropological literature about Haiti.[38]

Harrison puts his modernizationist foot further in his racist mouth when he concludes that neighboring Barbados is so much more successful than Haiti—apparently "approaching First World status"—because it has been able to de-Africanize its culture thanks largely to it remaining an English colony until 1966 by which time the African descent slaves had become "Afro-Saxons" and "black Englishmen."[39]

Development professionals should certainly consider whether certain assumptions, rituals, or identities, which are intertwined with religion including Haitian vodou, might be in need of change in order to advance economic growth but it is absurd to suggest that vodou writ large should be eliminated as a development strategy. The prohibition against usury by the Catholic Church was once a major impediment to the development of the financial sector in Europe but all that was required was working around and eventually lifting this ban rather than the eradication of Catholicism. In any event, Harrison's central argument boils down to an easily recognizable modernizationist formula whereby local culture is disparaged as a backward impediment to progress and Western culture is idealized, homogenized, and packaged as a development elixir: to improve an economy, just replace the traditional culture with the modern and stir.

A more updated and thus less obvious version of the modernizationist redux can be observed among some of the social development initiatives that are in vogue. In *The Will to Improve* Tania Murray Li described one such program spearheaded by the World Bank in Indonesia between 1998 and 2003. The chief architect of the Kecamatan Development Project (KDP), as it was called, was the US anthropologist Scott Guggenheim. According to Li, the backers of this $1 billion project (that was later cloned in the Philippines, East Timor, and Afghanistan) believed that Suharto's New Order had turned previously cohesive, capable, creative villagers into people who were passive, ignorant of their rights, accustomed to corruption, and diminished in their capacity to mobilize for their own resources—all qualities believed to impede economic development.

Certainly the New Order genocide had detrimental effects on Indonesian society. In *The Look of Silence*,[40] the documentary filmmaker Joshua Oppenheimer detailed how New Order assassins continue to be celebrated as national heroes and publically boast about their participation in the murder of hundreds of thousands of Chinese and communists. Moreover, they invoke the memories of these atrocities to bully, intimidate, and coerce the relatives of the victims of this genocide into accepting deplorable working conditions. Yet instead of addressing these histories and their obvious role in sustaining corruption, passivity, impunity, alienation, and ignorance in contemporary Indonesia, the backers of the KDP reasoned that such cultural defects, especially the lack of accountability, could be remedied by instructing villagers in a kind of Robert's Rules of Order.

> In order to access [project] funds villagers had to subscribe to a very detailed set of rules that obliged them to form committees, hold consultations, and interact with each other in new forums and new ways. The rules were elaborated in manuals, checklists, information sheets, and other documents. They were also presented verbally and reiterated constantly by the army of consultants and facilitators (over four thousand) hired by the project to work at village or subdistrict level, and by selected residents, a man and a woman from each village who received training and stipends for the work on project implementation.[41]

And so rather than work to build (or rebuild) accountability by holding those responsible for the genocide accountable, the World Bank effectively contributed to the silence and impunity by embracing a modernizationist-type solution of "improving" local culture by introducing Western-inspired administrative procedures into village organizational life.

KDP's rhetoric makes its modernizationist nature somewhat trickier to spot. Unlike Harrison above, the World Bank did not couch its imposition of external administrative procedures onto villagers in the crudely racist-colonial language of replacing backward Asian culture with European norms, habits, and values. Instead they claimed that they were merely trying to restore (not replace) a traditional culture that had been damaged by the New Order. Furthermore, their "overarching objective" was described as "creating participatory institutions and processes."[42] The development establishment is, of course, notorious for designing blueprints of change in which communities are given little or no say in the analysis of their problems or the formulation of the solutions that target them. The KDP, despite its assertions to the contrary, proved no different. In fact, rather than harness their ethnographic knowledge of Indonesian villages to facilitate cross-cultural understanding and collaborative dialogue and design, they used these insights as a marketing tool along the lines of business anthropology. In Li's words the project was "designed to *shape* desires and act on actions, setting the conditions so that people would behave as they ought. Neither the ends they sought to achieve nor the means were up for debate."[43]

The aficionados of the local are yet another strand of the modernizationist replay in that these celebrators of the indigenous conceptualize national/South/subaltern culture in binary opposition to the global/modern/West. Where they depart with the modernizationists is with respect to their valuation of these cultural poles. The local becomes the good and the global the bad. Ignoble savages become noble ones. Nederveen Pieterse put it this way:

> The tendency is to view local culture in terms of prelapsrian purity and unity, homogenizing the local community as the last stand of Gemeinschaft, in a manner reminiscent of the way ethnographers used to speak about 'their' villages, or their cultures, as cultural wholes or configurations.[44]

To varying degrees strands of this line of thinking have surfaced in policy circles, perhaps most notably in United Nations discussion papers. An example is a 2003 report titled *Culture and Development in Viet Nam*. In the executive summary, the authors state:

> [C]ulture is a key factor impacting on every stage of the development project. [. . .] The aim is to make development culturally sensitive, and to fully exploit potentials of culture in propelling and accelerating development, while avoiding any negative cultural factors. At the same time, one must be wary of the potentials of certain development models in eroding cultural identities, reducing cultural diversity, and inducing irretrievable losses to the national and local cultural heritage.[45]

To their credit the authors mention that there are "negative cultural factors." However, the report ultimately lends itself to the trope of local-culture-as-sacrosanct because these negatives are never specified or discussed and attention in the body of the report is placed exclusively on the positive qualities. The point here is not to advocate for high-modernist or assimilationist development schemes, something which these authors were obviously attempting to counter, but rather to caution against drawing on the binary logics of the modernizationists as a weapon in this struggle. The reality, of course, is that cultures, including those of subalterns, are vastly more complicated. One can safely assume that in any society or subculture there is an array of cultural elements that have a range of economic effects—negative, positive, neutral, and mixed. Consequently such platitudes about celebrating and cherishing local cultures, as espoused in the above-mentioned report, too glibly gloss over the fact that certain facets of a given culture may be in need of change (rather than commemoration) if economic progress is to be made.[46]

Critical Development Studies

Fortunately, there is another wing of the cultural turn in development studies that is distinct from that of the neo-modernizationists. Influenced by critical theory, post-structuralism, feminism, literary criticism, and subaltern studies, among other intellectual currents, these scholars do not conceptualize culture in dualistic terms, imagine it as a hermetically sealed island, or homogenize what is inevitably a heterogeneous and often contested terrain. Moreover, modernity and development are not equated with Westernization. Indeed there is an understanding that capitalisms and modernities have multiple forms.[47] Finally, and most importantly, they reject "economic essentialism or the assumption that there is a stable and universal distinction between economic and non-economic practices" in favor of the recognition that economic practices, relations and policies are "partly discursive."[48] In other words, they do not regard culture as a distinct sphere of society separate from economics and politics. These scholars hold that culture cannot be abstracted from the material and therefore capitalism is enmeshed with culture. Jacqueline Best and Matthew Peterson, described it this way:

> Karl Polanyi was simply wrong. The "disembedding" of markets never in fact detached markets from culture, . . . The idea of a "free market economy" may serve certain ideological purposes, but it is never in fact able to realize its utopia of a culture-free economy.[49]

One of the earliest examples of this scholarship that I came across was that of Victoria Lawson. In her ethnographic study of neoliberalism in Ecuador during the 1980s she demonstrated how researchers, such as David Harvey, had incorrectly theorized localities as over-determined by global capitalist forces. Lawson documented how the socio-cultural particularities of place, namely gender, mattered as well.[50]According to Lawson, the specific gender ideologies and practices in Ecuador enabled a liberalization of textile manufacturing to a degree that would have been impossible had women been included in unions during the era of import substitution industrialization or had their gendered identities as wives, mothers and household heads been differently constructed.

Like Lawson a number of feminists and other scholars working in the area of gender and development have mapped out many of the ways gender matters in different contexts and that gender and patriarchy often must be addressed, if not altered, for development to occur. These insights have had some limited impact on development policy. It is widely recognized, for example, that certain facets of gender inequality—such as the lack of parity in the education of girls and boys—must be addressed in order to advance economic growth. But to date scholars working in the area of gender and development have not been successful in prompting a broader cultural turn within development studies. Even with regards to gender specifically there is still a great deal of progress to be made. As Richard Wilk observes:

> Most economists persist in arguing against including housework in the measurement of the gross national product (GNP)! If a parent takes a day off and stays home to take care of a sick child, this is not counted as part of GNP, whereas if a parent pays a nephew to stay with the child, it does count. The reasons that work in the house is not considered "real work" are deeply cultural and historical; they are not based on objective scientific fact.[51]

As the cultural turn has unfolded, more and more research like Lawson's and Wilk's has been published detailing and highlighting the cultural dimensions of political economies. Presently there are a significant number of well-regarded scholars from a number of different disciplines and prestigious universities working under such labels as Cultural Political Economy, Identity Economics, Regional Modernities, Gender and Development, and Critical Development Studies. Yet despite this evolution, mainstream development studies continue to ignore or treat culture as nonessential. For this reason, to describe the recent consideration of culture as a turn is more aspirational than factual. Paradigm shifts are, to be sure, notoriously difficult to bring about within academic disciplines in part because gatekeepers in academic departments, disciplinary associations, and on editorial boards have staked their careers and reputations on certain assumptions and theories of the world. In the case of development studies, these barriers are heightened by the fact that much of the policy world, which helps to legitimate and fund development scholarship, is often beholden to acultural precepts as well.

Although these factors, to be sure, are significant impediments to the cultural turn becoming more widely accepted, scholars attempting to advance a cultural political economy share the blame for the marginalization of their ideas. Specifically, I believe that they have limited their impact on development studies by failing to engage with, if not outright shunning, the central goal of development studies: improving market economies. Area studies offer a good case in point. Scholars working in Asia have produced an impressive body of work delineating the intersections between culture and economies. Yet their objectives and goals have not centered on bettering development practice. They have been concerned with other aims such as shattering lingering colonial epistemologies that have constructed the West as the pinnacle and vanguard of modernity to be emulated. Some even hope to turn the tables and make the case that Eastern capitalism is more cosmopolitan than the Western version. For example, Timothy Brook and Hy V. Luong write in their edited volume *Culture and Economy* that "it seems inevitable that Eastern Asian cultures will shape, even remake, capitalism into a system of production and consumption beyond its original definition, letting it become something that is more genuinely universal than the European version."[52] Most, however, resist the temptation to claim the mantle of supremacy and instead make the case for alternative or regional modernities. That is, they offer detailed case studies of how local particularities in various parts of Asia have not been simply overwhelmed by capitalist-led globalization but instead have shaped how these forces have unfolded in a given society.[53] The point being that globalization is not a simple story of world homogenization but one in which there are various points of divergence as well.

If area studies have inadvertently skirted the central question of development studies because their concerns have been elsewhere, critical development scholars have done so deliberately. For instance, the editors of *On the Edges of Development* candidly announce in the introduction that "Our volume does not offer prescriptions or 'how-to' formulae for doing development."[54] In another example, James Ferguson, in *The Anti-Politics Machine*, openly states that his book "never intended or presumed to prescribe."[55] In yet another straightforward shunning of the applied, Tania Murray Li in *The Will to Improve* writes, "I [do not] offer a recipe for how improvement can be improved. I take a critical stance, one that seeks to prize open expert knowledge and expose its limits."[56] It is this "refusal to outline general programs of political action"[57] that has led many scholars, such as Sivaramakrishnan, Agrawal, and others, to characterize these "radical critics" as strong on critique and weak on construction.[58]

The lines, however, between critic and programmer are never so neatly siloed. Li goes on to explain one of her reasons for not offering development advice. In her experience as a development consultant she "observed the limited tolerance of elites for interventions that might actually restructure relations in favor of the poor."[59] The obvious policy implications being that such biases against the poor need to be altered in order to advance development. But as a self-identified critic, like many in critical development studies, she does not build on her insightful analysis with a discussion of the programmatic or policy implications of her findings.

This resistance to being prescriptive or to follow through with a consideration of the applied implications of their analyses has made it too easy for the mainstream development establishment to dismiss critical development scholars and their ideas. Envision, by way of analogy, that a group of carpenters were trying to figure out how to build better homes and someone who had studied construction techniques came along with ideas that called into question some of these carpenters' basic assumptions and construction methods. Certainly some of these builders would dismiss these ideas out of hand because they were unconventional and untested. But probably others would suspend their skepticism momentarily to hear the person out. Some of the more curious or open-minded ones might even be intrigued by the ideas and see their potential for improving housing construction. However, imagine if at this early stage in the discussion our fictitious innovator were to suddenly announce that she was only interested in critiquing current construction practices rather than proposing better ones because she believed that houses were bad for the environment and they limited peoples' freedoms. It is not hard to see how quickly the conversation would end regardless of the quality of her ideas. In a similar way I believe that critical development scholars have helped to limit their impact on development studies. By openly declaring that they are not interested in searching for ways to better market economies, they have made it easy for development scholars and practitioners to dismiss them out of hand. And in so doing they have managed to increase the odds that the cultural turn will remain marginal or digress into a full-blown modernizationist redux—something that is especially likely to occur given how much overlap there is between popular and modernizationist thought.

Popular Thought

In sharp contrast to mainstream development professionals, most laypeople see culture not only as relevant but also as determinant. The average citizen in Vietnam, Brazil, and the United States, I have found, tends to espouse a culturalist perspective. Charles Bergquist began his book, *Labor and the Course of American Democracy* (1996) with a similar observation: "Most US citizens, if pressed to explain why their country developed into a powerful industrial democracy while Latin American countries remain weak, unstable, and poor, would probably respond with vague references to different cultural values, including attitudes toward work."[60] Thus the United States and other publics, like modernizationists, tend to see culture as driving capitalist development and other facets of modernity. Furthermore, they often imagine culture in ways that have long been discredited in the social sciences. Jean-Pierre Olivier de Sardan observes:

> Lackadaisical references to "cultural factors" are more often than not oblivious not only of the existence of sub-cultures and internal cultural diversity within a given social group, but also of the influence of social cleavages (age, sex, social classes, among others) and of norms and behaviors.[61]

In addition to being viewed as discrete, static, and uncontested, they draw on the dualist assumptions outlined in the discussion of modernizationist thought. How often does one hear, for example, the tired tropes about Western and Eastern cultures as if they were innate, island-like universes that represented two adversarial poles devoid of any substantive overlap or internal diversity? And perhaps most disheartening, the supposed contours of these cultures are often perverse distortions, if not completely inaccurate simulations, of cultural realities.

Most people are familiar with the overplayed clichés regarding the "Asian" values of education, family, and hard work. In my experience, they are often invoked to explain the economic successes in East Asia or failures in countries like Brazil. I find the reference to work ethic especially flawed because I know how hard poor Brazilians toil and this has never led to their standard of living or the Brazilian economy improving. For instance, in one region where I conduct research, the Jequitinhonha Valley in Minas Gerais, 60 percent of the men leave their families for nine months of the year and work twelve-hour days cutting sugar cane to earn $400 a month. This is how one of the workers described the situation:

> My name is Antonio. I'm thirty-nine. I had to leave to work. I left with my two brothers. We went to Sao Paulo to cut sugarcane. . . . It was necessary because there is little work here. We earn too little. As many here say, slavery ended but only if you put "slavery" in quotation marks. Many work earning only $8 a day. This doesn't pay for anything especially if one has a large family. So people go to cut sugarcane in order to earn more money. I worked fifteen years cutting sugarcane. The first time I went was in 1987 with my dad. . . . It's hard work. One works from four in the morning until six in the evening. . . . Since I had little formal education, this was the only option available. I would cut more than one thousand meters of sugarcane each day. . . . At the minimum one had to cut ten thousand kilos a day or ten tons. I would cut thirty-three tons a day between March and November including Saturdays and Sundays. . . . It's awful to spend eight to nine months away from one's family. . . . It's awful but it's the only option we have.[62]

Obviously, then, if there were a causal relationship between hard work and wealth, the face of the well-off would be very different.

The value placed on education is one of the variables probably emphasized most in the popular press in Brazil. It is common to read articles or view featured news stories comparing Brazil with the prosperous East Asian countries such as South Korea. Inevitably the stories hinge on the importance placed on education. The long hours of studying and social pressure on students to excel are frequently mentioned. And the reason for this putatively heightened concern with education in East Asia, it is argued, has to do with the cultural values that stem from Confucianism.

Many observers have noted the irony of invoking Confucianism as the cause of development given that until recently it was theorized as the reason for East Asian economic retardation. Nevertheless, most agree that Confucianism served as the philosophical basis for the Mandarin mode of government that existed throughout most of the region for at least a millennium. Unlike feudal Europe, merit rather than blood was used to determine the appointment of civil servants. The primary measure of merit was an exam that was open to anyone who wanted to prepare for it. These exams, which were held once a year, were based on the memorization and mastery of the classics: Chinese poetry, literature, and philosophy. In *Lost Modernities* Alexander Woodside details this administrative system to make the point of how facets of modernity such as meritocratic administrative institutions emerged first outside of the West and independently of capitalism.

In Vietnam, the mandarinate was responsible for the establishment of a university system at least 500 years ago. Performance on exams determined one's position in government. The most successful students would move to *Duong Trang Thi* (Competition Street) in Hanoi to prepare for the PhD exam administered at the Temple of Literature. Even though the French dismantled the mandarinate in the early twentieth century, many villagers still celebrate the townspeople who passed these exams centuries ago. In Brazil the first university was established just 100 years ago.[63] However in contemporary Brazil many academics have gone on to become important political leaders—such as the sociologist Fernando Herinque Cardoso who was president of Brazil from 1995 until 2003—and also many streets and airports are named after famous artists and scholars (as is true in Vietnam as well). Muddying the waters further, many historians argue that Confucianism did not penetrate very deeply into mainstream Vietnamese society. For instance, Shawn McHale asserts in *Print and Power* that "Confucianism's impact on Vietnam has been exaggerated and misconceived."[64] Finally, 95 percent of Vietnamese had no formal education until the socialist revolution in the mid-twentieth century—this was lower than the literacy rate in Brazil at the time.

In both countries I have found that most parents desperately want their children to have the best education possible. If nothing else, they see it as a means of upward mobility. In Brazil, especially, I am always impressed by the heroic efforts I have witnessed as people attempt to further their children's or their own education: evening classes spent after ten-hour work days; months of separation from families in order to attend better schools; children braving gang violence and stray bullets in hopes of completing high school. At the Zumbi University in Sao Paulo, for example, all students work from 8 am until 5 pm and then study from 6 pm until 11 pm.

Complicating this issue further, most experts and persons I interviewed agree that the Vietnamese educational system is highly problematic if not dysfunctional. The learning—much like the Mandarin exams—is didactic and rote. Students are not taught to be independent, creative thinkers.[65] Applied knowledge is also lacking. So let us suppose that the value placed on education in Vietnam were higher than in Brazil and this in turn drives students to study harder. The outcome, then, would be that Vietnamese students are doing well in an education system that prepares them poorly for a twenty-first-century economy. Consequently the supposition that the value placed on education is driving economic growth becomes even less persuasive.

Interestingly the primary distinction between Brazil and Vietnam on this question of the value placed on education is rarely mentioned in these discussions. Although Brazilians value education for themselves and their children, the well-to-do do not see it as important for the *povo* (the people),[66] as the poor majority are often called. This is reminiscent of the dynamics in the United States—as documented by education researchers such as Jonathan Kozol—in which affluent, suburban communities favor spending robustly on schools in "their communities" but regard similar levels of investment in poorer, urban schools as a waste of money. Illinois Governor Tommy Thompson, in opposition to increasing funding for schools in Chicago in the late 1980s, put it this way: "We can't keep throwing money into a black hole."[67] One result of such discourses is that there is too little political support for improving the public education system in Brazil, whose student population—much like the public schools in Chicago—is mainly nonwhite. The predictable outcome is that most students attend impoverished, low quality schools. On this point Sebastian Edwards writes, "it is difficult to imagine a country with such a deficient system of schooling being able to turn itself into an economic force in the coming years. . . . Without a quality education system, it is difficult to foment an increase in productivity which, history has shown, undergirds economic growth that is both rapid and sustainable."[68]

Thus the value placed on education matters in Brazil but in a very different way than is typically implied or stated in the media or everyday conversations. The enhancement of human capital, productivity, and economic growth are hampered because of education values. However, it is not the worth that Brazilians place on their education or the education of their loved-ones that is at issue. Instead it is the importance that the rich and middle classes place on the education of the broader public that appears to be responsible for generating such a lamentable state of education in Brazil. And yet despite the hugely significant economic consequences of these values, how often are development monies targeted at creating initiatives or supporting existing organizations and individuals that have been working—often on a shoestring budget—to transform such attitudes in Brazil or elsewhere?

If nothing else, this brief discussion of education values should help to illuminate why critical development scholars, who offer an invaluable analytical framework for development studies, need to enter the fray and become interpretive economists. By distancing themselves from development practice, as discussed in the previous section, they remove themselves from the above sorts of debates about culture and development. In this way they contribute to an analytical void that is readily filled by the modernizationist-like arguments that reinforce rather than question the clichés and culturalism that dominate the public domain. As the reader will find in the next chapter, the social and economic consequences have been dire. These unchallenged stereotypes have helped to reproduce certain social hierarchies in Brazil, which in turn exacerbate poverty and limit economic growth.

Theoretical Black Boxes

A comparative study of East Asia and Latin America is a well-trod path in development studies. By studying and juxtaposing two regions that have had very different economic track records since WWII (East Asia remarkably impressive, Latin America unexpectedly mediocre to bad), researchers have sought to identify the causal factors (or what social scientists like to call independent variables) responsible for these different development trajectories. How *Cultures of Development* contributes to this tradition is by bringing a new case study (Vietnam) and a unique analytical perspective (interpretive economics), both of which allow me to make some important advances in development theory and practice.

Brazil has been studied and described at length within the comparative development literature. However, no studies, of which I am aware, have considered Vietnam. This is probably due to the fact that until recently Vietnam was an extremely poor country and so therefore did not fit the East Asian pattern of robust economic growth to which comparativists have been attracted. In addition to bringing a new case study to the comparative development literature, the Vietnamese case is very instructive for at least three other reasons.

First, there are doubts among some scholars, especially proponents of a robust interventionist state, as to whether a developmental state is still possible in the twenty-first century. In the edited volume *Putting Development First*, Kevin Gallagher notes, "There are growing concerns that additional [global trade commitments] will not give the developing world the 'policy space' to use the very instruments and tools that many industrialized nations took advantage of to reach their current levels of development."[69] Vietnam, which is a member of the World Trade Organization, demonstrates decisively that state-led capitalism is not only possible but also effective, even in the era of more extensive global trade rules and restrictions.[70]

Second, a better understanding of development in Vietnam may be especially valuable because it can offer insight as to which lessons can or should be gleaned from China. Given China's meteoric economic rise, there is understandably much interest in China. However, it is often hard to draw lessons from China for other developing countries primarily because of its size. With 20 percent of humanity, China can use its scale to achieve things that are simply unthinkable in other countries. Fortunately for development scholars, much of what is unfolding in China has also been taking place in Vietnam. Both societies are transitioning at their own pace and largely in their own terms from more insular, centrally-planned economies towards globally integrated, state-led market economies. But in the case of Vietnam we can better assess what works or is relevant—institutionally, socially, and culturally—in a developing society that does not have the advantage of China's size.

Third, and most importantly for the project at hand, Vietnam offers (especially when contrasted to Brazil) a powerful heuristic case for highlighting the significance of culture. This was, of course, what initially attracted me to this comparison. Missing in Vietnam are many of the institutional ingredients that many North Atlantic development experts presume are key to making development successful. There is no democratic polity or free press. Civil society, at least as measured by non-governmental organizations, is small. Civil servants are selected more by party affiliation than by merit and are widely criticized as corrupt. In Brazil the institutional landscape is much the opposite: all adults are required to vote in a competitive electoral system; many municipalities have impressive participatory democracies[72]; the federal government is at the vanguard of the international transparency movement[73]; the press is free of government control; and there are thousands of voluntary associations. In sum, the fact that the country with the "better" institutions (at least as defined by North Atlantic development experts) is being outperformed by the country with the "poorer" institutions should open up even some of the most ardent skeptics of interpretive economics to a consideration of the socio-cultural.

A way one could account for this anomaly would be to note that at present Brazil is much wealthier than Vietnam in terms of per capita income ($16,200 versus $5700 as of 2014).[74] However, it seems likely that this gap will continue to close in the coming decades much as has been the case throughout East Asia. In the 1950s few if any would have predicted that South Korea would surpass the Brazilian economy by the end of the century. Yet this is precisely what happened so that now the South Korean economy is more than twice as strong as the Brazilian one as measured by per capita income ($35,400 versus $16,200 as of 2014).[75] With the exception of North Korea, an eclectic mix of East Asian countries has experienced robust and sustained economic growth in the past half century, and most indicators suggest that Vietnam is following this regional pattern. In just thirty years it has gone from being one of the poorest countries in the world, in which the country imported rice and large segments of society were malnourished, to becoming one of the largest exporters of rice and having one of the lowest poverty rates in the world. Vietnam has also equaled if not surpassed most middle-income economies, such as Brazil and Thailand, in manufacturing output (as measured by percentage of world manufacturing). And if the growth trends of the past thirty years hold, Vietnam's per capita income will be higher than Brazil's in just twenty years.

Another potential explanation for this counter-intuitive relationship between institutions and economic performance in Vietnam and Brazil would be to argue that macro-economic policy is more important than institutions. That is, what really matters is the fact that Vietnam has been pursuing state-led development and Brazil has been following a more laissez-faire set of policies. This, however, ultimately brings one back to the question of why developmentalism failed in Latin America in the mid-twentieth century and has performed so well in East Asia. As discussed above, much of the comparative development literature, in attempting to answer this very question, has settled on the conclusion that the East Asian developmental state has been effective because of such factors as infant industrial policies that are driven by exports, monetary policies that prioritize capital improvements over inflation, tight controls on foreign direct investments, and government bureaucrats who are better paid, more insulated from the industrial and agricultural elites, and tend to be professional civil servants rather than political appointees. The major weakness with this answer, we have learned, is its analytical formalism. That is, the socio-cultural context is ignored or bracketed as a kind of dark matter. Even those scholars who recognize the significance of culture, such as Ben Schneider and Ha-Joon Chang discussed earlier, offer an insufficient operationalization of these influences and a lackluster theorization of how they lead to outcomes such as generating a higher degree of commitment among the elite and civil servants to societal interests.

The discussion of social diversity, which surfaces from time to time in the development literature (and even more so, at least in my experience, in popular thought), offers yet another example of how development theory tends to dissolve as it wades into cultural waters. T. J. Pempel argues, for instance, that East Asian states and their elites demonstrate a more genuine commitment to national development because of these societies are more socially homogenous. He writes, "the low levels of ethnic, religious, linguistic, racial, and other noneconomic divergences of Japan, South Korea, and Taiwan contrast starkly with conditions facing other developing countries, where such differences have often superseded any sense of overriding common nationhood. . . ."[76] Assuming for the moment that this empirical claim is true, there is a theoretical gap that still needs to be filled in. How does homogeneity lead to a common nationhood? Conversely how does heterogeneity, in places like Latin America, result in a weakened or more fragmented nation? In *What about Mozart? What about Murder?* Howard Becker describes this as a black box in which "we don't know what we most want to know: how what goes in (usually called the inputs) becomes what comes out at the other end (the outputs)."[77] Pempel never details what exactly about homogeneity and heterogeneity matters and in what particular ways. Is racism, multicultural movements, a clash of cultures, somatic distinctions, or something else about heterogeneity the issue? There is a great deal at stake in how we answer this question because if we conclude, for example, that cultural diversity is the problem, then the solution likely becomes one of trying to create a more homogenous society via restrictions on immigration, heavy-handed assimilation programs, and limitations on multicultural movements. Or if we decide that racism is the culprit, then we, as development practitioners, are suddenly tasked with generating and supporting various kinds of anti-racist initiatives.

If such theoretical shortcomings characterize the analyses of development scholars like T. J. Pempel, who, to their credit, give some consideration to the socio-cultural, then the reader will not be surprised to learn that the broader development literature, given its aculturalism, is littered with black boxes vis-à-vis some of its most fundamental development variables. Fortunately, interpretive economics offers a potent tool for filling in many of these explanatory holes. In the following chapters, I demonstrate how once development scholars take identities, symbols, discourses, and norms more seriously and draw on the sophisticated tools of cultural studies, it becomes clearer how certain inputs lead to preferred outputs that in turn allow us to identify effective solutions to development woes in places like Latin America.

Methodology

To state that culture is important is just the beginning. The next step—and the really hard work—is to sort out which facets of culture are economically important and why. This is no small task given how vast the cultural landscape can be in any society or subculture.

My method for identifying the economically relevant cultural variables began with my extensive knowledge of Brazil. When I formally started this project in November of 2003, thanks to a Luce Fellowship through the Asia Foundation in Hanoi, I had already spent several years conducting ethnographic research in both rural and urban regions of the states of Minas Gerais and Rio de Janeiro.[78] Thus, as I began my fieldwork in Vietnam, I let my instincts as an area studies expert, who had thought a lot about race, class, nation, and modernity in Brazil, guide me in uncovering key points of interest.

My other compass was the development literature, and especially the comparative development literature in which scholars had already thought a great deal about the differences between Latin America and East Asia. Their concerns with capacity-building, effective bureaucracies, social capital, participatory democracy, social inequality, and institutional monocropping allowed me to winnow down which cultural distinctions to privilege. For example, in parts of Brazil it is believed that if you put your butt on a watermelon seed when you plant it that it will grow big. This sort of cultural particularity is interesting but it is the kind of difference that I ignored because I did not see how it connected with any of the development variables identified by the comparativists.

Since 2003 I have spent a combined nine months in Vietnam conducting research and teaching. During the winter and spring of 2004 and summers of 2006, 2008, and 2010, the majority of my time was spent in Hanoi and the surrounding Red River Delta, but I also made brief visits and conducted some research in central Vietnam (primarily in and around Da Nang) and in the south (brief visits to Ho Chi Minh City, Long An, and Can Tho). While conducting fieldwork, I tried to stay as open as possible to discovery. I read a great deal of fiction, history, biographies, and social science literature. I viewed a number of Vietnamese films and documentaries. I talked informally with as many people as were willing to talk with me. I visited museums, read the English-language newspaper, and hung out in art galleries. I frequented the World Bank library and met with scholars, government officials, and development practitioners. I also sought out and reviewed any relevant survey data such as the World Values Survey.

As distinctions, themes, and patterns began to emerge, I used these inklings and insights to help craft the questions for my formal interviews (see Appendix A: Interview Schedule). Using a snowball sampling technique—which means that I asked anyone I knew if they or someone they knew would be amenable to being interviewed—I tried to talk with as diverse a mix of persons as I could find: teachers, taxi drivers, farmers, night watchmen, artists, architects, lawyers, doctors, administrative assistants, government employees, software developers, entrepreneurs, domestic servants, factory workers, and hotel managers (see Appendix B: Demographics of Interviewees).

The interviews were usually conducted with the help of a translator. The one advantage of this is that it gave me time to think about follow-up questions and bounce ideas off the translator who inevitably became a useful informant. I should add that even though I had official approval from the Vietnamese government to conduct these interviews, I later learned that many of the 2004 interviewees—and perhaps all of them—were questioned by the police (*canh sat chim*) about my research project and their answers to my questions. This chilling backdrop may have impacted how these interviewees responded to certain questions although I did not notice any differences between these people's responses and the ones I interviewed in subsequent years.

Over the course of conducting ethnographic work in Vietnam, I continued to return to Brazil to give academic talks, teach, and conduct research. Most of my fieldwork focused on completing a documentary, *From the Bottom Up*.[79] This film maps out the relationship between identities and socio-economic change in Aracuai, Minas Gerais, and is the case study of successful development cultural work detailed in Chapter 5. These trips—primarily to Rio de Janeiro and Aracuai during the summers of 2003, 2005, 2007, 2009, 2011, and 2013—allowed me to keep checking, testing, and nuancing my findings about what I believed to be the most economically relevant cultural differences between Brazil and Vietnam.

Figure 1.2 Author in Can Tho. Photograph by author, 2010

Despite having spent over fourteen years thinking about and conducting research in Vietnam, I still consider myself foremost a Brazilianist. Much of this has to do with formal training and language skills. At UC Berkeley, where I completed my PhD in sociology in 1997, I studied with some of the finest US Brazilianists: Linda Lewin, Peter Evans, Candice Slater, Nancy Scheper-Hughes. In contrast, virtually everything that I know about Vietnam has been self-taught. Moreover, I speak Portuguese well—or at least well enough to give academic talks and discuss anything I wish to—but the same is not true of Vietnamese. Despite always studying Vietnamese when I am in Vietnam, I would describe my language skills as somewhere in the second-year-college-level range.

Because of these factors there is a higher chance that I have misread or simply gotten wrong certain aspects of Vietnamese society. This possibility is enhanced by the fact that there is a lot less social scientific research on Vietnam than Brazil from which to draw in order to situate and confirm my findings. Much of the quality scholarship on Vietnam has been, at least until recently, historical.[80] This has much to do with the centrality of the anti-colonial, socialist revolution to the formation of contemporary Vietnam, which all but begged for an analysis of the origins, successes, and meanings of the revolution. Another reason for the historical emphasis has been that until recently Vietnam was a very closed society, at least for scholars located outside of the socialist bloc. This made ethnographic work virtually impossible. There are, fortunately, a growing number of excellent ethnographies but their numbers pale in comparison to Brazil. To date all of them focus on either Saigon or rural Vietnam, and none, to my knowledge, are based on fieldwork in Hanoi, which is a primary focus of this book.[81] Just the fact that this could be one of the few (if not the only!) post-colonial ethnographies of Hanoi speaks volumes. It would be unimaginable to make a similar claim about Rio de Janeiro or Sao Paulo. Despite all the caveats about my lack of formal training, language skills, and the relatively small social scientific literature with which to substantiate my empirical claims, I am confident that most area studies experts will find my description of the Vietnamese cultural terrain fairly non-controversial. Given that I have done extensive fieldwork and conducted scores of in-depth interviews I undoubtedly offer some original data to general understandings of Vietnamese society, but most Vietnamese experts will likely regard my central assertions about class, nation, the countryside, and modernity to be very much in line with conventional academic wisdom. Indeed this study's most original contribution to both Vietnamese and Brazilian studies stems much less from its empirical findings than from its contrapuntal reference. In a classic anthropological move, the juxtaposition of these societies helps to make the familiar strange. That is, that which is normally taken for granted, viewed as inevitable, or not regarded as particularly noteworthy within the confines of these area studies takes on a very different hue from a comparative vantage. For example, many Brazilianists assume that the poor will inevitably be disparaged by elites or national identities will be weakened by market-led globalization. A consideration of Vietnam, however, quickly demonstrates how such expectations are wrong. Area studies specialists will find, then, that this comparison helps to expose and unsettle a number of basic suppositions in their fields, which should ultimately lead to better understandings of key issues in both Brazil and Vietnam.

Finally, as a qualitative sociologist with a specialization in semiotics and discourse analysis, I have never fit neatly within the mainstream of US sociology, which tends to be more quantitative and positivistic. Nonetheless, in the book *Salsa Dancing into the Social Sciences*, Kristin Luker (who was also one of my mentors in graduate school) helped me to see how I am very much a sociologist of the times given my identity as a public scholar.[82] What this "public" means is that I am more interested in answering "the big questions that beset society and preoccupy ordinary people, not just those questions that are thought to be the straight line to prestige within a small coterie of social science scholars."[83] Development is, without a doubt, one of the enormous issues of the present era. The desire for better paying jobs and work conditions, higher quality health care and schools, nicer homes and modes of transportation—all of which is encapsulated in most peoples' minds with the idea of development—is universal on a scale unrivaled. Indeed the goal of development transcends or cuts across most religions, political ideologies, and nation states perhaps like no other. Moreover, it is a project around which unimaginable resources have been invested, human and physical landscapes completely remade, and countless lives altered beyond recognition and oftentimes for the worse. Thus, the paramount goal of *Cultures of Development* is to help enhance the prosperity and well-being of ordinary people throughout the world. This does not mean that academic debates are not advanced in the process—the reader will find that they most certainly are—but these scholastic, disciplinary, and professional concerns are secondary to my desire to figure out how to enhance economic well-being in countries like Vietnam and Brazil.

Overview

In the next chapter, "The Poison of Progress," I offer an answer to a troublesome human capital riddle in development studies. I argue that the significantly different levels of investment in capacity building in Vietnam and Brazil are a direct result of the discourses of class and countryside in the two countries. In Brazil I found that class was clear-cut, adversarial, and overlaid by race. The Vietnamese, in contrast, had notions of class that were much less mean-spirited and polarized. In interviews, persons of means were much more charitable toward the less affluent; something that was unusual in Brazil. Coupled with class and its meanings is the matter of rurality. In Brazil, rural spaces were referred to as the interior and imagined as a source of backwardness; whereas in Vietnam there were pejorative notions of the countryside but they were often balanced, if not outweighed, by an idealization of the countryside as the hearth of Vietnamese culture, nation, and anti-colonialism.

In Chapter 3, "Indigenizing Modernity," I point out how the institutional thesis in development studies, which posits a causal link between political democracy and degrees of institutional monocropping, does not hold for these two countries. The alternative explanation I forward hinges on different notions of tradition and modernity. I found that in Vietnam tradition was viewed as something to be preserved within the modern. Whereas Brazilians tended to see modernization as a racial-colonial project of replacing tradition with the modern. These distinct epistemologies of tradition and modernity, I argue, are what lead to more imitative development projects in Brazil and less institutional monocropping in Vietnam.

Chapter 4, "Corruption and the Commons," explores a number of aspects of society related to the broad theme of social capital. Trust and social solidarity, two of the hallmarks of social capital are in much shorter supply in Brazil than in Vietnam. Brazilianists often attribute the low levels of social capital in Brazil to an underdeveloped individualism. With Vietnam as the referent such a thesis makes little sense because individualism is not more developed in Vietnam than

Brazil and yet, social solidarity and trust are more vibrant in Vietnam. The alternative explanation and policy prescriptions that I propose revolve around efforts to bring honor codes in line with ethics and the law, build more currency for the metanarrative of nation through anti-racist interventions, and reduce violence through measures like police reform and challenging crime narratives.

What emerges in Chapters 2, 3 and 4 is a keen sense of how certain facets of culture impede economic growth in Brazil. In the context of these chapters, the labor of various artists, social scientists, activists, and educators can be seen for the development work that it is—a central point of Chapter 5. More specifically, the economic importance of the cultural work that pedagogues, church choirs, and ethnographers have being doing in the Jequitinhonha Valley of Minas Gerais over the past three decades—a region that in the 1960s was considered by UNESCO to be one of the poorest in the world—is rendered visible in "Development Lore." This case study also allows me to give a concrete face to the cultural work of development and demonstrate its feasibility and cost-effectiveness, a concern often raised by development practitioners once they begin to take culture seriously.

In the final chapter, "Trade Tips," I offer some suggestions for development scholars and practitioners who wish to begin incorporating culture into their analysis and add cultural work to their menu of applied options. The aim of these recommendations is to entice and help guide future interpretive economists. My hope is that by attracting and mentoring more development scholars in the science of cultural studies I can help to foster a collective effort to advance the cultural turn within development circles in the direction of interpretive economics.

Notes

1 Freire, *Pedagogy of the Oppressed*, 32.
2 Sivaramakrishnan and Agrawal, "Regional Modernities in Stories and Practices of Development," 23.
3 Ernst, *Forging a Fateful Alliance*.
4 This has changed some in recent years with the gradual implementation of race and class based affirmative action admission policies at most federal universities. See Htun, "From 'Racial Democracy' to Affirmative Action," 60–89.
5 Laderman, *Tours of Vietnam*; and Masina, *Vietnam's Development Strategies*.
6 Gainsborough, *Vietnam*, 56.
7 Gainsborough, *Vietnam*; Fforde and De Vylder, *From Plan to Market*; and Masina, *Vietnam's Development Strategies*.
8 Babb, *Managing Mexico*, xiv.
9 BRICS is the acronym for the five emerging national economies (Brazil, Russia, India, China, and South Africa) that was coined by the chairman of Goldman Sachs Asset Management, Jim O'Neill in 2001. BRICS are distinguished by their large, sometimes fast growing economies and significant influence on regional and global affairs. Since 2010, the BRICS nations have met annually at formal submits.
10 See *Life and Debt*, directed by Stephanie Black, New York Films, 2001. 80 minutes.
11 Hira, *An East Asian Model for Latin American Success*.
12 Kerstenetzky, "The Brazilian Developmental State," 182.
13 Gallagher and Porzecanski, *The Dragon in the Room*, 15.
14 Baer, "Dois dilemas no caminho" (Two dilemmas on the path), 78.
15 Pessoa, "Estamos errados" (We are wrong), 44.

16 Gallagher and Porzecanski, *The Dragon in the Room*, 48–49.
17 Gallagher and Porzecanski, *The Dragon in the Room*, 56.
18 Cimoli and Katz, "Structural Reforms, Technological Gaps and Economic Development."
19 Taylor, "Two Theories of Modernity," 178.
20 Rational choice theories have been adapted, to varying degrees, by a number of the other social science disciplines, in particular political science and international studies, to explain not only market economies but also politics and society. I agree with Bruce Cumings' observation that the effect of this "colonization" of the social sciences by "the historically limited and contingent theory of the rational, interest-maximizing individual" has been to "abolish them as creators of worthwhile knowledge."
21 See, for instance, Kahneman and Tversky (Eds.), *Choices, Values, and Frames*. The one notable exception to this rule is *Identity Economics* by George A. Akerlof and Rachael Kranton.
22 Epstein, *Forbidden Grounds*, 10–11.
23 Alexander, *The New Jim Crow*; Nelson, *Volunteer Slavery*; Darity and Myers, *Persistent Disparity*; Singh, *Black is a Country*; Lubiano, *The House that Race Built*; Brown, et al. *Whitewashing Race*.
24 Ha-Joon Chang makes a similar point in *Kicking Away the Ladder*.
25 Campbell, "Post-Autistic Economics," 1.
26 Akerlof and Kranton, *Identity Economics,* 10.
27 For an excellent genealogy and critique of the neoliberal wing of the good governance movement within development studies see *Is Good Governance Good for Development?* Summarizing the research on the relationship between good governance and economic growth, Sundaram and Chowdhury note "there is little convincing evidence that improved or good governance accelerates growth" (10).
28 Wade, *Governing the Market*, 111.
29 Johnson, "The Developmental State," 40. See also Anil Hira's *An East Asian Model for Latin American Success*.
30 Evans, *Embedded Autonomy*.
31 Rafael, *White Love*, 107–108 .
32 Schneider, "The *Desarrollista* State in Brazil and Mexico," 293.
33 Ibid., 303.
34 Chang, "The East Asian Model of Economic Policy," 208.
35 Radcliffe, (Ed.), *Culture and Development in a Globalizing World*, 2.
36 Pieterse, *Development Theory*, 64.
37 Fairbank, Reischauer, and Craig, *East Asia*.
38 Harrison, "Do Some Religions Do Better than Others?," 15. See also "Haiti and the Voodoo Curse," *The Wall Street Journal*, February 6, 2010: A13.
39 Ibid., 16.
40 *The Look of Silence*, Oppenheimer.
41 Li, *The Will to Improve*, 248.
42 Ibid.
43 Li, *The Will to Improve*, 231 and 249.
44 Pieterse, *Development Theory*, 68.
45 United Nations Country Team Viet Nam, *Culture and Development in Viet Nam*, i.
46 The authors of this report were invoking idealized notions of the local in part an attempt to counter the racism against the 15 percent of the population that is viewed as culturally and linguistically distinct in Vietnam. This "noble savage" move has been a common anti-racist strategy in many parts of the world over the past two hundred years but it is ultimately a deeply flawed one because it hinges upon a racist conceptual grid. Most contemporary critical race scholars agree that it is much wiser to address racism head-on. In Vietnam this would mean identifying, denouncing, and working to reform Kinh racism against ethnic minorities rather than focusing energies on a romanticized celebration of minorities' cultures.

47 Amable, *The Diversity of Modern Capitalism.*
48 Jessop and Oosterlynck, "Cultural Political Economy," 1168.
49 Best and Paterson, *Cultural Political Economy*, 3.
50 Lawson, "Beyond the Firm."
51 Wilk, *Economies and Cultures*, 17.
52 Brook and Luong, *Culture and Economy*, 19–20.
53 See Wilson, *The Intimate Economies of Bangkok.*
54 Bhavnani, et al., *On the Edges of Development*, 5.
55 Ferguson, *The Anti-Politics Machine*, 279.
56 Li, *The Will to Improve*, 2.
57 Sivaramakrishnan and Agrawal, "Regional Modernities in Stories and Practices of Development," 31.
58 Pieterse, *Development Theory*, 73.
59 Li, *The Will to Improve*, 2.
60 Bergquist, *Labor and the Course of American Democracy*, 9.
61 Olivier de Sardan, *Anthropology and Development*, 28.
62 Antonio Cosme, thirty-nine-year-old sugar cane cutter. Interviewed by Jonathan Warren in Aracuai, Brazil, 2011.
63 The first university was founded in Parana in 1912, but it only survived for three years. Afterwards the Federal University of Rio de Janeiro was established in 1920. It began as a military and engineering school in 1792 and then added a medical school in 1808. The next oldest university in Brazil is the University of Sao Paulo which began in 1934.
64 McHale, *Print and Power*, 67.
65 St. George, "Reimagining the Role of Education for Development in Vietnam, 2015 Vietnam Update," Australian National University, November 12, 2015.
66 "People" does not have the same meaning in English as it does in Brazil. In Brazilian Portuguese it invokes the poorer, non-elite popular sectors that are predominantly of color. In much of the English-speaking world, "people" does not have such specific class and racial connotations. Therefore to avoid confusion, I use *povo* instead of people throughout the book.
67 Kozol, *Savage Inequalities*, 53.
68 Edwards, "Uma nova China?" (A new China?), 38.
69 Gallagher (Ed.), *Putting Development First*, 1.
70 Masina, *Vietnam's Development Strategies.*
71 See Hannah, "The Mutual Colonization of State and Civil Society Organizations in Vietnam"; Kerkvliet, Nguyen, and Sinh, "Forms of Engagement Between State Agencies & Civil Society Organizations in Vietnam."
72 Baiocchi, *Militants and Citizens.*
73 Alves and Heller, "Accountability from the Top Down?"
74 Central Intelligence Agency. *The World Factbook.* www.cia.gov/library/publications/the-world-fact-book. Accessed July 26, 2015.
75 Ibid.
76 Pempel, "The Developmental Regime in a Changing World Economy," 168.
77 Becker, *What about Mozart? What about Murder?* 62.
78 Warren, *Racial Revolutions.*
79 Macklin and Warren, *From the Bottom Up.*
80 Ninh, *A World Transformed: The Politics of Culture in Revolutionary Vietnam, 1945–1965*; Malarney, *Culture, Ritual and Revolution in Vietnam*; Pelley, *Postcolonial Vietnam*; Kerkvliet, *The Power of Everyday Politics*; Giebel, *Imagined Ancestries of Vietnamese Communism*; and McHale, *Print and Power.*
81 Malarney, *Culture, Ritual and Revolution in Vietnam*; Taylor, *Fragments of the Present*; Harms, *Saigon's Edge*; and Nguyen-Vo, *The Ironies of Freedom.*
82 Luker, *Salsa Dancing Into the Social Sciences*, 17.
83 Ibid., 17.

Bibliography

Akerlof, George A., and Rachael Kranton. *Identity Economics: How our Identities Shape Our Work, Wages and Well-Being*. Princeton, NJ: Princeton University Press, 2010.

Alexander, Michelle. *The New Jim Crow: Mass Incarceration in the Age of Colorblindness*. New York: The New Press, 2010.

Alves, Jorge Antonio, and Patrick Heller. "Accountability From the Top Down? Brazil's Advances in Budget Accountability Despite a Lack of Popular Mobilization." In *Open Budgets: The Political Economy of Transparency, Participation and Accountability*, Sanjeev Khagram, Archon Fung, and Paolo de Renzio (Eds.), 76–104. Washington, DC: The Brookings Institution, 2013.

Amable, Bruno. *The Diversity of Modern Capitalism*. New York: Oxford University Press, 2003.

Amsden, Alice. *Asia's Next Giant: South Korea and Late Industrialization*. Oxford: Oxford University Press, 1989.

Babb, Sarah L. *Managing Mexico: Economists from Nationalism to Neoliberalism*. Princeton, NJ: Princeton University Press, 2001.

Baer, Werner. "Dois dilemas no caminho" (Two dilemmas on the path). *Exame CEO* (October 2010): 76–79.

Baiocchi, Gianpaolo. *Militants and Citizens: The Politics of Participatory Democracy in Porto Alegre*. Palo Alto, CA: Stanford University Press, 2005.

Becker, Howard. *What about Mozart? What about Murder? Reasoning from Cases*. Chicago, IL: The University of Chicago Press, 2014.

Bergquist, Charles. *Labor and the Course of American Democracy: US History in Latin American Perspective*. New York: Verso, 1996.

Best, Jacqueline, and Matthew Paterson (Eds.). *Cultural Political Economy*. New York: Routledge, 2010.

Bhavnani, Kum-Kum, John Foran, Priya A. Kurian, and Debashish Munshi. "Introduction: From the Edges of Development." In *On the Edges of Development: Cultural Interventions*, Kum-Kum Bhavnani, John Foran, Priya A. Kurian, and Debashish Munshi (Eds.), 1–12. New York: Routledge, 2009.

Brook, Timothy, and Hy V. Luong (Eds.). *Culture and Economy: The Shaping of Capitalism in Eastern Asia*. Ann Arbor, MI: University of Michigan Press, 1999.

Brown, Michael K., Martin Carnoy, Elliot Currie, Troy Duster, David B. Oppenheimer, Marjorie M. Shultz, and David Wellman. *Whitewashing Race: The Myth of a Color-Blind Society*. Berkeley, CA: University of California Press, 2003.

Campbell, Deborah. "Post-Autistic Economics." *True Cost Economics*. April 11, 2006. www.adbusters.org/metas/eco/truecosteconomics/post-autistic.html. Accessed July 15, 2009.

Cardoso, Fernando Henrique. *Capitalismo e escravidão no Brasil meridional: O negro na sociedade escravocrata do Rio Grande do Su* (Capitalism and slavery in southern Brazil: slave society in Rio Grande do Sul). Sao Paulo: Difusao Europeia do Livro, 1962.

Central Intelligence Agency (CIA). *The World Factbook*. www.cia.gov/library/publications/the-world-fact-book. Accessed July 26, 2015.

Chang, Ha-Joon. "The East Asian Model of Economic Policy." In *Models of Capitalism: Lessons from Latin America*, Evelyn Huber (Ed.), 197–236. University Park, PA: The Pennsylvania State University Press, 2002.

Chang, Ha-Joon. *Kicking Away the Ladder: Development Strategy in Historical Perspective*. London: Anthem Press. 2002.

Cimoli, Mario, and Jorge Katz. "Structural Reforms, Technological Gaps and Economic Development: A Latin American Perspective." *Industrial and Corporate Change* 12, no. 2 (2003): 387–411.

Cumings, Bruce. "Boundary Displacement: The State, the Foundations, and Area Studies during and after the Cold War." In *Learning Places: The Afterlives of Area Studies*, Masao Miyoshi and H.D. Harootunian (Eds.), 261–302. Durham, NC: Duke University Press, 2002.

Darity, William A. Jr., and Samuel L. Myers, Jr. *Persistent Disparity: Race and Economic Inequality in the United States Since 1945*. Cheltenham, UK: Edward Elgar Publishing Company, 1998.

Degler, Carl N. *Neither Black nor White: Slavery and Race Relations in Brazil and the United States*. New York: Macmillan, 1971.

Edwards, Sebastian. "Uma nova China?" (A new China?). *CEO Exame* (October 2010): 34–38.

Epstein, Richard Allen. *Forbidden Grounds: The Case against Employment Discrimination Laws*. Cambridge, MA: Harvard University Press, 1992.

Ernst, John. *Forging a Fateful Alliance: Michigan State University and the Vietnam War*. East Lansing, MI: Michigan State University Press, 1998.

Evans, Peter B. *Embedded Autonomy: States and Industrial Transformation*. Princeton, NJ: Princeton University Press, 1995.

Fairbank, John K., Edwin O. Reischauer, and Albert M. Craig. *East Asia: Tradition and Transformation*. Boston, MA: Houghton Mifflin, 1978.

Ferguson, James. *The Anti-Politics Machine: Development, Depoliticization, and Bureaucratic Power in Lesotho*. Minneapolis, MN: University of Minnesota Press, 1994.

Fforde, Adam, and Stefan De Vylder. *From Plan to Market: The Economic Transition in Vietnam*. Boulder, CO: Westview Press, 1996.

From the Bottom Up (*De baixo para cima*). Directed by Angelica Macklin and Jonathan Warren. San Francisco, CA: Kanopy, 2016.

Freire, Paulo. *Pedagogy of the Oppressed*. New York: Continuum, 1993 (1970).

Gainsborough, Martin. *Vietnam: Rethinking the State*. Chiang Mai, Thailand: Zed-Silkworm Books, 2010.

Gallagher, Kevin P. (Ed.). *Putting Development First: The Importance of Policy Space in the WTO and International Financial Institutions*. New York: Zed Books, 2005.

Gallagher, Kevin P., and Roberto Porzecanski. *The Dragon in the Room: China and the Future of Latin American Industrialization*. Stanford, CA: Stanford University Press, 2010.

Giebel, Christoph. *Imagined Ancestries of Vietnamese Communism*. Seattle, WA: University of Washington Press, 2004.

Hannah, Joseph J. "The Mutual Colonization of State and Civil Society Organizations in Vietnam." In *Local Organizations and Urban Governance in East and Southeast Asia: Straddling State and Society*, Benjamin L. Read and Robert Pekkanen (Eds.), 84–100. New York: Routledge, 2009.

Harms, Erik. *Saigon's Edge: On the Margins of Ho Chi Minh City*. Minneapolis, MN: University of Minnesota Press, 2011.

Harrison, Lawrence E. "Do Some Religions Do Better Than Others?" In *The Hidden Form of Capital: Spiritual Influences in Societal Progress*, Peter L. Berger and Gordon Redding (Eds.), 15–28. London: Anthem Press, 2010.

Harrison, Lawrence E. "Haiti and the Voodoo Curse," *The Wall Street Journal*, February 6, 2010: A13.

Hira, Anil. *An East Asian Model for Latin American Success: A New Path*. Aldershot, UK: Ashgate Publishing Limited, 2007.

Htun, Mala. "From 'Racial Democracy' to Affirmative Action: Changing State Policy on Race in Brazil." *Latin American Research Review* 39, no. 1 (2004): 60–89.

Jessop, Bob, and Stijn Oosterlynck. "Cultural Political Economy: On Making the Cultural Turn without Falling into Soft Economic Sociology." *Geoforum* 39 (2008): 1155–1169.

Johnson, Chalmers. "The Developmental State: Odyssey of a Concept." In *The Developmental State*, Meredith Woo-Cumings (Ed.) 32–60. Ithaca, NY: Cornell University Press, 1999.

Kahneman, Daniel, and Amos Tversky (Eds.). *Choices, Values, and Frames*. Cambridge, UK: Cambridge University Press, 2000.

Kerkvliet, Benedict J. Tria. *The Power of Everyday Politics: How Vietnamese Peasants Transformed National Policy*. Ithaca, NY: Cornell University Press, 2005.

Kerkvliet, Benedict J. Tria, Quang A. Nguyen, and Baeh Tan Sinh. "Forms of Engagement Between State Agencies & Civil Society Organizations in Vietnam" (study report). VUFO-NGO Resource Center, Hanoi, Vietnam, December 2008.

Kerstenetzky, Celia Lessa. "The Brazilian Developmental State: A Progressive Agenda in a (Still) Conservative Political Economy." In *The End of the Developmental State?*, Michelle Williams (Ed.), 172–196. New York: Routledge, 2014.

Klein, Naomi. *The Shock Doctrine: The Rise of Disaster Capitalism*. New York: Picador, 2007.

Kozol, Jonathan. *Savage Inequalities: Children in America's Schools*. New York: Crown Publishers, 1991.

Laderman, Scott. *Tours of Vietnam: War, Travel Guides, and Memory*. Durham, NC: Duke University Press, 2009.

Lawson, Victoria. "Beyond the Firm: Restructuring Gender Divisions of Labor in Quito's Garment Industry under Austerity." *Environment and Planning D: Society and Space* 13, no. 4 (1995): 415–444.

Li, Tania Murray. *The Will to Improve: Governmentality, Development, and the Practice of Politics*. Durham, NC: Duke University Press, 2007.

Life and Debt. Directed by Stephanie Black. New York Films, 2001.

Look of Silence, The. Directed by Joshua Oppenheimer. Final Cut for Real, 2014.

Lubiano, Wahneema (Ed.) *The House that Race Built*. New York: Vintage Press, 1998.

Luker, Kristin. *Salsa Dancing into the Social Sciences: Research in the Age of Info-Glut*. Cambridge, MA: Harvard University Press, 2008.

McHale, Shawn Frederick. *Print and Power: Confucianism, Communism, and Buddhism in the Making of Modern Vietnam*. Honolulu: University of Hawai'i Press, 2004.

Malarney, Shaun. *Culture, Ritual and Revolution in Vietnam*. 1st ed. London: Routledge, 2002.

Masina, Pietro. *Vietnam's Development Strategies*. New York: Routledge, 2006.

Nelson, Jill. *Volunteer Slavery: My Authentic Negro Experience*. New York: Penguin Press, 1993.

Nguyen-Vo, Thu-Huong. *The Ironies of Freedom: Sex, Culture, and Neoliberal Governance in Vietnam*. Seattle, WA: University of Washington Press, 2008.

Ninh, Kim N. B. *A World Transformed: The Politics of Culture in Revolutionary Vietnam, 1945–1965*. Ann Arbor, MI: University of Michigan Press, 2002.

Olivier de Sardan, Jean-Pierre. *Anthropology and Development: Understanding Contemporary Social Change*. London: Zed Books, 2005.

Pelley, Patricia M. *Postcolonial Vietnam: New Histories of the National Past*. 1st ed. Durham, NC: Duke University Press, 2002.

Pempel, T. J. "The Developmental Regime in a Changing World Economy." In *The Developmental State*, Meredith Woo-Cumings (Ed.), 137–181. Ithaca, NY: Cornell University Press, 1999.

Pessoa, Samuel. "Estamos errados" (We are wrong). *Exame CEO* (October 2010): 40–44.
Pieterse, Jan Nederveen. *Development Theory*. 2nd ed. London: Sage Publications, 2010.
Radcliffe, Sarah A. (Ed.). *Culture and Development in a Globalizing World: Geographies, Actors and Paradigms*. New York: Routledge, 2006.
Rafael, Vincent L. *White Love and Other Events in Filipino History*. Durham, NC: Duke University Press, 2000.
Schneider, Ben Ross. "The *Desarrollista* State in Brazil and Mexico." In *The Developmental State*, Meredith Woo-Cumings (Ed.), 276–305. Ithaca, NY: Cornell University Press, 1999.
Schwarz, Roberto. *Misplaced Ideas: Essays on Brazilian Culture: Critical Studies in Latin American Culture*. London/New York: Verso, 1992.
Singh, Nikhil. *Black is a Country: Race and the Unfinished Struggle for Democracy*. Cambridge, MA: Harvard University Press, 2004.
Sivaramakrishnan, K., and Arun Agrawal. "Regional Modernities in Stories and Practices of Development." In *Regional Modernities: The Cultural Politics of Development in India*, K. Sivaramakrishnan and A. Agrawal (Eds.), 1–61. New York: Oxford University Press, 2003.
St. George, Elisabeth. "Reimagining the Role of Education for Development in Vietnam, 2015 Vietnam Update." Australian National University. November 12, 2015.
Sundaram, Jomo Kwame, and Anis Chowdhury (Eds.). *Is Good Governance Good for Development?* New York: Bloomsbury, 2012.
Taylor, Charles. "Two Theories of Modernity." In *Alternative Modernities*, Dilip Parameshwar Gaonkar (Ed.), 172–196. Durham, NC: Duke University Press. 2001.
Taylor, Philip. *Fragments of the Present: Searching for Modernity in Vietnam's South*. Honolulu: University of Hawai'i Press, 2000.
United Nations Country Team Viet Nam. *Culture and Development in Viet Nam*. Discussion Paper No. 4 (December 2003).
Wade, Robert. *Governing the Market: Economic Theory and the Role of Government in East Asian Industrialization*. Princeton, NJ: Princeton University Press, 2003.
Warren, Jonathan. *Racial Revolutions: Antiracism and Indian Resurgence in Brazil*. Durham, NC: Duke University Press, 2001.
Wilk, Richard R. *Economies and Cultures: Foundations of Economic Anthropology*. Boulder, CO: Westview Press, 1996.
Wilson, Ara. *The Intimate Economies of Bangkok: Tomboys, Tycoons, and Avon Ladies in the Global City*. 1st ed. Berkeley, CA: University of California Press, 2004.
Woodside, Alexander. *Lost Modernities: China, Vietnam, Korea and the Hazards of World History*. Cambridge, MA: Harvard University Press, 2006.
World Bank. www.data.worldbank.org. Accessed March 27, 2014.

2 The Poison of Progress

> Our fathers told their children:
> When you eat a bowl of rice, you must think of the labor of farmers. When you don garments, you must think of the toil of weavers.
>
> Hoang Dao Thuy (1862–1945)[1]

This chapter attempts to solve a puzzle that has dogged development scholars for at least two decades. There is widespread recognition that investment in capacity-building—education, infrastructure, healthcare, and scientific research—is essential for economic growth. It impacts levels of creativity, productivity, and employability; all are seen as foundational for development. Therefore the healthier and better educated the general population is and the more access it has to quality infrastructure, the more efficient and competent it will be as a workforce. Moreover such a society of highly capacitated citizens will be more apt to build and support the kinds of quality governmental and nongovernmental institutions that are often regarded as fundamental for economic well being.

Given the importance of human capital for development, most comparativists point to the unequal levels of human capital in Latin America and East Asia as a leading cause of the contrasting economic outcomes in the regions. What these development scholars have yet to sort out is why fewer resources—usually measured as percentage of GDP—get placed into health care, education, transportation, and other capacity-building endeavors in Latin America. The closest that they get to an explanation is along the lines of the one forwarded by E. V. K. Fitzgerald:

> [O]ne of the main differences between Asian developmental states and their less successful counterparts in Latin America is the inability of the latter to tax their own elites, despite the fact that elites in Latin America appropriate larger shares of the collective national product for themselves. Having the organization capacity and political will necessary to collect adequate revenue was the prerequisite to investing in both capacity expansion and industrial transformation.[2]

The supposition that better organization capacity and more political support for progressive taxation are the reasons for different levels of human capital is ultimately, however, an incomplete thesis. We do not know what we most need to know: why are there varying degrees of organization capacities and political will? As discussed in the previous chapter, most development scholars are ill prepared to fill in these sorts of theoretical black boxes because they ignore or avoid the socio-cultural altogether. And yet even among those who address culture we find, at best, opaque references to "lower levels of social divergence," "fiercer nationalism," or "revolutionary-like development ideology." Hong Yung Lee offers another example of this analytical fuzziness. In the introduction to *A Comparative Study of East Asian Capitalism*, he argues there is less political support for progressive taxation and resource allocation in Latin America because the elite, when compared to the East Asian elite, is more sectarian and less able to understand the long-term interests of society.[3] As is so often the case in the development literature when culture is broached, Lee does not continue on and explain why he believes that the Latin American elite is more sectarian or what may be the basis of this sectarianism, or what in particular about sectarianism is the issue. Moreover, no evidence is offered to back up the assertion that the Latin American elite is less capable of comprehending their societies' long-term interests. Are we to presume that they are less intelligent or attend inferior schools? The point here is not to undress the various comments, musings, and clichés like Lee's that pepper the development literature. Instead I wish merely to further illustrate and highlight the analytical voids that permeate the writings of even those development scholars who show some cultural awareness.

In this chapter I offer a solution to the human capital riddle. I deploy interpretative economics to provide an explanation of why there have been disparate degrees of political support for taxing elites and investing this increased revenue more equitably. In Brazil, as I detail below, I found a racially inflected elitism that was very different from how the Vietnamese interviewed thought about class and the poor. I demonstrate that as a consequence of this social imaginary there has been a formidable anti-poor bias among politicians, bureaucrats, elites, and large segments of the middle and working classes that has resulted in insufficient investments in capacity-building, irrespective of political regime or macroeconomic policy. The implications for development policy are clear-cut: these elitist features of the Brazilian cultural terrain must be undone if human capital is to be increased to the levels that most development economists agree is necessary in order to ensure robust economic growth. To make my case, I begin with a discussion of the emic concepts of class. In Brazil, class identities tended to be adversarial and uncharitable. In Vietnam, in contrast, the reader will discover a spirit of inter-class benevolence often prevailed.

Veneration of the Bourgeoisie

deal of debate among contemporary historians of Vietnam as to
.st two thousand years are best characterized as a remarkably

harmonious relationship between China and Vietnam or a conflict-laden one marked by dogged Vietnamese resistance to repeated Chinese aggressions.[4] Indeed some historians, such as Liam Kelley, have called into question whether there were even any meaningful distinctions between "Chinese" and "Vietnamese" in pre-colonial times, given how identified elites in the Red River Delta were with the Middle Kingdom.[5] Regardless of one's take on this history, no one disputes that the society that became Vietnam was profoundly shaped by China. Sinitic civilization has influenced, to varying degrees, most aspects of Vietnamese society: its cuisine, religion, philosophy, language, art, and medicine.[6]

One of the most notable Chinese legacies in Vietnam, at least until the early twentieth century, was the Mandarinate mode of government. For centuries Vietnamese society was governed by Confucian scholar-officials, who were meritocratically selected based on how well they performed on exams that tested one's mastery of the humanities. In terms of social status, farmers, craftsmen and lastly, merchants or traders followed the literati administrators. Of the three lower classes, only the merchants were stigmatized. Most business practices, according to the orthodox ethics of the Mandarinate era, were understood to be in tension with morality. For example, humanitarianism (*nhan*) and righteousness (*nghia*) were seen as largely incompatible with self-interest and profit (*loi*). It was not that wealth was considered bad per se, but rather it was seen as unlikely that one could be caring and maintain ethical rectitude if one prioritized making money. In this way trade was associated with immorality. This is why scholars, such as Hoang Dao Thuy, have argued that in pre-colonial Vietnam "[t]he trader was regarded as not worth one's esteem. He did not always show self-respect and often told lies. As a result, he was the object of universal contempt."[7] Although an oversimplification of what must have been a very complex and contested symbolic terrain, this certainly represented an important current in Vietnamese thought at the time.

French colonialism, which began in Saigon in 1862 and ended with the military defeat of the French by the communist-led Viet Minh in 1954, threatened to turn this social order on its head. Entrepreneurs—especially those who sold French manufactured goods or produced and secured primary commodities for the French market—were richly rewarded, esteemed, and celebrated by the French colons. David Marr writes that "books and articles were published bearing such evocative titles as 'Paragons of How to Get Rich,' 'Buying Cheap and Selling Dear,' 'Forty-one Occupations Requiring Little Capital,' and 'Wealth is Better than Nobility.' "[8] To traditionalists, these values and priorities were revolting. Knowledge and self-cultivation—not the "crass pursuit of wealth"[9]—should determine status and ruler. Thus from a pre-colonial vantage, moral standards were perceived as having degenerated to the point where "those who have gathered the most money could achieve the greatest power."[10]

The academic literature on class in contemporary Vietnam is very nascent. The few examples of this budding scholarship are Huong Le Thu's and Catherine Earl's studies of the middle class in Hanoi and Ho Chi Minh City.[11] When I began my fieldwork in 2004, however, there was no such research to inform or nuance my expectations. Therefore, I anticipated that the long-standing, historical prejudice against the merchant class, which had been stoked and burnished by the socialist revolution's well-known vilification of the bourgeoisie, would hold some currency. To my surprise, however, even the few disgruntled service and blue-collar workers interviewed—those who saw their workplace treatment as unfair and disrespectful—never drew from this discursive tradition to vent or critique their employers or entrepreneurs in general. Instead business owners and private-sector entrepreneurs were generally held in high regard. The effusive adjectives frequently used were active, intelligent, open-minded, and creative.

I eventually came to see that one reason for this rosy imaginary of private-sector entrepreneurs is that it offers people a coded way of expressing their dissatisfaction with the government. In Vietnam—as in many parts of the world—the private sector is symbolically juxtaposed to the public sector. Consequently in lauding one pole, the other is impugned. In my experience, many Vietnamese are deeply dissatisfied with the Communist Party Vietnam (CPV) controlled government, which is widely viewed as corrupt and inefficient. To take one example, everyone with whom I spoke assumed that the state-owned enterprises (SOEs) that dominate the Vietnamese economy were controlled by individuals with connections to the upper echelon of the CPV rather than by hardworking, qualified managers. Moreover these enterprises were perceived as unjustly receiving and squandering vast amounts of public treasure. Given that public criticism of the government and the CPV is discouraged or prohibited means that disapproving views of government officials, policies, and practices tend to be expressed in private or indirectly. The point here is that the bubbly image of private entrepreneurs should be seen, at least in part, as something that James Scott[12] and Benedict Kerkvliet[13] would recognize as a discourse of dissent. The semiotics are such that a favorable construction of the businessman or woman simultaneously offers an opportunity to invoke the notion of the wasteful, rent-seeking, and unproductive public official. And so, in praising private sector entrepreneurs one can publically vent and draw unfavorable attention to the cronyism and malfeasance of the CPV-controlled government without risk of censure. Given this symbolic backdrop, I sensed that many people heaped on more praise of the private sector than they might have otherwise had it not afforded them a chance to critique the government and the CPV.

Class Antagonisms

As intriguing as the cultural politics of the adulation of private sector entrepreneurs may be, especially given the history of ideas about traders and the bourgeoisie in Vietnam, what I found most noteworthy as a Brazilianist was how muted class hierarchies and imaginings were in Vietnam. To be clear, I am not arguing or attempting to imply that class does not matter. In the context of choosing a mate, various women were blunt that a man's income and wealth was one of the most important factors impacting their willingness to date and marry. For them it trumped ompatibility or kindness. Some men noted that their wives' families against their marriage because the groom's family was poor. I also nual workers were, at times, referred to as brutish and ill mannered.

This is likely why one small business owner who I interviewed, Chau, felt he had taken a step backwards professionally by quitting his job as a general manager of a small hotel in order to start his own motor-bike business, even though he made a great deal more money and had much more free time. His attire symbolized his social descent. One evening while sharing a beer he pointed in obvious disgust to his clothes, which were soiled from repairing bikes, and noted bitterly how he no longer wore a button-down shirt and tie. One further example of the class biases in Vietnam, a few interviewees like Giang, a twenty-four-year-old woman involved in the tourist industry in Hanoi, used Marx's justification of a socialist revolution—the need to overturn capitalism's dehumanizing effects on the proletariat—and twisted it into a rationalization for the belittlement and workplace abuse of blue-collar workers. This daughter of a local Communist party cadre told me in 2004, "The working class is stupid because their work is rote and dehumanizing. Therefore employers have to treat them badly."

Figure 2.1 A Blue-Collar Worker with Her Daughter. Photograph by author, 2010

Despite the presence of these sorts of class prejudices and antagonisms in Vietnam, when one compares Vietnam to Brazil, class is barely perceivable. Unprompted, Brazilians often self-identify and frame their society as divided into two distinct, adversarial sectors: the people or popular sector, on one side, and the elite, big ones, or colonels on the other. The significance of this gulf is such that this gap shapes and influences almost every facet of Brazilian society. Criminal and civil laws apply very differently to the wealthy. It is common to read news stories about middle-class youth killing, burning, or raping someone from the working classes and then having their sentences waived even if found guilty.[14] Zoning or basic infrastructure, such as sewage treatment, often do not extend to the periphery or *favelas*.[15] Middle- and upper-class residences have service elevators and entrances so that the commoners who work in the buildings are kept spatially segregated. Policing takes a very different form in the *popular* neighborhoods.[16] Gang warfare festers, and when the police respond they do so with scorched-earth tactics so that many innocent people end up wounded or killed—an approach that would be unthinkable in middle- and upper-class neighborhoods. It is no wonder, then, that most observers of Brazil have described Brazilian society in dualistic terms. For example, in 1974 the economist Edmar Bacha dubbed Brazil "Belindia," a Belgium-sized island of prosperity in a sea of India-like poverty—a moniker that has stuck because it well captures the social reality of Brazil.

Contrast this brief sketch of Brazil with how Cuong, a twenty-seven-year-old English teacher from Ha Tinh in central Vietnam, describes Vietnam in 2006:

> There are not sharp class distinctions in Vietnam. You can't tell class status by accent or behavior. There is not much stigma against the poor. People don't want to be poor but we don't treat someone badly because they are poor. We don't talk about "the upper class" or "the lower class." We just don't use this language in Vietnam. There are not sharp class distinctions. In India I think there are sharp class distinctions but not here. We don't have much class distinctions in Vietnam—things like slaves.

In general, class was a framework that did not come easily to interviewees in Vietnam. I often felt as if my questioning about class was imposing an alien perspective. The categories that all of my interviewees eventually settled upon, albeit usually after some nudging by me, were rich, poor, and middle income.[17] According to the interviewees the rich were those who lived in a big house, wore designer clothes, ate at expensive restaurants, traveled abroad, and drove a luxury car—most people in contemporary, urban Vietnam drive motorbikes. The poor were defined in two ways. A small minority of interviewees defined the poor as those who lived at or below the subsistence level, or as one interviewee described them, "Those who have to eat corn because they do not have rice," and who were believed to be disproportionately concentrated in central Vietnam and the mountainous regions close to Laos and China where ethnic minorities predominate. From this perspective, then, the poor were effectively racialized as ethnic minorities or non-Kinh people. Most interviewees, however, equated the poor with rural inhabitants or peasants. Thus, from one vantage point, the poor were the 10 to 20 percent of the population that were at or below the poverty level and believed to be living primarily in regions with a high concentration of ethnic minorities; whereas other interviewees, a much higher percentage of respondents, equated the poor with rural farmers, who make up about 70 percent of the country and are imagined to be predominantly ethnic Kinh, the majority ethnic group in Vietnam

Interestingly, everyone I interviewed, from domestic servants to successful professionals, identified themselves as "middle income." This meant that they did not consider themselves rich or poor. When pushed to quantify what middle income was, most defined it as someone who earns at least 500,000 VND or $33 per month in 2004. The words used to describe middle income varied—*binh thuong*, *binh dan*, *trung binh*—but the basic meaning was ordinary, middle level, everyday, or normal. The few that were familiar with the term middle class as used in the United States were quick to point out, as Hoa (a thirty-three-year-old administrative assistant in Hanoi) does below in 2008, that it would be a mistake to interpret *binh thuong* as the middle class in the US sense of the word.

> *Binh thuong* are the people in between rich and poor. It is not really middle class. To translate it as middle class would be misleading because it implies a level of wealth that *binh thuong* people do not have. The meaning is not middle class. The connotations are not the same. The "middle level people" or "the people in the middle" are better translations. Most people [in Vietnam] are *binh thuong*. Many think of it as "ordinary people." *Binh thuong* are ordinary people without much money. They may go to a restaurant but a very cheap one; nothing fancy or special.

One reason that everyone identified as "ordinary" may have to do with what Ly, a Hanoian in her late twenties who studies history in the United States, described as a pressure to downplay, rather than accentuate distinctions. She explained to me in 2013 that there is a common expression whose meaning is that "if everyone is in the same low or difficult situation, it's better than if there's one person who is better off." She used this saying to make her point:

> In a classroom or in an organization or in a village, it's better to be an ordinary person rather than a better student or wealthier farmer. Otherwise people may get jealous and pull you down (*Xau deu hon tot loi*). It can be risky to be too different without at least first testing to see if others are alright with you being more successful. In general one doesn't want to stand out. One wants to be ordinary . . . a common person. You could destroy your reputation and that of your family if you stand out. This is why many—including myself—try to be an ordinary, common person.[18]

Perhaps the most noteworthy distinction from Brazil, on this issue of class, was how not one person with whom I spoke viewed those who were outside of their social class as ontologically distinct. In Brazil, in contrast, the more elite sectors imagine the poor, urban neighborhoods and the people who inhabit them in starkly different terms. Let me offer one example. Over the past twenty years, I have frequently resided in a *favela* in Rio de Janeiro called Babilonia. Like many *favelas*, Babilonia has, at times, been terrorized by gang and police violence. But Babilonia is overwhelmingly populated by lower-middle class and blue-collar workers, who hold steady jobs, struggle to ensure the best education possible for their kids, have satellite TV, indoor plumbing and laptop computers, routinely attend church, do not drink alcohol let alone use other types of drugs, and have no connection to gangs. Yet for those who do not reside in *favelas* they tend to imagine them in ways that are perhaps best captured in the film, *City of God*.[19] It is a world portrayed as being dominated by parentless, alienated, drug-addicted children who kill and commit atrocities without compunction. Even though this portrait does not even faintly resemble Babilonia, several well-heeled Brazilians have sternly told me that this film accurately captures the reality of *favela* life.

Related to this is the way in which I have been described at times in more elite circles. After stating my name, I am forthwith introduced as "The gringo who lived in a *favela*." It is true, as noted above, that I have spent time in a *favela* but this is not the nomenclature I would select for myself. My list might include "the North American who speaks Portuguese, knows a lot about Brazil, has two kids, is a professor, lives in Seattle, or practices Taekwondo," but never this. Yet, for the elites, *favelas* are envisioned as profoundly distinct from the white, modern, moral, and nonviolent locales, which they imagine that they inhabit. I have on more than one occasion heard the privileged describe *favelas* as a socio-cultural extension

Figure 2.2 People of Babilonia. Photograph by Nando Neves, 2015

of Africa as opposed to their "European-like" neighborhoods. It is as if the elite imagine a journey from "their" space to *favelas* as a trip from modern to primitive, civilization to savagery, Europe to Africa. From this standpoint, then, a white North American who embodies the civilized pole of the social binary and actually ventures into and inhabits the space of this Other is exotic, newsworthy and deserving of the title, *favela gringo*.

In Vietnam class simply does not conjure up notions of such sharp socio-cultural distinctions or differences. One of the downsides to this is that it can create anxieties of the sorts that wealthy Brazilians do not have to face. In Hanoi during the summer of 2010 a story circulated widely of the domestic servant who seduced and eventually runs off with and marries the man of the household. Several people with whom I spoke commented that this possibility was generating worries for a number of married Hanoian women well off enough to have a domestic servant. In Brazil there is a long history of sexual relations between masters and servants. However, there are no story lines in soap operas or quotidian chatter, of which I am aware, of this relationship maturing into a legitimate relationship. Such an outcome is simply not considered plausible because the social divide is too great.

Not only is class seen as less distinct in Vietnam than Brazil, it is also understood in less adversarial terms. Of those I interviewed, government employees who were rich were viewed with contempt because they were perceived as having amassed wealth through corruption—a point I return to in Chapter 4. The view of the private-sector rich, in contrast, was favorable. As noted above, they were assumed to be innovative and hard-working entrepreneurs. The poor, too, were seen in empathetic terms. Remarkably, every interviewee expressed concern rather than callousness towards the poor. All agreed that poverty was largely due to the overall poverty of the country, in which there was a general lack of quality jobs and educational opportunities. They did not theorize poverty as a consequence of the motivational or moral shortcomings of the poor. In 2010, the opinion of Duy, a software engineer in Hanoi, was typical, "Everybody in the countryside works hard." Poverty was attributed instead to the existence of few opportunities. Or as many theorized, much like Van, a thirty-eight-year-old language teacher in Hanoi in 2004, "Poverty is due to a lack of resources."

In Brazil, the attitude of the middle and upper classes is much less generous. Maureen O'Dougherty's ethnography of middle-class *Paulistas* offers a window into these sentiments. In Sao Paulo she found the poor, who were often referred to as *nordestinos* (Northeasterners), routinely chastised as unintelligent, lazy, dirty, alien, and physically distinct (e.g., "flat headed"—*cabeca achatada*).[20] Moreover, the overall tone was extremely unsympathetic as illustrated by one heated conversation she had during her fieldwork:

> An intellectual friend who brought me to a party presented me to a friend of hers by saying we both had been married to Northeasterners. "So like Northeasterners," I badly joked. She said, "Not at all," and how violent they were. The discussion turned to how Nordest judiced against Paulistas, and how they came here to live but

money back in Bahia. . . . On the way home, I confided to the academic contact that I had been shocked by the discussion because in my mind it sounded like a racist discourse. The acquaintance immediately launched into a venomous diatribe against Northeasterners, repeating that "they" are prejudiced against "us," "they" do not like São Paulo, "they" talk up the Northeast," "they" have wealth. I responded that São Paulo is their city by now as well, they are Brazilians, and after all Brazil is one country (I said this fully aware of the "two Brazils" construct). The woman laughed derisively, saying, "That's an old story." I repeated the point I had tried to make at the party, that in the US, negative views such as these are often stated of poor minority ethnic groups. This attempt to draw parallels was "too theoretical," said the acquaintance, who added, as the evening reached a grand finale of heated argument, that I knew nothing of Brazil, its history, and in particular, nothing of the realities in São Paulo and having to live with "those people" on an everyday basis.[21]

My experiences with the middle and upper classes in Rio de Janeiro and Minas Gerais have been similar. Poverty and various social problems are often minimized and, if acknowledged, blamed on the poor. To my surprise, given the vast *favelas* that dominate the cityscape in Rio de Janeiro, some of my acquaintances would deny the existence of poverty. One friend, Sonia, a *Carioca* (resident of the city of Rio de Janeiro) pediatrician in her forties, held that one could eat well on fifty cents a day. Therefore, if there was poverty, it was because those individuals were not using their resources wisely. An executive of the Brazilian Development Bank, Enrique, assured me in 2008 that the violence in the *favelas* was an inevitable outcome of overpopulation—due to poor peoples' inability to control their bodies via birth control and their penchant for hypersexuality. Therefore the high death rates that resulted were, in his opinion, positive for it reduced this population and therefore the causes of violence. A biology professor at Universidade Federal de Rio de Janeiro (UFRJ), Cedinha, blamed gang warfare on a Brazilian culture that did not have a tradition of being well organized like cultures in Europe or the United States. In short, poor peoples' inability to behave in a civilized, ordered manner was the reason for the violence.

These contrasting opinions of the poor are magnified when one considers the material realities. Brazil is a much more unequal society than Vietnam. It has long ranked as one of worst countries in the world in terms of distribution of wealth. On the Gini index it scores a 51.9 as compared to Vietnam's 37.6 in 2012. Or put differently, in Brazil 42.9 percent of the wealth is controlled by 10 percent of the population and the lowest 10 percent control .08 percent of this treasure. In Vietnam the ratio is 30.2 percent for the top 10 percent and 3.2 percent for the lowest 10 percent in 2012. Furthermore, Vietnam is much poorer than Brazil (Vietnam's per capita income is $5600 compared to $16,100 in Brazil in 2014), and yet has a poverty rate (11.3 percent) that is about half of that of Brazil (21.4 percent).[22] Thus, even though the actual investment in the poor is much lower in Brazil than Vietnam, such investment is still considered excessive, if not wasteful, by people of means because poverty is viewed as either non-existent or the fault of the poor.

Figure 2.3 *Favela* in Rio de Janeiro. Photograph by Nando Neves, 2015

Conversely, in Vietnam many openly fretted about what impact various government initiatives were having on the poor, and everyone whom I interviewed argued that the government should be doing more to assist the poor. As Kien, a hotel doorman in his late twenties in Hanoi put it in 2010, "The government needs to better support the poor by giving them access to education, health care and employment."

Tales of Twentieth-Century Rupture

Development professionals sometimes attribute the relative equality and classlessness in Vietnam to the socialist revolution. The Viet Minh, after all, defined the revolution as a war against not only colonialism but also social hierarchies in general.[23] And there is little doubt that the communist-led revolution was instrumental in ending the establishment of a planter class, white supremacy, and urban elitism. Absent a broader historical perspective, however, it is easy to miss or overlook how Vietnam has long been a relatively equitable society. Pre-colonial villages—where the vast majority resided—were sharply hierarchical in terms of gender and age but not vis-à-vis social class. The Mandarins did not fashion themselves as a hereditary elite in opposition to an ignoble peasantry. Rice farmers were not demonized, pathologized, or otherized by the Mandarins but instead enjoyed a relatively esteemed status that sometimes even superseded the position of scholar-officials. This was the message of at least one maxim from the pre-colonial era: "When we run out of rice, farmers become number one. (*Nhat si nhi nong, het gao chay rong, nhat nong nhi si*)." Moreover poverty was widely believed to be the consequence of politics or government mismanagement rather than the shortcomings of the poor.[24] Not coincidentally, a system of social welfare was advocated and frequently experimented with by government officials centuries earlier in Vietnam than in Europe, where such interventions were not initiated until the nineteenth century, once the feudal order and its perceptions of the poor as subhuman were in decline.

It was only under French rule that social inequalities ballooned dramatically in Vietnam. David Marr summarized the shift from the pre-colonial to the colonial era as a dramatic increase in the

> concentration of wealth, land alienation and growth of a class of landless and land-poor Vietnamese. . . . Communal lands—traditionally the basis of village social welfare palliatives, as well as providing modest support for local temples, schools, and routine administrative tasks—now increasingly became the private property of several well-placed families or even under control of non-village members. . . . Peasant families . . . found themselves being evicted or converted into tenants, perhaps simply because they had not learned the new administrative rules as quickly as others.[25]

Moreover, more sophisticated dike methods created vast new tracts of lands, which were then converted into large plantations. The colonial elite and a small indigenous minority, who were obedient to them, appropriated the spoils of these innovations and did not share them. By the end of French colonial rule, the disparities became so extreme in the south that "less than one percent of the total population owned over half the cultivated land."[26] And much of this land belonged to "absentee landlords who controlled the fates of hundreds or thousands of local people without ever having to meet them face to face, or, perhaps even more upsetting, showing up only at rent- or loan-collection times."[27] It was not until the socialist revolution prevailed that these unprecedented levels of socio-economic inequalities were reversed and brought back in line with pre-colonial practices and sensibilities.

Among development scholars working in East Asia this broader historical perspective of continuity is often overshadowed by a tale of rupture. Perhaps most famously, Chalmers Johnson in *MITI and the Japanese Miracle* argued that the extraordinary events of the twentieth century gave birth to the overarching, revolutionary-like goal of development throughout the region. In *State-Directed Development* Atul Kohli's historiography is also a saga of radical change. He credits Japanese colonialism with Korea's economic success by helping to bring an end to the traditional aristocratic or *yangban* class as well as creating a state able to impose its development goals on both the elite and working classes. And still others, like Ben Schneider, have emphasized how developmentalism, as an ideology, enjoyed more urgency in East Asia because the communist threat was more intense there than in Latin America. On this point he writes, "the Cuban revolution sent adrenaline through the veins of cold warriors and developmentalists in Latin America, but neither the fear was enduring nor the threat as close as it was in divided Korea and Taiwan/China."[28]

In conversations with development practitioners in Vietnam I encountered a similar historical perspective. For example, a World Bank economist, Rob Swinkle, credited the socialist revolution for the pro-poor sentiments of government officials in an interview in Hanoi in 2004.

> ROB SWINKLE: When we show the government that there's growing inequality, they get very worried. They clearly don't want this. There is a genuine concern about the poor and there are concrete outcomes. Schools are in every area. And also health clinics . . . there are also problems with them. Preventative care has been very, very successful. Malaria and education in very remote areas in the past 15 years has been very good. The same with schools. Enrollment numbers are much higher than in many other countries. So generally social outcomes are very good which reflect government commitment to service delivery, *which is of course the ideology—socialist, communist—ideas of equality and getting everyone the same assets, education and land.* That's been one of the driving forces, so to say, for proper growth in the 1990s. . . . There are very few other governments in the world that are so committed to the poor. Any meeting on poverty, they come and they listen. They are very, very interested. You don't have to put it on the agenda. it is on the agenda. It's in the newspapers, it's on everybody's minds. [T]hey are obsessed with bringing poverty down.

JONATHAN: Are they getting grassroots pressure for this or is this being driven by their own ideology and principles?

ROB SWINKLE: It would be better if it were driven by grassroots pressure but it isn't. . . . It's not based on good accountability or good involvement or discussion at the local level including the poor who are left out. *It's more the ideology that this is part of the system and they have to do this* [emphasis added].[29]

Swinkle and I agree that there is a genuine concern for the poor that translates into significant investments in human capital. Where we differ is with respect to how much credit socialism deserves for this. I am dubious about the importance of socialist ideology in part because I cannot recall one conversation in which someone (including government officials) seemed to know very much about, let alone have a commitment to, socialist ideology. Moreover, as I briefly sketched above, a strong case can be made that the pro-poor ideology of the revolution was largely a repackaging in socialist garb of deep-seated pre-colonial ethics, norms, and practices rather than the brainchild of the communist-led revolution. This is why it is probable that social inequalities would still have been brought down to their current levels in Vietnam if the French had been defeated by a non-socialist regime. Further evidence of the insignificance of socialist ideology, in my opinion, is the fact that many East Asian countries that have non- or anti-socialist governments have equally low Gini coefficients: Japan 37.6 (2008), Vietnam 37.6 (2008), Taiwan 34.2 (2011), Korea 31.1 (2011).[30]

The main point of this section is not to set the record straight about the impact of socialist ideology or the socialist revolution on attitudes toward the poor (this I will leave for historians to sort out) but instead to raise questions about the historiography of rupture that is prevalent in development studies. The stakes are high because if we accept that extraordinary, macro-global forces created the key development ingredients in East Asia, then the implication is that little can be done by development practitioners elsewhere in the world. Surely no one would propose a development prescription of immiseration in which, for example, a brutal Japanese-like colonialism or a bloody anti-colonial, socialist revolution should be advanced in order to boost economic growth in Brazil. Nonetheless, this is an implication of the rupture thesis.

In Chapter 4, I return to the theme of revolutionary nationalism and detail how many of its economically beneficial effects, such as social capital, can be had in Brazil without such cataclysmic events. And in this chapter I have shown that the relatively pro-poor values in Vietnam predated the tsunami-like macro-forces that traumatized East Asia in the twentieth century. What is needed to produce similar concerns about and investments in the poor will, of course, vary by context. But it will be much less likely to happen if development scholars and practitioners continue to hold that the East Asian cultural field was produced by and therefore can only be had through catastrophic wars and revolutions. At least with regards to the more equitable leanings found in Vietnam, this is clearly false given that they existed well before French colonialism and the socialist revolution of the twentieth-century. Moreover, as I detail in Chapter 5, fairer and less elitist commitments have been generated in a few Brazilian municipalities in recent decades—further evidence that these facets of cultures of development can be had absent the horrors of twentieth-century East Asia.

Countryside People

If class was noticeable for its relative absence in Vietnam, the same cannot be said of the rural–urban divide. Even though many urbanites are, at most, one generation removed from the countryside, city dwellers reserve a number of clichés about rural Vietnamese such as "backwards" (*lac hau*), "frank" (*ngay thang*), "friendly" (*than thien*) and "simple" (*don gian*). One interviewee, a thirty-nine-year-old lawyer from the city of Vinh in central Vietnam, described rural backwardness as an inability to concentrate on doing a job well and not valuing education for girls. "Parents in the countryside don't want their daughters well educated," Due claimed. "They marry the girls off young. They don't care about education." Phillip Taylor, based on his ethnography in South Vietnam, summarized the urban perspective of rural Vietnam as a world of "limited horizons, low education and life experiences limited to rice and fruit growing and the drinking of home brewed rice wine."[31] Indeed one of the biggest insults one can throw at the *nouveau riche*, a thirty-two-year-old software programmer in Ho Chi Minh City told me, is to call them a peasant. According to Khai this is apt to provoke fisticuffs.

What caught my attention were not these stereotypes (such urban chauvinism is common throughout much of the world) but rather how they were balanced, if not outweighed, by a number of positive ones. Official and popular narratives of anti-colonialism laud the peasants as the nation's historical vanguard. The narratives give the peasants credit for having carried on the tradition of sacred resistance against foreign aggression or invasion (*Khang chien than thanh chong ngoai xam*). Everyone I met concurred with this and many agreed with Tan, a forty-seven-year-old street barber, who straightforwardly stated, "The peasants saved Vietnam." What Tan and others meant was that it was the rural farmers who bore the brunt of the twentieth-century wars, which took well over three million lives, and that without their sacrifice Vietnam would likely not be reunified or independent.

Rural Vietnam is also widely regarded as the wellspring of Vietnamese culture and traditions. According to official historiography, the countryside is where the ancient Vietnamese culture predominates: the culture of the Bronze Age rice civilization (~1000 BC–179 BC) that predated Chinese invasions, Indian influences and French colonialism. A number of widely circulated historical and education materials echo this perspective. In *Wandering through Vietnamese Culture*, for example, Huu Ngoc writes, "To understand the soul of traditional Vietnam, you must go to the countryside. There lies the village, the social cell and the administrative, economic and spiritual unit, that is the depository of [Vietnam's] oldest cultural values."[32] Indeed the countryside is so "welded" with Vietnameseness in popular thought in contemporary Vietnam, according to Nguyen-vo Thu-huong, that prostitutes often feel pressured to embody or perform rurality in order to appeal to urban Vietnamese men's desire to consume Vietnam's authentic soul.[33]

These symbolic equations of ruralness with national essence and heroic patriotism closely parallel Maoist constructions of the peasants. Rural Chinese, or at least the Han who resided in the countryside, were defined in revolutionary

Figure 2.4 Farmers in Hung Yen. Photograph by author, 2010

narratives as the vanguard of socialist development and the source of authentic Chinese culture because Han peasants, the Communist Party instructed, had tirelessly resisted foreign invasion and contamination. In post-socialist China, at least according to the anthropologist Yan Hairong, peasants are no longer viewed as a source of valued knowledge and practices but instead are repositioned in urban, upper-class discourses. They are no longer viewed as a source of valued knowledge and practices but instead are defined as lacking the proper qualities (*suzhi*), such as self-discipline, required for modernity. Unlike the urban working classes—who are considered irredeemably damaged by socialism—rural Chinese are seen by the urban elite as capable of modernity, but only if they work as employees for the professional, urban employers who have already achieved modern traits. It is through this mode of contact that the rural Chinese overcome their deficits and acquire the requisite qualities that will allow rural inhabitants and the nation to develop.[34]

Strikingly different in Vietnam is how post-socialist modernization narratives, even among city-dwellers interviewed, have not significantly reworked the relationship of peasants to modernity. Peasants are certainly considered deficient in certain regards: unsophisticated, naïve, dirty, isolated, superstitious, and so on. But their deficiencies—like those of the poor—are largely considered structural rather than essentialist in nature by the urbanites with whom I spoke. That is, their shortcomings are due to their lack of exposure to the larger world, poor education, and poverty—not something innate or deeply rooted in their character or culture. And so it is believed that if the rural people had decent jobs and access to a good education, they would quickly overcome any unsavory qualities that they might have.

Moreover, interviewees constructed rural Vietnamese as the source of a number of values and practices considered essential for Vietnam's successful modernization. As I develop in the next chapter, modernization was widely regarded by those with whom I spoke as a process of molding Western modernities to a Vietnamese culture. Merely emulating Western modernities was considered inappropriate and ill-advised. This places the countryside in a pivotal role. As the source of Vietnamese culture the rural sectors bring certain assets to the modernization table beyond their labor power. Rural communities are the font of the Vietnamese culture, the keepers of traditions, people that should be consulted and turned to for guidance as Vietnam modernizes.

The rural as a treasured cultural touchstone ideology was evident among the professionals I met. Painters in Hanoi told me that in art school, they were required to spend several months residing in and studying the countryside. It was there that they would come to better know the soul of Vietnam—its landscapes and culture—so that their art would not become too detached from Vietnamese culture as they matured as painters and experimented with artistic forms developed elsewhere. A fashion designer I spoke with in Saigon said that he routinely returned to his village to get ideas and inspiration for his clothing line. One well-known architect in Hanoi said he often visited and studied village architecture in order to ensure that his modern high-rises would be adequately infused with traditional Vietnamese architectural styles.

Figure 2.5 Hanoian Architect. Photograph by author, 2010

In sum, I found that peasants were not regarded as merely deficient subjects in need of resocialization. They had both shortcomings and assets. The limitations were largely regarded as environmental and therefore could be overcome via expanded opportunities. Their strengths, in contrast, were more essentialized. As the holders of tradition they were seen as foundational to the realization of a successful Vietnamese modernity. The countryside was a cultural compass that should guide the modernization process. It was not a way of life to be simply shunned and negated as a means of becoming modern. Instead progress was realized by including and nurturing various aspects of rural culture—a point I return to and develop further in Chapter 3.

Unlike Yan Hairong's portrait of contemporary China, then, modernity is not conceptualized as a process of bringing rural people to the city so that they can acquire a particular quality (*suzhi*) required for national development. Everyone with whom I spoke—again mainly Hanoians—preferred that the sustenance and incorporation of the traditional within the modern be actualized by bringing jobs and educational opportunities to the countryside rather than rural people to the cities. Urbanization was seen as a much more risky prospect—one that could lead to an erosion of Vietnamese culture. These sentiments were echoed in most cinematic and artistic depictions of rural-to-urban migration, which tell a story of decline rather than of personal or societal uplift. Innocent men are transformed into money-obsessed malcontents who have little time for their families. Righteous women

Figure 2.6 *Open* by Nguyen Cong Cu, 2004. Printed with permission from Nguyen Cong Cu

80 x 100

Figure 2.7 *Vision 4* by Nguyen Cong Cu, 2008. Printed with permission from Nguyen Cong Cu

turn to crime and become sexually promiscuous. Nguyen Cong Cu's paintings offer an example of this widely held perspective. In one series of paintings (2004), new migrants are painted as wide-eyed and innocent, who are able to articulate just a few words such as "open" or "no." In his next series (2008), the same figures are consumed with work. They are money obsessed; their throats are toilets, and they have no time for family or relationships.

Neoslave Developments

In at least one respect, then, Brazil resembles contemporary China more than Vietnam in that modernization has been conceptualized as a process of encouraging rural populations to become more like urban professionals. There have been attempts to challenge this urban-centricism such as Walter Salle's *Central Station.*[35] In this film, Rio de Janeiro is juxtaposed to the rural backlands of the Northeast. It is in this countryside—not urban Rio—where family, community, humanistic ethics, and happiness exist. The main protagonists are transformed by their journey away from the city to the countryside. Yet this recipe for progress remains a weak countercurrent in Brazil. Development and modernity are, for most, conceptualized as a process of moving from the "backward" countryside to the "modern" metropole.

The parallels between Brazil and China end here. One important distinction is the way in which race is configured in Brazil. Throughout East Asia, race underpins ideas of nation and Asia as distinct from the West. The poor, including peasants, are considered part of the same Kinh or Han racial group as the people with economic and political power—something that would not be true in Vietnam had French colonialism prevailed.[36] When the French ruled, they set up a social order in which race figured centrally. The Vietnamese or "natives," as they were called, suffered countless acts of racial belittlement and discrimination. Physical and verbal abuse, in which the Vietnamese were kicked, hit, and called names such as boy, dumb bugger, animal, and slave, was commonplace. Shawn McHale's juxtaposition of the two vignettes from this era succinctly depicts this hierarchy:

> The unfairness of this racial domination was underlined by the unequal punishments meted out to French and "natives" who violated the law. Two contemporaneous incidents in 1929 illustrate this point. After slapping a plainclothes police officer by mistake—the officer had grabbed his identity papers and he tried to grab them back—the erudite radical Phan Van Hum was hauled off for questioning (and eventually jailed). When Nguyen An Ninh came to the defense of Hum, he too was punished with a jail term. In contrast, when a Frenchman in Soc Trang shot dead his foreman Ninh and invoked the right to self-defense, he was cleared of any wrong.[37]

In contemporary Vietnam, the more elite social sectors do not consider themselves as racially distinct from the general population. Except with respect to the roughly 15 percent of the population that are non-Kinh, such racial slights are nonexistent. In Brazil, this sort of racial distinction and discrimination is commonplace. The middle and upper classes view the popular sectors as racial others. Discussions of the *nordestinos*, *favelados*, and *povo* are also code for "morenos or pardos; colored, not white."[38] And to be nonwhite in Brazil is similar to being "native" in colonial Vietnam.

One way that racism manifests in Brazil is that modernization is widely understood as a racialization project. Progress is achieved through racial transformation. In the early twentieth century the emphasis was placed on biological whitening. The intelligentsia, persuaded as they were by the tenets of scientific racism, believed that Brazil could only become modern if the dominant blood group of the nation were white.[39] Racial mixing was the solution they concocted to solve this race problem. It was their hope that in one or two generations, blackness would be bleached away. The comments of Joao Batista de Lacerda at the First Universal Races Congress in London in 1911 offer a window into this worldview:

> The children of [bi-racial people] have been found, in the third generation, to present all physical characters of the white race. . . . the influence of sexual selection . . . removes from the descendants of the metis all the characteristic features of the black race. . . . In virtue of this process of ethnic reduction, it is logical to expect that in the course of another century the metis will have disappeared from Brazil. This will coincide with the parallel extinction of the black race in our midst.[40]

Residue of this ideology persists in popular thought today. It is not uncommon for nonwhites to explicitly state that they chose lighter-skinned mates in the hopes that their children would be whiter. This racial logic also often shapes identities, memories, and everyday practices. As a means of elevating oneself, if not nation, Brazilians often actively attempt to whiten their racial identification, distance themselves from non-white ancestries and histories, and adopt cultural practices that are racialized as white.[41]

Challenges have been leveled against whitening. Conceicao Evaristo, for one, has argued for the embrace of black communities, biographies, cultures, and identities as the path toward modernity. In her novel, *Poncia Vicencio*, the two main protagonists leave their black village, which is controlled by whites, in order to attempt to improve their lives. In the end they realize that "the move to the city simply means replacing the squalor of the country for the violence and indignities of the *favelas*."[42] Progress, they come to learn, can only be achieved through blackness rather than by distancing oneself from it. Anderson Sa, the co-founder of Afro-Reggae in Rio de Janeiro, also challenges whitening. It is by accepting and embracing one's identity as a *favelado*, by celebrating and claiming black culture, that one's humanity is realized, violence reduced, and development achieved.[43] These black-to-modernity forays, however, continue to represent a marginal, albeit growing, counterpublic in Brazilian society.

In many respects, Brazil is a neofeudal society much more in the European than East Asian tradition. "Europeans," Alexander Woodside writes, "were predisposed for many centuries to think of the poor as contemptible idlers; or (in mercantilist thought) as economic traitors to the national economy."[44] East Asia, in contrast, generally held much less pejorative imaginings of the poor. As mentioned before, poverty was viewed as an outgrowth of government mismanagement rather than the fault of the poor. In Brazil, like feudal Europe, social class is understood in more biological terms or what social scientists today often label racial essentialism. For centuries, European commoners were viewed as being from a different stock than the aristocracy. One's achievements, no matter how impressive, could not trump blood. East Asian peasants, in contrast, were not seen in such "racial" terms. As we have seen, the scholar-officials, many of whom came from peasant backgrounds, were selected by merit not birth.

Of course the particular contours of social distinction were and are different in Brazil than Europe. One important distinction is that just as various movements aimed at weakening and breaking down the feudal social order in Europe were gaining the upper hand, much the opposite was occurring in Brazil. In the eighteenth century, for example, the Enlightenment revolutionized not only France but also much of Western Europe. In *The Roads to Modernity*, Gertrude Himmelfarb maps out how John Wesley and the broader Methodist movement helped to socially democratize England by advancing the then-radical assumption that everyone, including slaves and the poor, had a soul and were therefore worthy of benevolence rather than scorn. One specific facet of English common sense that the Methodists attacked was the assumption that the poor were lazy. Citing his own experiences among the poor in London Wesley wrote:

> I found some in their cells underground, others in their garrets, but I found not one of them unemployed who was able to crawl about the room. So wickedly, devilishly false is that common objection, they are poor only because they are idle.[45]

Other kinds of social democratic movements emerged and flourished throughout most of nineteenth-century Europe. The 1848 revolutions, motivated by the ideas of democracy, liberalism, nationalism, and socialism, foreshadowed the many changes that would eventually sweep through and radically transform the continent in the next century. In Latvia, to take one example, German barons owned most of the land and governed the country. They represented civilization—much as do whites in contemporary Brazil. "Social mobility involved assimilation into the Baltic German classes"[46] and a disassociation with the Latvian or non-German people and countryside. According to Vieda Skultans, to embrace a Latvian identity was considered a revolutionary act—much like asserting a black identity in contemporary Brazil. By the early twentieth century a Latvian nationalist movement emerged, led by folklorists, religious leaders, musicians, and writers, that successfully redefined the rural, non-Germanic spaces, cultures, and peoples.[47] Today, Latvians typically imagine the countryside as bucolic rather than backward. In Skultans' words:

> My image of the Latvian countryside belongs to fairy tales. It is of a sparsely populated, undulating and magical landscape. There is a perfect balance of wild forest and cultivated fields and lonely farmsteads; between wild animals such as wolves and wild-boars and much loved farm animals. It is never boring because it has the right mixture of ingredients, the right proportion of land to water. . . . It is an intimate country of perfect scale and proportion.[48]

As the social order was being leveled in Europe, in Brazil the social hierarchies of colonialism, conquest, and slavery were being elaborated and hardened. When King John VI fled to Rio de Janeiro in 1808, in advance of Napoleon's invasion of Portugal, he did not privilege the humanitarian ideas of the Enlightenment but rather called for a "Just War" against the indigenous inhabitants of the forbidden zone of Minas Gerais. Moreover, he and his court accommodated rather than challenged slavery. In *Empire Adrift*, Patrick Wilcken writes:

> The court could clean out the city, set up new cultural institutions, encourage education, but no matter what gloss of refinement they brought to Rio, they could not escape the less savory aspects of Portugal's imperial legacy. Even with its choirs, orchestras and theatres, Rio de Janeiro was still essentially an enormous slave market town—by far the biggest in the Americas. . . . Every aspect of life in Rio was touched by slavery, from the central districts filled by day with African laborers, to the massively serviced households of rich Brazilians. . . . As memories of their former lives in Lisbon receded, the royal family and their retinue became . . . slave owners in their own right, and court life took on the flavor of a city state in antiquity. A dozen slaves dressed in red livery carried Dom Joao in his sedan chair around Rio. Royal barges glided across the bay, powered by rows of slave oarsman. On special occasions slave musicians provided court entertainment. The palace received gifts of slaves as tribute from wealthy planters. And all the while the public works went on, with chain-gangs cutting roads through forested hills that surrounded the city, sweating teams hauling granite blocks from nearby quarries and slave laborers laying the foundation stones for the new Rio.[49]

A half-century later, as revolutions were pulsating through Europe and the traditional landed-elite were barely clinging to power, the slave-owning barons of the Brazilian backlands were consolidating their power further. For instance, a law was passed in 1850 that required landholders to register their land, usually hundreds of miles away, in Rio de Janeiro. The costs of such a journey prohibited most small landholders from acquiring title to their holdings. Without title the barons and colonels of the interior were able to appropriate the lands of small, mostly mestizo landholders and force them to live on the peripheries of plantations as tenant farmers or sharecroppers in near slave-like conditions.

Even the few significant challenges to this social order during the past two centuries were matched, if not bested, by powerful reactionary forces. When Brazil became the last country in the Americas to abolish slavery in 1888, to take one example, the oligarchic elite were able to ensure that the majority of freed slaves had few options but to continue to live in the same slave quarters and work for their formers masters in the same jobs for subsistence wages. As one of my interviewees, Luiz, a seventy-three-year-old cobbler, summed it up, "When abolition happened, they said, 'You're free!' Right? 'Everyone's free.' But those slaves there, where would they go? They're free, but what will they do?"[50] Rather than funding programs to help the liberated slaves transition to freedom, the political and economic elite subsidized European immigration in the hopes of whitening Brazil.[51] These immigrants, mainly peasants from southern Europe, quickly filled most of the more skilled trades and better-paid manufacturing jobs. The result was few employment opportunities for Brazilians of color outside of domestic and agricultural work. Hence a neoslave social order was established in the wake of abolition.

It was not until one hundred years later, in 1988, that Brazil achieved universal suffrage. As the Brazilian anthropologist Teresa Caldeira observed, "many social groups . . . reacted negatively to the enlargement of the political arena and the expansion of rights" and used the issue of crime as a way of articulating their opposition and in the process delegitimize civil citizenship.[52] She found that crime narratives, which constructed criminals as evil incarnate, led to massive human rights violations, the destruction of public space, the segregation of social groups, and the destabilization of the rule of law. Ironically, then, "political democracy . . . brought with it not respect for rights, justice, and human life, but their exact opposites," or what she and James Holston called "disjunctive democracy."[53]

Thus in Europe, as social democratic movements of various stripes made inroads over the course of three centuries, much the opposite occurred in Brazil. Roberto Schwarz summed up these different trajectories well when he wrote that in Brazil:

> The combination of *latifundia* and unfree labor . . . stood firm through Colony, Emperors, and Regencies, through Abolition, the First Republic, and even now is a matter of debate and bullets. . . . The *latifundia*, little changed, saw the baroque, neoclassic, romantic, naturalist and modernist cultures pass by, cultures which in Europe reflected immense transformations in its social order.[54]

These basic neoslave social relationships have proved remarkably tenacious and enduring in Brazil. Not surprisingly, then, by almost any measure social disparities are much more pronounced in Brazil than in Europe. And as we will now see, it is not just subalterns who suffer but the society and its economy as a whole.

Narratives and Human Capital

The question with which I began this chapter was why have there been such regionally different degrees of political support for investing in human capital.

At this juncture an answer should be coming into view. It has to do with the sorts of narratives detailed above. We have seen that in Vietnam the poor, rural sectors, which make up approximately 70 percent of the population, are not blamed for their marginalization. In fact, they are lauded as having saved Vietnam from colonialism. Moreover, as the embodiment of Vietnamese culture, they are regarded as vital to Vietnam's modernization. This is very distinct from Brazil where the *povo*, the roughly 70 percent of the population which lives in the *favelas*, periphery, or countryside, are disparaged as immoral aliens who are largely to blame for their marginalization. Progress is imagined as a process of molding these putatively backward, racial others in the image of urban, professional, whites.

Given these contrasting cultural landscapes, one would anticipate a pattern of government initiatives that is more progressive or pro-poor in Vietnam than in Brazil. Indeed this is what one finds. Land reform in Vietnam in the 1980s and 90s is a case in point. In 1985, Vietnam was one of the world's five poorest countries with a per capita index of US$130 per year. The CPV responded to this crisis with the adoption of the *Doi Moi* (renovation) policy reforms. At the Sixth Congress of the Communist Party, held in December 1986, the government explicitly adopted the goal of replacing central planning with a regulated market economy. A series of fundamental policy changes were quickly implemented in the following years, and one of the most important ones was Decree Number 10 that was issued in April 1988. This decree dismantled agricultural cooperatives and divided up agricultural land among rural households that had worked on these cooperatives.

Martin Ravallion and Dominque van de Walle found that the privatization of these communes was carried out in a very equitable fashion. According to them there was

> no evidence that land allocation unduly favored households with government or semigovernment jobs. . . . [The] decentralized reform achieved a more equitable outcome than one would have expected from a consumption-efficient allocation, as would have been achieved by free markets. Our results suggest an effort to protect the poorest and reduce overall inequality, at the expense of aggregate consumption. The solution that was arrived at entailed an equity-efficiency trade off, indicating that both objectives were valued positively.[55]

The imperative to minimize inequality and consider, if not privilege, the interests of the poor, most of whom are rural farm workers, has been noted by many observers. Paul Glewwe, like Rob Swinkle quoted earlier, noted that "Vietnamese policymakers are genuinely concerned about inequality" and poverty.[56] Consequently, this emphasis has featured in several other policy initiatives since *Doi Moi*. Examples include the *Comprehensive Poverty Reduction and Growth Strategy* that was released by the Vietnamese government in May 2002.[57]

Even though most interviewees felt that the Vietnamese government should do more to help the rural sectors, most also thought that it had been very generous toward farmers. The degree to which this is empirically true is open to debate and a question I do not wish to resolve here. Instead my point is that relative to Brazil, Vietnamese policies have been much more fair and evenhanded, which lends support to my central argument about the links between discourses and human capital. In Brazil there is a long-standing and well-documented tradition of government interventions, which neglect and disadvantage the working classes and poor, even when they are intended to benefit those populations. For instance, the *Sistema Financeiro de Habitacao* was created specifically to promote the construction and financing of homes for low-income families. However, because the poor could not meet the underwriting policies, the loans went overwhelmingly to the middle classes. The result was that

> the middle classes were getting cheap mortgages subsidized by the government, and the working classes, who could not afford to buy on the formal market and who only rarely met the BNH requirements for a loan application, were building their houses by themselves on the periphery without any public financial help.[58]

When Luiz Inacio Lula da Silva, a former shoeshine boy from the Northeast, union leader, and founding father of the Workers' Party (PT), was elected President of the Republic in 2002, there was great hope that this dynamic would change. And to some degree it has. Thanks in part to a handful of progressive government initiatives,[59] social inequalities and poverty had declined and thousands of Brazilians have improved their standard of living until the recession in 2015.[60] Not surprisingly, however, the socio-cultural sinews of society have proven resilient in the face of pressure for change. This is perhaps most visible in the megaprojects that were constructed in preparation for the 2014 World Cup and 2016 Olympics. Billions of dollars were invested in infrastructure, which overwhelmingly favored the elite. The schools, health care, and infrastructure projects that service the *povo* received little attention. Instead the airport was renovated, and existing transportation networks were improved so that one could pass more readily between the airport and elite neighborhoods (especially Baja da Tijuca) without having to notice urban blight. The *popular* sectors were rarely consulted or included in the decision making process for these megaprojects.[61] And many became their victims. In the center of Rio de Janeiro, for instance, thousands of working-class residents were displaced by the renovation of the port. Adding insult to injury, this project was funded largely by revenue from a payroll tax in which the funds generated were earmarked for infrastructure improvements that were supposed to benefit the *povo*—and not the elites.[62]

These megaprojects are eerily reminiscent of what occurred a century earlier when Rio de Janeiro underwent a series of urban reforms in an explicit attempt to more closely resemble Paris as a means to signal its level of civilization.[63] In the process, thousands of servants, vendors, craftsmen, and merchants, most of whom were the descendants of slaves, were displaced to the peripheries where they created some of Brazil's first *favelas*. Unlike at the turn of the last century, the latest round of regressive urban renewal projects has sparked a wave of mass demonstrations against the government, but this movement has yet to fundamentally alter much the dynamics that have characterized Brazilian public policy for centuries.

My central contention is that this status quo is due to the socio-cultural field outlined in this chapter—what John H. Coatsworth describes as an heirloom of Brazil's ignoble past:

> The legacy of slavery can be seen in many aspects of Brazilian society, but the greatest damage to the economy came from the failure to invest in human beings, that is, in the education and training of slaves and their descendants. Until recently, Brazil not only lagged behind the developed world but much of Latin America in developing its human capital. A big part of the educational gap came from the failure to invest in schools for the children of poorer citizens in states, cities and neighborhoods where the Afro-Brazilian population predominates.[64]

The salience of this racist, anti-poor legacy is perhaps most on display in the political backlash to even modest attempts at reform such as that against *Bolsa Familia*. This social program has proven to be one of the most successful progressive policies to come out of the Cardoso (1995–2002) and da Silva (2003–2011) administrations. It has been lauded by a wide range of development experts both within and outside of Brazil and emulated by various other governments including Mexico. *Bolsa Familia*, probably more than any other government policy, has helped to mute the most extreme forms of poverty in Brazil, where, according to Pauline Bartolone,

> 47 percent of Brazil's land is owned by just 1 percent of the population, making the country's land distribution the second most unequal in the world. As a result, a class of four and a half million people is left on the verge of starvation, without land of their own.[65]

Bolsa Familia provides a small stipend of $R80 ($60) a month to such families, if they keep their children in school and have them vaccinated. This pales in comparison to the large subsidies that the more advantaged receive through pensions, tax breaks, higher education subsidies and urban renewal projects.[66] Nonetheless I *repeatedly* heard harsh comments by the middle and upper classes about how the program is "a waste of money" and that beneficiaries of this program "should not be allowed to vote." From their vantage it is perpetuating "a paternalistic culture of dependency" and is a form of electoral corruption. Such reactions are especially illuminating when juxtaposed to Vietnam, where every urban resident whom I interviewed complained that the government was not doing enough to assist the rural poor even though they believed that the government

Table 2.1 Infrastructure, Investment, and Life Expectancy

	Brazil	*Vietnam*
Internet Users per 100 (2013)	49.8	39.5
Average Life Expectancy (2013)	73	75
Public Spending on Education (% of GDP in 2010)	5.8	6.8
Mobile Phones per 100 (2013)	125	149
Access to Improved Sanitation Facilities, Urban, 2013 (%)	87	93

Source: The World Bank. Accessed March 27, 2014. www.data.worldbank.org.

already prioritized these sectors.

Thus interpretive economics has allowed me to provide a compelling explanation of why there have been such different kinds and levels of commitment to capacity-building in places like Vietnam and Brazil. Vietnam is a country that is more than three times poorer than Brazil. Its per capita income is $5600 compared to Brazil, which is $16,100.[67] Yet rates of infant mortality, literacy, life expectancy, and quality of infrastructure, such as schools, sewage treatment, roads, hospitals, and so on, are on par if not better in Vietnam than in Brazil. Perhaps most telling of all are poverty rates and the distribution of wealth and income. The percent who are poor in Vietnam is just 11.3 percent—about half that of Brazil at 21.4 percent. The lowest 10 percent of the population had 3.1 percent of the nation's income in Vietnam in 2006; whereas the wealthiest 10 percent had 29.8 percent of the nation's income. In Brazil 1.1 percent of Brazil's income was in the hands of the lowest 10 percent of the population while 43 percent—nearly half—was controlled by the richest 10 percent of the population, indicating a tremendously unequal pattern of income distribution. The Gini coefficient in Brazil was 0.51 compared to 0.37 in Vietnam in 2013.[68] I believe such outcomes are in large measure due to the very different ways that certain sectors of society are imagined. And yet development experts rarely consider narratives and semiotics, let alone target them for change. Instead they discuss economies as if cultures that disparage and marginalize the poor, *favelados*, blacks and other social groups were immaterial.

Culture and Power

In addition to the aculturalism of development studies, another reason that the cultural variables addressed in this chapter have been overlooked has to do with the simple fact that development scholars and technicians tend to ignore power altogether. The Nobel Prize-winning economist Amartya Sen noted this bent among admirers of China's extraordinary economic growth. He observed that

> [t]he Maoist policies of land reform, expansion of literacy, enlargement of public health care, and so on had a very favorable effect on economic growth. . . . [They had built] the social foundations of a market economy and capitalist

expansion.[69]

According to Sen these changes greatly enhanced human capacity and capital by improving, among other things, the "productivity and employability of the people involved." Sen concluded that there is therefore a "need for greater recognition" of "the extent to which post-reform China draws on the results of pre-reform China."

The failure to acknowledge the ties between equality, capacity-building, and development extends far beyond considerations of the Maoist origins of China's economic successes. Power and its links to economic well-being are rarely if ever addressed by pundits, publics, and policymakers throughout the world. For instance, in a speech in Seattle in 2005, the then outgoing Mexican President Vicente Fox proudly boasted that he was leaving Mexico with its economic fundamentals in sound condition because tariffs had been reduced, inflation was under control, deficit spending had ceased, the public sector had been downsized, and credit markets had been liberalized. No mention was made of the hyper-marginalization of indigenous people and their descendants, or the fact that most Mexicans earned at most $100 a day while the top 10 percent were fabulously wealthy—indeed Mexico produces more billionaires than any other country in the world.[70] This decoupling of socio-economic inequalities from market fundamentals is reminiscent of how Joseph Stiglitz described US lawmakers: "Politicians typically talk about rising inequality and the sluggish recovery as separate phenomenon, when they are in fact intertwined. Inequality stifles, restrains, [and] holds back [US] growth."[71]

Unfortunately, as critical development scholars have repeatedly pointed out, such power-evasiveness is also common among development professionals.[72] Much like President Fox and US politicians, they frequently assume that economic growth can be had absent a reckoning with racism, patriarchy, and poverty or what Paul Farmer has labeled "structures of violence."[73] This power-evasiveness is why James Ferguson long ago dubbed the development establishment "the anti-politics machine."[74] Ferguson pointed out that development scholars and practitioners frequently discuss economies and propose development strategies as if socio-economic orders and disparities were irrelevant. He explained how this depoliticization of development is often achieved through a technocratic move. That is, development is reduced to a narrow process of building a road, extending credit, or setting up proper accounting practices without considering, let alone addressing, the social hierarchies, divides, and interests that exist in any society.

In *Aiding Violence*, Peter Uvin detailed this practice in Rwanda in the 1980s and early 1990s. Development experts ignored the salient racial divisions and racist rhetoric that was constructing the Tutsi minority as subhuman impediments to societal progress. They proceeded as if the state were simply a neutral arbitrator impartially looking out for the best interests of all its citizens. In reality, however, the Hutus held the levers of power and were using development grants and loans to advance Hutu power and marginalize the Tutsi population. Monies for a bridge would be used to build political patronage by awarding Hutus construction contracts and jobs, eliminate or marginalize Tutsi dwellings based on where the bridge or road was located, and legitimate Hutu politicians by demonstrating that they enjoyed the support of international organizations despite their venomous anti-Tutsi propaganda at the time. In the end, Uvin demonstrates how the development establishment unwittingly became a handmaiden to genocide by not addressing race and power.

Uvin offered a number of insightful explanations for the failure of development practitioners in places like Rwanda to reckon with social inequalities. Reminiscent of Edward Said's critique of Western journalism,[75] he observed that many development entities and their agents

> have little in-depth knowledge of the social, political, and historical background of the countries they work in; training in these matters is not usually considered a major issue by the agencies that send them, nor is knowledge of local language. . . . As a result, most (though not all) of the people in the foreign aid system are incapable of even noticing the political stakes and abuses of their actions. . . . To the extent that some people at some point do realize the political and social stakes and abuses that surround development aid and its projects, they often choose not to react. This has various causes, including fear of rocking the boat, of making enemies, of losing jobs; a desire to get on with the job of development (defined as independent from political and social processes); a sense of powerlessness and incapacity to promote the kind of change required; and a complacent, racist attitude of low expectations.[76]

If the majority of development professionals are oblivious to the discourses that generate and sustain power for the simple reason that they do not see or choose to react to political and social processes, then how do we explain the aculturalism among the subset of development scholars who are not power-evasive? In these instances cultural-blindness usually stems from a different source: social determinism. Epistemological cousins of the instrumentalists discussed in Chapter 1, socio-economic groups are presumed to have fixed interests that transcend culture (recall that the instrumentalists made this assumption about individuals rather than social groups). This is why scholars such as Joel Migdal, in *Strong Societies and Weak States*, forward no cultural analysis. Power is an uncomplicated calculus of group size. States are strong and therefore effective if certain social classes, such as the landed elite, industrialists, or commodity-barons, are small and therefore weak. There is no consideration of how a specific social group may have different identities, ambitions, and perceived interests across time and place, which might in turn affect their relative strength and political orientations. A manufacturer or worker in Vietnam can be expected to think and behave in similar ways to a manufacturer or worker in Brazil. Development is thus theorized as a straightforward endeavor of attempting to enhance or reduce the size of a particular socio-economic group in order to ensure a strong and therefore non-predatory developmental state.

This perspective—along with the historiography of twentieth-century rupture—is reflected in Migdal's observations of why parts of East Asia have enjoyed such rapid economic growth. He writes:

> The most common sort of twentieth-century dislocation leading to the emergence of strong Third World states has been a devastating combination of war and/or revolution, sometimes associated with massive migration. For China, Korea, and Vietnam, the succession of brutal war and revolution after the 1930s led to catastrophic organizational changes in everyday life. Landlords fled, and labor became scarce in all cases, thus changing the most fundamental basis of social control in society.[77]

Strong states, from this vantage, are a clear-cut by-product of an eliminated landlord class and reduced labor supply. There is no mention of transformed discourses, identities, or sensibilities. The existence or size of particular social groups is all that matters. Thus power is addressed (unlike most development scholars and practitioners), but culture does not figure as a variable to be considered, studied, or changed.

Such a theory of development should be recognizable to readers familiar with the Marxist revolutions of the twentieth century. Mao Zedong, Vladimir Lenin, Pol Pot, Fidel Castro, and Ho Chi Minh all asserted, to varying degrees, that progress and prosperity was a simple process of purging the feudal, colonial and/or bourgeois classes. Such social determinist prescriptions led to what the CPV eventually admitted was an error. Landlords, many of whom had supported the revolution, were killed or tortured simply because they were or had been landlords. In *The Sacred Willow*, Duong Van Mai Elliot describes how one of her relatives, a high-ranking Mandarin and landlord, was threatened with execution, stripped of his home, and brutally humiliated, even though he had supported the Viet Minh and land reform policies. Furthermore, the most marginalized were touted as the pillars of land reform irrespective of their ethics, patriotism, politics, reputation, or capacities. Elliot described it as a "reverse form of class prejudice, the more destitute a peasant, the more worthy he or she appeared in the eyes of the Party. . . . Poor peasants who could neither read nor write, and who had no leadership skills, were given power."[78]

Thus most, if not all, twentieth-century revolutions that were inspired by Marxism were built upon and attempted to advance social determinist ideas and policies. As noted above, social location was presumed to determine interests as if group interests were fixed, acultural givens. Culture, when considered, was viewed as a reflex of social class. In this way, subjectivities, discourses, morality, and emotions—let alone free will—were rendered analytically unimportant. Like pool balls struck by a cue ball, semiotics and interpretative frameworks were the predictable consequence of social locations. No cultural diagnosis was required. The only germane issue was the existence and size of certain socio-economic classes; not how these sectors might imagine nation, modernity, self, other, the state, subalterns, the metaphysical, and interests.

With the benefit of hindsight, it is easy to recognize the errors of these Marxist projects but it would be a mistake to assume that this kind of aculturalism is a relic of the twentieth century. For example, one finds traces of these background assumptions in Paul Farmer's widely read and highly influential book, *Pathologies of Power* (2003). In an attempt to sensitize development agents to the question of power and address structural violence in ways that move beyond liberal ideals of formal inclusion in institutional processes, he posits a remedy that hints at social determinism. Farmer writes, "The central thesis of this book is that human rights abuses are best understood (that is, most accurately and comprehensively grasped) from the point of the view of the poor." Following through with Farmer's logic, he would predict that black and white sharecroppers in Arkansas would give us the best insight into human rights abuses in that part of the United States. In reality, however, they would give us radically different perspectives. In trying, then, to correct the wide-spread exclusion of subalterns from the formulation of development goals and strategies, Farmer forwards a solution that presumes consciousness is the unmediated product of socio-economic location. Consequently, he renders identities, values, discourses, and norms dependent variables and thus irrelevant as sites of analysis or intervention. Or in Farmer's words, "[C]ulture should enjoy an exceedingly limited role in explaining the distribution of misery."[79]

The problem with Farmer's analysis is that misery is—as has been persuasively argued by such luminaries as Michel Foucault, Stuart Hall, Raymond Williams, Antonio Gramsci, Jurgen Habermas, and Pierre Bourdieu, among others—the outgrowth of both the material and cultural. Discourses, sensibilities, and symbols play as large a role as the socio-material in determining the distribution of wretchedness and suffering. Consequently any project that attempts to diminish social inequalities, something upon which economic growth hinges, *must* take culture seriously. This is why Vik Muniz, the world-renowned Brazilian artist, asserted in the documentary film *Waste Land*, "Elitism is the poison of Brazil. The elite truly believe that they are better than others in Brazil."[80] The problem, in his opinion, is not with the elite per se but rather the attitude of superiority that prevails among the elite. Further complicating matters is the fact that this poison is not simply confined to the haves. It saturates the consciousness of the poor majority in Brazil, many of whom have internalized ideas of black inferiority, whitening, *favelado* qua criminal, and littleness. This fact alone should help the reader to appreciate why it is a mistake to assume that the poor will inevitably have a more critical consciousness or superior understanding of structural violence simply because they are marginalized and oppressed. It would, of course, make development practice much simpler if all we had to do was give voice to the poor, but this ignores the independence of culture. Semiotics, worldview, and identities are not free-floating and untethered from the socio-material but they are not determined by it either. Culture cannot be side-stepped by operationalizing it as the reflexive by-product of the social. Instead it must be studied, theorized, and certain aspects of it targeted for change—and not simply uncritically voiced—in order to reduce social inequalities and advance economic growth in societies like Brazil.

Notes

1 Hoang Dao Thuy, *Ha Noi thanh lich* (Han Noi, the City of Refinement and Elegance). Education Pub., 1996. Translated by and cited in Huu Ngoc in *Wandering Through Vietnamese Culture*, 1004–1005.
2 Cited in Evans, "The Developmental State," 232.
3 Lee, "Precis," 25.
4 Taylor, *A History of the Vietnamese*.
5 Kelley, *Beyond the Bronze Pillars*.
6 Taylor, *A History of the Vietnamese*, 621.
7 Hoang Dao Thuy, *Ha Noi thanh lich* (Han Noi, the City of Refinement and Elegance). Education Pub., 1996. Translated by and cited in Huu Ngoc in *Wandering Through Vietnamese Culture*, 1006.
8 Marr, *Vietnamese Tradition on Trial, 1920–1945*, 123.
9 Duiker, *Sacred War*, 255.
10 Marr, *Vietnamese Tradition on Trial, 1920–1945*, 124.
11 Le, "The Middle Class in Hanoi"; and Earl, *Vietnam's New Middle Classes*.
12 Scott, *Weapons of the Weak*.
13 Kerkvliet, *The Power of Everyday Politics*.
14 Aziz Filho and Eliane Cobato, "Marginais da classe media," 68–72; and Warren, *Racial Revolutions*, 5–8.
15 Unlike cities in the United States, poor people are usually concentrated in the suburbs or periphery of the cities in Brazil. These poorer neighborhoods or slums are commonly referred to as *favelas*.
16 "Popular," like people, does not translate neatly into English. In Brazilian Portuguese it connotes the poorer, predominantly nonwhite segments of society. For example, popular culture in English means a kind of mass media, consumer culture; whereas, in Portuguese it refers to the culture of the non-elites. Therefore when I use it in its Brazilian sense, I italicize the term to help distinguish it from its English meaning.
17 According to conventional social scientific definitions of class (e.g., daily spending of 10–100 USD), there were about 12 million middle-class people in Vietnam in 2012—a number that is supposed to grow to 33 million by 2020. This means that by 2020 about one-third of the population will be middle class (given that the population is estimated to be 97 million by that year) and most of the remaining population will be above the poverty line but still earn less than 300 USD per month. Thu, "The Middle Class in Hanoi."
18 Ibid.
19 *Cidade de Deus* (City of God), directed by Walter Salles, Donald Ranvaud, Andrea Barata Ribeiro, 2003.
20 When manufacturing took off in Sao Paulo in the mid-twentieth century, thanks to the developmental state, thousands of landless people from the countryside, most of who were the descendants of slaves and lived in slave-like conditions, moved to Sao Paulo in hopes of bettering their lives. Migrants came largely from the interior of Sao Paulo, Minas Gerais, and the so-called Northeast. However in everyday parlance, these migrants and their descendants are all lumped together and labeled "nordestinos" or Northeasterners.
21 O'Dougherty, *Consumption Intensified*, 179.
22 Central Intelligence Agency (CIA). *The World Factbook*. www.cia.gov/library/publications/the-world-factbook/rankorder/2004rank.html?countryName=Brazil&countryCode=br&regionCode=soa&rank=103#br. Accessed February 8, 2013.
23 Viet Minh is an abbreviation for Viet Nam Doc Lap Dong Minh Hoi (League for the Independence of Vietnam) that was initially led and then eventually usurped by the Communist Party Vietnam. This coalition originally formed to end French colonialism

and then later directed its attention towards the reunification of Vietnam, after the Republic of Vietnam and its backer, the United States, refused to comply with the 1954 Geneva Accords in which general elections were to be held in 1956.

24 Woodside, *Lost Modernities*.
25 Marr, *Vietnamese Tradition on Trial*, 4.
26 Duiker, *Sacred War*, 109.
27 Marr, *Vietnamese Tradition on Trial*, 4.
28 Schneider, "The *Desarrollista* State in Brazil and Mexico," 303–304.
29 Swinkle, World Bank economist. Interviewed by Jonathan Warren, 2004 in Hanoi.
30 Central Intelligence Agency (CIA). The World Factbook. www.cia.gov/library/publications/the-world-factbook/rankorder/2004rank.html?countryName=Brazil&countryCode=br&regionCode=soa&rank=103#br. Accessed February 8, 2013.
31 Taylor, *Fragments of the Present*, 161.
32 Ngoc, *Wandering Through Vietnamese Culture*, 170.
33 Nguyen-Vo, *The Ironies of Freedom*, 51–60.
34 Yan, "Self-Development of Migrant Women and the Production of *Suzhi* (Quality) as Surplus Value."
35 Central do brasil (Central Station). Director Walter Salles, 1998. Audiovisual Development Bureau, Ministerio de Cultura, Brasilia.
36 The Han and Kinh are the dominant ethnic groups in China and Vietnam, respectively. In both countries, there are officially fifty-four distinct ethnic groups. The Han make up about 90 percent of the population in China and 85 percent of the population in Vietnam are Kinh. In neither country are peasants seen as racially or ethnically distinct from the economic and political elite. In Vietnam merchants were historically racialized as Chinese, and mountainous people were viewed, as they are today, as ethnically distinct.
37 McHale, *Print and Power*, 44.
38 Caldeira, *City of Walls*, 383.
39 Skidmore, *Black into White*.
40 Ibid., 66.
41 Sheriff, *Dreaming Equality*; Hanchard, *Orpheus and Power*; Twine, *Racism in a Racial Democracy*; Warren, *Racial Revolutions*; and Telles, *Race in Another America*.
42 Evaristo, *Poncia Vicencio*, iii.
43 Neate and Platt, *Culture is our Weapon*; and *Favela Rising*, directed by Jeff Zimbalist and Matt Mochary, 2009.
44 Woodside, *Lost Modernities*, 59.
45 Himmelfarb, *The Roads to Modernity*, 121.
46 Skultans, *The Testimony of Lives*, 165.
47 Another example of a similar socio-cultural movement in Europe was Grundtvigism in Denmark, which emerged in the early 19th century and emphasized a valuation of land, country, God, and ordinary people or folk.
48 Skultans, *The Testimony of Lives*, 2.
49 Wilcken, *Empire Adrift*, 182–188.
50 Luiz, seventy-three-year-old retired cobbler, Aracuai, Minas Gerais. Interview by author, 2009.
51 Andrews, *Blacks and Whites in Sao Paulo Brazil, 1888–1988*.
52 Caldeira, *City of Walls*, 51–52.
53 Ibid. A parallel kind of anti-democratic backlash happened in the US in the wake of the civil rights movement's successes in the 1960s. Racialized crime narratives began circulating widely among whites and in the white media in the 1970s and 1980s. These have been credited with helping to fuel mass incarceration in the United States. See Alexander, *The New Jim Crow*.
54 Schwarz, *Misplaced Ideas*, 27.
55 Ravallion and van de Walle, *Land in Transition*, 176.

56 Glewwe, "An Overview of Economic Growth and Household Welfare in Vietnam in the 1990s," 7.
57 Masina, *Vietnam's Development Strategies*, 95–100.
58 Caldeira, *City of Walls*, 227.
59 The other major factors were a growing economy spurred by a commodity boom and the loosening of access to credit to the general public.
60 Kerstenetzky, "The Brazilian Developmental State."
61 Novais, "Rio de Janeiro."
62 Galiza, "Grandes Eventos, Obras e Remocoes na Cidade do Rio de Janeiro, do Seculo XIX ao XXI."
63 Fischer, *A Poverty of Rights*.
64 Coatsworth, "ReVista," 7.
65 Bartolone, "Land for Those Who Work It."
66 Education monies are distributed heavily in favor of higher education and thus in favor of the elite. Over 360 billion USD (12 percent of GDP) was spent on pensions in 2015, the primary benefactors being retired judges and military officers—again individuals disproportionately from the privileged sectors of society—versus 9 billion USD (2.5 percent of GDP) spent on *Bolsa Familia*. Finally, at least 2 billion USD has been spent on port renovations in Rio de Janerio that have displaced large poor communities and eliminated important historical sites (e.g., the largest slave auction pen in the world) in order to offer subsidies to developers like Donald Trump. Helena da Rosa Galiza, "Mega Events, Building Works, and Population Removal in Rio de Janeiro between 19th and 21st Centuries."
67 Central Intelligence Agency (CIA). *The World Factbook*. www.cia.gov/library/publications/the-world-factbook/rankorder/2004rank.html?countryName=Brazil&countryCode=br&regionCode=soa&rank=103#br. Accessed February 8, 2013.
68 Central Intelligence Agency (CIA). The World Factbook. www.cia.gov/library/publications/the-world-factbook/rankorder/2004rank.html?countryName=Brazil&countryCode=br&regionCode=soa&rank=103#br. Accessed February 8, 2013.
69 Sen, *Development as Freedom*, 260.
70 Sue, *Land of the Cosmic Race*.
71 Stiglitz, "In No One We Trust," A 21.
72 Examples include Ferguson, *The Anti-Politics Machine*; Lawson, *Making Development Geography*; Uvin, *Aiding Violence*; Escobar, *Encountering Development*.
73 Farmer, *Pathologies of Power*.
74 Ferguson, *The Anti-Politics Machine*.
75 Said, *Covering Islam*.
76 Uvin, *Aiding Violence*, 156.
77 Migdal, *Strong Societies and Weak States*, 270.
78 Elliott, *The Sacred Willow*, 348.
79 Farmer, *Pathologies of Power*, 49.
80 *Waste Land*, directed by Lucy Walker, 2011.

Bibliography

Alexander, Michelle. *The New Jim Crow: Mass Incarceration in the Age of Colorblindness*. New York: The New Press, 2010.

Andrews, George Reid. *Blacks and Whites in Sao Paulo Brazil, 1888–1988*. Pittsburg, PA: Pittsburg University Press, 1991.

Caldeira, Teresa P. R. *City of Walls: Crime, Segregation, and Citizenship in São Paulo*. Berkeley, CA: University of California Press, 2000.

Central Intelligence Agency (CIA). *The World Factbook*. www.cia.gov/library/publications/the-world-factbook/rankorder/2004rank.html?countryName=Brazil&countryCode=br&regionCode=soa&rank=103#br. Accessed February 8, 2013.

Cidade de Deus (City of God). Directed by Walter Salles, Donald Ranvaud, Andrea Barata Ribeiro, et al., O2 Filmes. Distributed by Buena Vista Home Entertainment, Inc. São Paulo, Brazil/Burbank, CA, 2003.

Coatsworth, John H. "ReVista." *Harvard Review of Latin America* (Spring, 2007): 7–13.

Conceicao Evaristo. *Ponciá Vicencio*. Austin, TX: Host Publications, 2007.

Duiker, William. *Sacred War: Nationalism and Revolution in A Divided Vietnam*. 1st ed. New York: McGraw-Hill, 1994.

Earl, Catherine. *Vietnam's New Middle Classes: Gender, Career, City*. Copenhagen: NIAS Press.

Elliott, Duong Van Mai. *The Sacred Willow: Four Generations in the Life of a Vietnamese Family*. Oxford: Oxford University Press, 2000.

Escobar, Arturo. *Encountering Development: The Making and Unmaking of the Third World*. Princeton, NJ: Princeton University Press, 2011

Evans, Peter. "The Developmental State: Divergent Responses to Modern Economic Theory and the Twenty-First-Century Economy." In *The End of the Developmental State?*, Michelle Williams (Ed.), 220–240. New York: Routledge, 2014.

Farmer, Paul. *Pathologies of Power: Health, Human Rights, and the New War on the Poor*. Berkeley, CA: University of California Press, 2003.

Favela Rising. Directed by Jeff Zimbalist and Matt Mochary. THINKfilm and HBO/Cinemax Documentary Films. USA, 2009.

Ferguson, James. *The Anti-Politics Machine: Development, Depoliticization, and Bureaucratic Power in Lesotho*. Minneapolis, MN: University of Minnesota Press, 1994.

Filho, Aziz, and Eliane Cobato. "Marginais da classe media" (The outcasts of the middle class). *Isto É* (July 4, 2007): 68–72.

Fischer, Brodwyn. *A Poverty of Rights: Citizenship and Inequality in Twentieth-Century Rio de Janeiro*. Palo Alto, CA: Stanford University Press, 2008.

Galiza, Helena. "Grandes Eventos, Obras e Remocoes na Cidade do Rio de Janeiro, do Século XIX ao XXI" [Big events, public works, and gentrification in Rio de Janeiro, 19th through 21st centuries). II Conferencia Internacional Megaeventos e Cidades, do Ettern/Ippur/UFRJ (coordenado pelo Prof. Carlos Vainer), 2013.

Glewwe, Paul. "An Overview of Economic Growth and Household Welfare in Vietnam in the 1990s." In *Economic Growth, Poverty and Household Welfare in Vietnam*, Paul Glewwe, Nisha Agrawal, and David Dollar (Eds.), 1–26. Washington, DC: The World Bank, 2004.

Hanchard, Michael. *Orpheus and Power: The Movement to Negro of Rio de Janerio and Sao Paulo, Brazil, 1945–1988*. Princeton, NJ: Princeton University Press, 1994.

Himmelfarb, Gertrude. *The Roads to Modernity: The British, French, and American Enlightenments*. New York: Vintage Books, 2005.

Johnson, Chalmers. *MITI and the Japanese Miracle: The Growth of Industrial Policy 1925–1975*. Palo Alto, CA: Stanford University Press, 1982.

Kelley, Liam C. *Beyond the Bronze Pillars: Envoy Poetry and the Sino-Vietnamese Relationship*. Honolulu, HI: University of Hawai'i Press, 2005.

Kerkvliet, Benedict J. Tria. *The Power of Everyday Politics: How Vietnamese Peasants Transformed National Policy*. Ithaca, NY: Cornell University Press, 2005.

Kerstenetzky, Celia Lessa. "The Brazilian Developmental State: A Progressive Agenda in a (Still) Conservative Political Economy." In *The End of the Developmental State?*, Michelle Williams (Ed.), 172–196. New York: Routledge, 2014.

Kohli, Atul. *State-Directed Development: Political Power and Industrialization in the Global Periphery*. Cambridge, UK: Cambridge University Press, 2004.

Lawson, Victoria. "Beyond the Firm: Restructuring Gender Divisions of Labor in Quito's Garment Industry under Austerity." *Environment and Planning D: Society and Space* 13, no. 4 (1995): 415–444.

Lawson, Victoria. *Making Development Geography*. London: Hodder Education, 2007.

Le, Thu Huong . "The Middle Class in Hanoi: Vulnerability and Concerns—Analysis." *Eurasia Review*. www.eurasiareview.com/10032015-the-middle-class-in-hanoi-vulnera bility-and-concerns-analysis/. Accessed March 10, 2015.

Lee, Hong Yung. "Précis." In *A Comparative Study of East Asian Capitalism*, Hong Yung Lee (Ed.), 1–10. Berkeley, CA: Institute of East Asian Studies, 2014.

McHale, Shawn Frederick. *Print and Power: Confucianism, Communism, and Buddhism in the Making of Modern Vietnam*. Honolulu, HI: University of Hawai'i Press, 2004.

Marr, David G. *Vietnamese Tradition on Trial, 1920–1945*. Berkeley, CA: University of California Press, 1984.

Masina, Pietro. *Vietnam's Development Strategies*. New York: Routledge, 2006.

Migdal, Joel S. *Strong Societies and Weak States: State–Society Relations and State Capabilities in the Third World*. Princeton, NJ: Princeton University Press, 1988.

Neate, Patrick, and Damian Platt. *Culture Is Our Weapon: Making Music and Changing Lives in Rio de Janeiro*. New York: Penguin Books, 2010.

Ngoc, Huu. *Wandering Through Vietnamese Culture*. Hanoi: The Gioi Publishers, 2008.

Nguyen-vo , Thu-Huong. *The Ironies of Freedom: Sex, Culture, and Neoliberal Governance in Vietnam*. Seattle, WA: University of Washington Press, 2008.

Novais, Pedro. "Rio de Janeiro: Urbanistic Challenges/Experiments for a City at a Crossroads." In *Transforming Distressed Global Communities: Making Inclusive, Safe, Resilient, and Sustainable Cities*, Fritz Wagner, Riad Mahayni, and Andreas G. Piller (Eds.), 139–160. New York: Routledge, 2016

O'Dougherty, Maureen. *Consumption Intensified: The Politics of Middle-Class Daily Life in Brazil*. Durham, NC: Duke University Press, 2002.

Ravallion, Martin, and Dominique van de Walle. *Land in Transition: Reform and Poverty in Rural Vietnam*. New York: Palgrave Macmillan, 2008.

Said, Edward W. *Covering Islam: How the Media and the Experts Determine How We See the Rest of the World*. New York: Pantheon Books, 1981.

Schneider, Ben Ross. "The Desarrollista State in Brazil and Mexico." In *The Developmental State*, Meredith Woo-Cummings (Ed.), 276–305. Ithaca, NY: Cornell University Press, 1999.

Schwarz, Roberto. *Misplaced Ideas: Essays on Brazilian Culture*. London/New York: Verso, 1992.

Scott, James C. *Weapons of the Weak: Everyday Forms of Peasant Resistance*. New Haven, CT: Yale University Press, 1985.

Scott, James C. *Domination and the Arts of Resistance: Hidden Transcripts*. New Haven, CT: Yale University Press, 1990.

Sen, Amartya Kumar. *Development as Freedom*. New Delhi/Oxford: Oxford University Press, 2000.

Sheriff, Robin E. *Dreaming Equality: Color, Race, and Racism in Brazil*. New Brunswick, NJ: Rutgers University Press, 2001.

Skidmore, Thomas E. *Black into White: Race and Nationality in Brazilian Thought*. Durham, NC: Duke University Press, 1993.

Skultans, Vieda. *The Testimony of Lives: Narrative and Memory in Post-Soviet Latvia*. London: Routledge, 1997.

Stiglitz, Joseph E. "In No One We Trust." *New York Times*. December 22, 2013, A21.

Sue, Christina A. *Land of the Cosmic Race: Race Mixture, Racism, and Blackness in Mexico*. New York: Oxford Press, 2013.

Taylor, Keith W. *A History of the Vietnamese*. Cambridge: Cambridge University Press, 2013.

Taylor, Philip. *Fragments of the Present: Searching for Modernity in Vietnam's South*. Honolulu, HI: University of Hawai'i Press, 2000.

Telles, Edward. *Race in Another America: The Significance of Skin Color in Brazil*. Princeton, NJ: Princeton University Press, 2004.

Twine, France Winddance. *Racism in a Racial Democracy: The Maintenance of White Supremacy in Brazil*. New Brunswick, NJ: Rutgers University Press, 1997.

Uvin, Peter. *Aiding Violence: The Development Enterprise in Rwanda*. West Hartford, CT: Kumarian Press, 1998.

Warren, Jonathan. *Racial Revolutions: Antiracism and Indian Resurgence in Brazil*. Durham, NC: Duke University Press, 2001.

Waste Land. Directed by Lucy Walker. New Video Group. United States, 2011.

Wilcken, Patrick. *Empire Adrift: The Portuguese Court in Rio De Janeiro: 1808–1821*. New Edition. London: Bloomsbury, 2005.

Woodside, Alexander. *Lost Modernities: China, Vietnam, Korea, and the Hazards of World History*. Cambridge, MA: Harvard University Press, 2006.

Yan, Hairong. "Self-Development of Migrant Women and the Production of Suzhi (Quality) as Surplus Value." In *Everyday Modernity in China*, Madeleine Yue Dong, and Joshua Goldstein (Eds.), 227–259. Seattle, WA: University of Washington Press, 2006.

3 Indigenizing Modernity

> We Brazilians and other Latin Americans constantly experience the artificial, inauthentic, and imitative nature of our cultural life.
>
> Roberto Schwarz (b. 1938)[1]

In 1999, I participated in some of the marches surrounding the World Trade Organization (WTO) talks taking place in Seattle. Much to my chagrin protestors like me were cast as opponents to globalization. I was uncomfortable with the anti-globalization label because I did not view globalization as the problem. Instead, I was concerned with process and who had the power to define the terms of globalization. More bluntly, I was against the global economic rules being written by unelected technocrats of a predictable pedigree, i.e., well-to-do individuals who believed in the validity of neoclassical economics and too often mistook elite interests for those of the common good. Thus, what was at stake for me was not globalization per se, but rather the kind of globalization.

I suspect that many, if not most, of the other protestors shared my position. The anti-globalization tag, however, was not merely a figment of the media's imagination. Many activists and opinion makers were and continue to be, anti-globalization advocates. For instance, Walden Bello, has argued that any global institution, democratic or not, is prone to fall victim to "the same Jurassic trap that ensnared organizations as different as IBM . . . and the Soviet state," namely the imposition of a monolithic system of universal rules by an overly centralized bureaucratic structure that is unable "to tolerate and profit from diversity."[2] Consequently Bello advocates deglobalization as the best method for advancing economic development. In his opinion the more global institutions are weakened, such as the WTO and Bretton Woods organizations, the more developing countries will be able to tailor strategies to their particularities of their societies, and thus the more effective these initiatives will be.[3] Developing countries do not need a centralized global institution such as the WTO, he argues, but rather "the deconcentration and decentralization of institutional power and the creation of a pluralistic system of institutions and organizations interacting with one another, guided by broad and flexible agreements and understandings."[4]

Bello's anti-globalization stance is predicated upon a critique of "'mono-economics'—the idea that there is a single set of economic laws applicable at all times and in all places."[5] That is, he believes that a one-size-fits-all development approach is a recipe for economic failure because markets and societies are not monolithic. And indeed this is increasingly the position of a number of development experts, who argue that the imposition of foreign-inspired blueprints—what some call "institutional monocropping"[6]—impairs economic development.[7] In their opinion, development projects will only be successful if they are informed and shaped by local knowledge, skills, and thus fit to the contours of the society in question.

If more organic, locally attuned development institutions are important parts of the formula for economic success, then one question that arises is how much space is available for developing countries to create their own, indigenized brand of capitalism, especially given the constraints imposed by international trade agreements such as the WTO. Ha-Joon Chang thinks that there is much more room for maneuverability than is commonly assumed.[8] He writes, "the constraints [of the WTO] are not as widespread and binding as they are usually argued to be."[9] Although developing countries may have "to exercise a considerable amount of policy ingenuity and administrative and diplomatic skill" to maintain infant industrial policies, East Asia countries offer proof that it is possible under the current global governance system.[10] It is undeniably true that East Asian governments, despite being signatories to the WTO, have created their own models of capitalism that have, probably because of this, performed exceptionally well. Peter Evans observes, for example, "the star performers in terms of sheer economic growth during the last ten years—e.g., China, Vietnam, and Malaysia—exhibit institutional patterns that are embarrassingly hybrid relative to the monocropping ideal."[11]

If tailoring institutions to local contexts is both preferable and possible, then what facilitates or impedes this process besides weakening global institutions along the lines of Bello's recommendations? To this important economic question, development scholars do not have many satisfactory answers. One of the few that I am familiar with comes from a subset of institutionalists who argue that building more democratic modes of governmentality—"participatory political institutions,"[12] "empowered participatory governance,"[13] and "deliberative democracy"[14]—will reduce, if not prevent, monocropping development practices. In *Seeing Like a State*, James Scott nicely articulates their reasoning: "[D]emocracy itself is based on the assumption that the metis [a local knowledge born of experience in a given context] of its citizenry should, in mediated form, continually modify the laws and the policies of the land."[15] That is, if people are given the political mechanisms to shape policies and regulations (e.g., through direct elections, participatory institutions, and other democratic processes), then government initiatives, laws, and organizations will be better adapted to that society.

Coming from the United States, with its long-standing liberal political tradition, such a theory makes a great deal of intuitive sense. The problem with respect to the cases of Vietnam and Brazil, however, is that the democracy-will-mitigate-against-monocropping thesis does not hold up to the empirical realities of these societies. As we have seen, Vietnam's institutions are more hybrid than Brazil's, remarkably so according to Evans, despite the Vietnamese government being much less participatory and democratic than Brazil's. Clearly, then, the key independent variable, at least in these instances, is not the degree of political democracy.

While searching for an alternative explanation of why economic institutions were more hybrid or custom-made in Vietnam than Brazil, I came across Gary Hamilton's article on *guanxi* capitalism in Taiwan. Hamilton observed that while Taiwan was transitioning to democratic rule in the mid-1990s, government bureaucrats and policymakers attempted to recreate certain perceived strengths of the Japanese economy: large-sized, government-sponsored trading companies, business lending via the formal banking sector, vertically integrated and more permanent subcontracting systems, and a world-class export-oriented car manufacturing industry. These initiatives failed, according to Hamilton, because they cut against the grain of the *guanxi* social networks upon which Taiwanese capitalism had been built. For example, it was customary to rely on one's social network of friends, family, schoolmates, fellow villagers, and neighbors to generate the capital needed to start or expand a business. And so, according to Hamilton, the attempt to shift lending to a formal banking system—like in Japan—did not succeed because it ignored the *guanxi* character of the Taiwanese society and economy.

Although this description was helpful in offering another example of the indigenizing impulse in East Asia, it was his analysis of state agency that proved so valuable to me. While speculating on why unelected government officials in Taiwan abandoned their attempts to recreate facets of the Japanese model, Hamilton theorized that "the Taiwan state has to contend with and ultimately to accept the established patterns and economic momentum that exist within the society, the very patterns that arise out of Taiwan's horizontal economic networks."[16] And here the reader gets to see the value of comparative studies because as a Latin Americanist this made absolutely no sense to me. Why would the state *have* to contend with and ultimately accept established patterns in a society—especially an authoritarian one? Indeed I anticipated much an opposite outcome, one that went something like this:

> The well-meaning Taiwanese officials, who are concerned with and responsible for improving the nation's economy, conclude that they should double down and push forward with the development strategies that more closely parallel the Japanese model despite initial failures and setbacks. The problem, they reason, is not a defect with the model—given that the model works exceptionally well in Japan—but with the societal context that is impeding its successful execution. Thus the domestic patterns of *guanxi* social practices should be targeted for change or elimination (and certainly not respected!) because they are barriers to the economic growth that the superior, Japanese model promises to deliver.

This hypothetical scenario ran through my head because this is what typically happens in Brazil. The inclination of government bureaucrats (appointed or not), policymakers (elected or not), and the general public (at least a large percentage of it) is to blame society rather than the imported economic formulas. Thus the clash of Hamilton's thesis of state behavior with my Brazil-informed expectations allowed me to see, for the first time, regionally distinct levels of respect for native norms and customs that appears to influence the degree of institutional monocropping. Given the potential utility of this insight for development practitioners, in particular those looking to indigenize economic institutions, I began looking for what might lie beneath the relative disdain or concern for domestic patterns.

What I eventually uncovered were different epistemologies of modernization. "Modernity," Charles Taylor writes, "always unfolds within a specific cultural or civilizational context . . . [which] interact in specific ways under the exigencies of history and politics to produce alternative modernities. . . ."[17] In this chapter I argue that a key feature of this cultural context, at least in the cases of Vietnam and Brazil, is the background assumptions of modernization. More specifically, I contend that how a society believes the process of modernization will or should occur powerfully impacts the extent to which economic institutions are tailored to local conditions. As I detail below, I found that modernization is largely thought of as a practice of imitation in Brazil. Echoing how modernizationist theorists conceptualized this process (as discussed in Chapter One), home-grown traditions tend to be regarded as impediments to progress that will or should be discarded in order to make room for the implantation of a first world modernity. In Vietnam, the reader will find, modernization is understood in very different terms. If and when done properly, Western modernities are to be domesticated or assimilated such that a Vietnamese cultural core is left largely unscathed. Unlike Brazil, the metis of the citizenry is not viewed as something to be casually discarded as the price of progress but rather it is highly prized and therefore all efforts should and must be made to protect and incorporate it within the new.

Domesticating Modernity

Among the Vietnamese I interviewed, most gave the Communist Party of Vietnam (CPV) credit for successfully decolonizing Vietnam and reuniting the country. The CPV also received high marks for its stewardship of economic development since the late 1980s. But these positive sentiments were offset by a deep frustration with the CPV. The primary grievance did not hinge on questions of democracy, such as the limitations of personal expression, human rights violations, or the absence of a competitive electoral system. What irritated, if not enraged, the Vietnamese with whom I spoke was cronyism, police extortion, and the perceived bilking of the public treasure and everyday citizens. In this context, embracing globalization, such as joining the WTO, was overwhelmingly favored by those I interviewed because it was hoped that such steps would help to mute, if not remedy, government corruption and in the process bring higher levels of economic growth. It was reasoned, for instance, that the egregious levels of embezzlement and government mismanagement, especially within the state-owned enterprises (SOEs), would not be sustainable. Most interviewees believed that corruption would lessen within SOEs as pressures to compete in the global marketplace increased and certain internationally recognized "best practices"—such as independent auditing procedures—became more widely adopted.

Even though those I interviewed viewed globalization as a tool for reducing government graft, they did not frame globalization in utopian terms. Indeed, most Vietnamese with whom I spoke fretted aloud their concerns about what they perceived as the potential risks and dangers involved with globalizing the Vietnamese economy and society. For example Thuy, a thirty-five-year-old administrative assistant from Hanoi, observed:

> I'm very happy about [joining the WTO].[18] We'll have lots of chances now. There will be more foreign direct investment and we will also learn about newer technologies. This is good for Vietnam. There will be some bad effects as well. Many small companies in Vietnam will likely die. If they continue to pay low salaries and fail to improve their procedures, they will perish. Or at least a number of smaller companies will be forced to merge into larger, foreign-controlled companies in order to survive.

Figure 3.1 Hanoian Entrepreneurs. Photograph by author, 2015

Thuy's sentiments were typical.[19] Even though she believed that the political and economic impact of globalization would be on balance advantageous, she was not insensitive to the financial difficulties it would cause for some, especially during the transition period. Interviewees were even less sanguine about the socio-cultural effects. A number of individuals identified, often with great consternation, the impact that Western-inflected modernization may have on Vietnamese culture. The comments of Ha, a twenty-six-year-old internet technology developer working in Hanoi in 2006, were typical. After extolling the positive impact that Vietnam's entry into the WTO was apt to have for the economy, I asked whether she was worried about the social and cultural impact of the WTO and globalization more generally.

HA: Sometimes people say it's dangerous, especially for the young people, because they can be influenced by the culture from other countries. There is a real danger because we are an Eastern people that could be affected by the Western lifestyle and other things. For me, it's no problem because I'm no longer young. I'm twenty-six. I can adapt to a new environment but retain the basic culture of Vietnam.

JONATHAN: Are most people like you or will most forget their Vietnamese culture and become Western?

HA: Fifty percent. But I think that young people who are well educated by their families or the university will not be too greatly impacted.

JONATHAN: What's an example of someone who has been too heavily influenced by globalization?

HA: For example, some people, some students, they think that Vietnam is a poor country with a low living standard and so they want to go abroad and never return to Vietnam. They only think about the higher standard of living in the West and so they neglect their families and they don't want to conform to certain traditions. They want to live abroad and they don't appreciate traditional Vietnamese music or some other tradition. Or they don't want to live with their family and maybe practice the new lifestyle. They like to dye their hair and dress like Western people. If we go to a formal meeting or some ceremony, we need to wear a formal suit. But they can come with a T-shirt or shorts. And they don't like traditional Vietnamese music—only pop and rock. They can have a baby without a family—it's a Western not a traditional Vietnamese behavior. Sexual relationships are increasing among young people. They are being influenced by the mass media from the West and other countries.

JONATHAN: You see lots of this? Is this common?

HA: Not many; just some.

JONATHAN: And you believe this can be mitigated if they have a good education from the family or schools.

HA: Yes.

JONATHAN: And do most people have a good education?

HA: Yes.[20]

Initially Ha argues that Vietnamese traditions are in grave jeopardy, given that 50 percent of the population is already "too Western." She then backtracks, claiming that the traditions are not really in danger given that most Vietnamese are properly educated. Therefore Vietnamese traditions will not be too greatly impacted by modernization. This narrative was common in many of the interviews: a preliminary assertion that Vietnamese culture was on the brink, followed by an upbeat conclusion that most Vietnamese traditional values and practices would endure, given some concerted attention and effort to the matter. Consequently I interpreted Ha's and others' assessment that large chunks of the Vietnamese population were already too Western as a political, rather than sociological statement, aimed at motivating themselves and other Vietnamese to be on guard against the possible erosion of Vietnamese traditions as Vietnam underwent globalization.

Interestingly, there was a high degree of consensus among the interviewees as to what constituted the central contours of Vietnamese traditions and the evidence of their erosion. Interviewees frequently raised the issue of aesthetics, such as hair coloring and clothing, to indicate a decline of Vietnamese culture. A number of so-called immoral practices, in particular illicit drug use, out of wedlock births, and casual or premarital sex, were invoked as examples of Westernization. Interviewees also mentioned excessive individualism and materialism as indicators of cultural contamination. All concurred that Vietnamese/Asian people placed affinities to community and family above individual desires or material enrichment. Hence, Ha's observation that some Vietnamese prioritized self above nation and family—they were abandoning Vietnam and their families in pursuit of a higher standard of living abroad—was meant as an especially cutting criticism of these individuals.

Ha's comments also raise the specter of Asian orientalism, or perhaps more accurately, occidentalism. Much like the rest of East Asia, the Vietnamese, or at least the ones I interviewed, imagine Asia and the West as ontologically distinct in terms of both culture and blood. Aihwa Ong, for one, discussed how this Asian orientalism has been strategically used to rationalize authoritarian regimes in Singapore and Malaysia. Political leaders in these countries sometimes contend that their societies can modernize without the political changes associated with liberalism in the West because, their reasoning goes, "We are Asian."[21] The fact that government leaders can—and do—use orientalism to legitimate repressive political regimes testifies to its currency in the region.

In Vietnam I never encountered an orientalist defense of authoritarian rule, but I did frequently hear the expression *qua tay*—"too Western." Often transgressive women or rebellious young people were singled out as being *qua tay*. But this label was not limited to gender or generational politics. This condemnation was also frequently leveled, according to interviewees, by others in society against Vietnamese whom neighbors, friends, colleagues, or strangers perceived as deviating too much from core Vietnamese traditions. Thuy, as mentioned above, enthusiastically embraced globalization. She also identified herself as a traditionalist and considered 70 percent of Vietnamese to be *qua tay*. Not everyone, or even most people with whom I spoke, identified as a traditionalist—but a surprisingly large number of interviewees did. And even if they did not explicitly identify as a traditionalist they agreed that a number of Vietnamese were excessively Westernized. Again, this usually meant individuals who dressed a bit eccentrically, deviated too radically from conventional gender scripts, used foreign words too frequently, prioritized the self over family, or valued money above other concerns such as being a good person or spending time with one's spouse and children.

All of this helped me to identify tradition as the epistemological equivalent of modernity in contemporary Vietnam. In *Fragments of the Present*, Phillip Taylor observes that modernity is one of the "most important experiential categories" in Vietnam. "The symbolism of modernity," he writes, "[has been] widely incorporated into people's self-conceptions and [has become] a charter for diverse projects of self-actualization. An imagined relationship to the modern [has] informed a great variety of attempts . . . to enforce change, as well as to accommodate and resist it."[22] The comments of my interviewees indicate that the same can be said for tradition. That is, tradition, like modernity, is a core anchor of identities and politics in Vietnam and is often employed to advance or hinder societal and policy changes.

A historical example of the valence of tradition is how some in the south responded to their subaltern status in the aftermath of the American War. The CPV defined allies of the Republic of Vietnam (RVN) as traitors who had backed foreigners committed to colonizing and dividing the nation. Moreover, supporters of the RVN were officially described as being so socially and culturally contaminated by colonialism and capitalism that they posed a threat to the realization of modernity both locally and nationally.[23] A common strategy used to counter this pariah status and the socio-economic polices of the new regime was by describing the CPV and their development programs as anti-traditional. On this point, Taylor writes:

> Criticism of the new regime's approach to intellectuals, seniority, gender relations, and religion were directed at the violence done in the building of a "new life" at the expense of cultural traditions. . . . Many saw the new regime's campaign to sweep away the "alien," "noxious," and "mongrel vestiges of neo-colonial culture" as quite the opposite: that is, a campaign aimed at eliminating Vietnamese culture and replacing it with foreign contents and forms.[24]

Obviously, if tradition were not highly valued in Vietnam, then it would make little sense to attempt to discredit the CPV and their policies in such terms.

The fact that these initiatives were officially reversed in 1986 suggests that this line of criticism packs a powerful punch. Of course, it is impossible to prove a causal link between *Doi Moi* in 1986 and the discourses positioning the CPV's policies as anti-traditionalist, but this narrative's on-going circulation indicates that many believe in its political efficacy. Indeed, whenever I am in Ho Chi Minh

City, I am always struck by the wide-spread presence of this set of discourses. Much like what Taylor documented among Saigon intellectuals in an earlier generation, I find that people continue to use this reasoning to chide and critique the CPV. For instance, when asking polite questions about how things are going, many seize the opportunity to remark about how various social ills, such as crime, prostitution, and drug use, are on the rise, and then conclude by noting how all of this was the predictable outcome of the CPV's assaults on the family, religion, and other Vietnamese traditions after the war.

Figure 3.2 Doctor of Traditional Chinese Medicine. Photograph by author, 2010

One further example of the symbolic heft of tradition in Vietnam was how artists in northern Vietnam used it to loosen the constraints on artistic expression in the 1980s. During the high socialist era in North Vietnam (1954–1982), only social realist forms of art were permitted—expressionist, surrealist, or abstract styles were considered bourgeois, decadent, and therefore prohibited. The painter Nguyen Tu Nghiem, born in Nghe An Province in 1922, figured out an ingenious way around these restrictions. He experimented with expressionist styles but took as his subject matter various icons of Vietnamese "tradition"—symbols of the lunar calendar, village life, and traditional folk festivals or dances. Thus by choosing "tradition" as his subject matter, he and eventually other painters successfully inoculated themselves against the government censors. Nora Taylor described how this move helped to open up space for painters to work with different artistic genres.

> Since abstraction and surrealism were forbidden, artists had not used motifs found in their native culture to express "modern" artistic concepts. Nguyen Tu Nghiem changed that. . . . Like the African sculptures incorporated by European modernists into their works, the village carvings that Nguyen Tu Nghiem employed were removed from their original culture context. He was merely employing what he thought to be their interesting forms, not paying particular attention to the meaning of their content. The younger generation of artists found his idea brilliant. Imitating Nghiem allowed them to experiment with semiabstract shapes without deviating from their indigenous cultural sphere. They could maintain national identity while still attempting to experiment with other forms. *Sustaining "tradition," so to speak, also gave them a guarantee against potential criticism from the Arts Association* [emphasis added].[25]

The ability, then, to claim the mantle of tradition allowed artists to expand the limits of politically acceptable artistic forms. The central point here being that if tradition were not a valued category in Vietnam, then Nguyen Tu Nghiem's and others' attempts to alter the Vietnamese artistic canon in this manner would most likely have failed.

I believe that the esteemed position that tradition enjoys in Vietnam, as illustrated above, translates into an editing posture vis-à-vis development practice—a factor that development scholars, even those concerned with institutional monocropping, have failed to grasp. That is, adapting modernities (which are broadly considered to be Western in origin) to Vietnamese traditions is regarded as preferable if not inevitable, a kind of ontological imperative. Indeed I found a widespread belief that to copy wholesale a Western-derived modernity to an Asian/Vietnamese context was both unpatriotic and unnatural—a violation of nation and race. Consequently, economic development may entail Westernization, but only to a certain degree and in particular ways. Some changes were viewed as inevitable and even desired. Nonetheless, all modernization endeavors, including sought-after ones, should be altered to protect core Vietnamese traditions as much as possible. Among those

Figure 3.3 Roosters by Nguyen Tu Nghiem, 2005. Author's collection

with whom I spoke, it was considered the obligation of both the government and individual citizens to mold globalization to the contours of certain foundational Asian/Vietnamese values and practices.

For reasons that will become clearer in the next section, most were optimistic that this would occur. Comments by Dinh, a fifty-two-year-old taxi driver in Ho Chi Minh City in 2008, succinctly capture this confidence: "There will be some downsides to modernization, hair coloring, short skirts, and drugs, but overall the traditional will be maintained as Vietnam modernizes."[26] In other words, most of those I interviewed were convinced that with just a little attention, core Vietnamese cultural values and customs would survive globalization. In this way, the Vietnamese in my study were reminiscent of the Japanese who, according to Koichi Iwabuchi, fashion themselves as artful domesticators of Western modernities.[27] The people I interviewed saw themselves as skillfully indigenizing or editing (Western) modernities so that core Vietnamese sensibilities, ethics, and practices would be left intact. A thirty-three-year-old food vendor in Hanoi, Mai, summarized the process like this in 2010: "As we modernize, we'll be affected by a Western way of life. We'll take the advantages of the West but not the disadvantages."[28] Thus the positive facets of (Western) modernities—such as more efficient business practices, meritocracy-based institutions, new technologies and know-how, and more practical and less didactic educational systems—would be adopted, but the disadvantages, which interviewees always defined in contradistinction to core Vietnamese traditions, would be limited, if not completely filtered out.

Post-Colonial Subjects

In my reading of Vietnamese history, the consensus around an editing posture toward modernization appears to be a relatively recent phenomenon. The initial response to European encroachments on Vietnam was to circle the wagons and reject anything associated with Europeans. Ultimately this approach was widely discredited because it proved so ineffective—French colonialism being the painful evidence.

Early in the twentieth century, at the height of French colonialism and North Atlantic power, Vietnamese intellectuals, activists and the broader population faced two options: (1) an imitative or (2) an editing approach to modernization. Calls for replication among sectors of the intelligentsia were forceful and must have been especially compelling, given the backdrop of European hegemony. Neil Jamieson observed that in the 1930s the Self-Strength Literacy movement advocated a replacement of the old with the new, in which one followed one's inner moral compass, even when it contradicted a number of conventional social expectations surrounding marriage and filial piety. In perhaps the most famous novel from this movement, *Breaking the Ties* (1935) by To Nguyen Tuong Tam, the main protagonist, Loan, says to her mother-in-law, "You are a person and I am a person. Neither of us is any better or worse than the other."[29] In effect Loan was placing self before duty. She was calling into question the conventional obligations to both family and elders, which were to supersede individual desires. Jamieson put it in more dramatic terms: "With these two short lines, the entire socio-cultural system of tradition was declared to be invalid."[30]

Although Loan had thousands of passionate supporters, Jamieson notes that there was significant push back against the call for such a radical break with tradition. The direct rebuke to the above novel was *Miss Minh, the Schoolteacher* (1936) by Nguyen Cong Hoan. Minh was placed in a similar difficult position as Loan—an unfulfilling marriage and abusive mother-in-law. At the moment that she is about to leave her husband's family, Minh asks herself:

> "Should I really follow European ideas to smash an Asian family? . . . People fear the new because the. . . ." Minh hesitated, then pressed her hand against her chest. "Because they hate it, they resent the new. People think the new is something altogether bad." She bounded to her feet. "But the new isn't bad. It's very good, better than the old. If we want to avoid having a bad

> reputation for being new, what we have to do is get the old to respect the new." . . . "In the heat of the moment I almost debased the new. Breaking the ties with the old family is a selfish thing to do. It leads people to ridicule the new, to be repulsed by it, to resent it. Whether one follows the old or the new, the goodness of the person is what is important."[31]

Even among those who were advocating the new over the old, such as Nguyen Cong Hoan, few argued that it should come via an abrupt departure from the old. Vietnamese traditions could, over time, be modified and integrated with the new, but they should not be too hastily rejected—if rejected at all—in the rush to modernize. In the end, an Asian family should take precedent over European ideals.

It is worth recalling that at moments the CPV, the party that eventually took power in Vietnam, teetered more toward an emulative than an editing approach to modernization. Almost everything that most Vietnamese would have defined as traditional—prioritization of family and the village, ideas of the metaphysical, artistic expressions, and economic practices—the CPV labeled as either feudal or colonial and targeted them for change, if not eradication. But even the CPV, at its most zealous high-modernist moments still consistently attempted to bolster its legitimacy by claiming to be the heir and protector of certain ancient traditions. It was, the CPV declared and repeatedly reminded the Vietnamese public, the entity carrying on Vietnam's putatively long tradition of sacred resistance to foreign invaders.

We see, then, that the vast majority of opinion makers, government officials and the general public never desired to become "yellow-skinned Europeans."[32] Even during the heyday of colonialism and the socialist revolution, tradition may have been on trial, as David Marr put it,[33] but the ultimate verdict was mixed: certain traditions should be ended, others reformed, and others maintained and protected.[34] Thus the objective was rarely if ever to simply replace the old with the new, to substitute modernity for tradition. And this editing posture only intensified in the second half of the twentieth century, as the self-confidence of the Vietnamese people grew.

Delight in Defeat

In contemporary Vietnam it is hard to appreciate how culturally and psychologically deep colonialism must have run under French rule. Even though French colonialism never produced, at least on a large scale, the radically colonized subjectivities described by Frantz Fanon and Albert Memmi in North Africa, it undoubtedly left marks. Many of the more educated, urban Vietnamese "had come to see themselves as the French saw them: members of a poor, backward, and subjugated race."[35] Thus, Vietnamese confidence had been shaken to its core. Surprise and shock at seeing Frenchmen pleading for help or at seeing them beaten by Asians with impunity, when the Japanese took over Vietnam briefly in 1940, offer a glimpse of how deeply ideas of European/white superiority had penetrated the Vietnamese psyche.[36]

One whiff I got of this racist-colonial moment was a conversation I had with a Vietnamese American woman, Amy, who lived in Hanoi in 2008. With complete sincerity, she questioned whether I thought it was really possible for the Vietnamese to build a developed economy. I was caught off guard by her doubt. The Vietnamese, as almost every contemporary commentator on the country has remarked, have a deep faith in their ability to accomplish almost anything to which they set their minds. This self-assuredness is pervasive and infectious. Thus statements anchored in a belief in Vietnamese inferiority—as if they were somehow culturally, socially, if not biologically, incapable of becoming an economically developed nation like Japan, Germany or the United States—are noteworthy because of how unusual such sentiments are.

I suspect that this self-belief is, at least in part, a consequence of the wars that the Vietnamese fought and won in the twentieth century. In Hanoi I spent some time with the generation that had participated in the anti-colonial struggle against the French. Many of these former revolutionaries suffered from bitterness and depression. They felt that a Leninist party apparatus had betrayed the ideals and hopes of the revolution. And of course they were right. The anti-democratic brutality of the CPV is undeniable. It has been particularly hard on intellectuals and artists because, at least until recently, their options were limited to propaganda, silence, or exile. Nonetheless what they did not fully appreciate, I believe, was the degree to which their efforts and sacrifices had been successful in that these revolutionaries helped to birth a post-colonial nation.

One hugely significant watershed moment was the military victory at Dien Bien Phu in 1954. The Viet Minh, seemingly against all odds, decisively defeated the French at this remote border garrison. This was not only the turning point in the war but also a tremendously important cultural event for the Vietnamese. The sense of inferiority, which French colonialism and Western technological, economic and military superiority had fostered, was unsettled. The event helped to produce a national pride and self-confidence that many, even those who supported the French, experienced.[37] These sentiments were intensified and more firmly consolidated by the defeat of the US military approximately twenty years later.

In reading a number of accounts of the fall of Saigon in 1975 I was, at least initially, perplexed by the fact that those fighting the Viet Minh took a great deal of pride in defeat. Remember that most of the Vietnamese who were allied with the Americans maintained that they were fighting a civil war. But their postwar sentiments betray a much more complex set of meanings surrounding the war.

In my experience, many Vietnamese who were allied with the Americans against the Viet Minh were, and still are, bitter towards the United States for having, in their opinion, abandoned them. In memoirs such as *The Sacred Willow*[38] and in my conversations with Vietnamese Americans who lived in Vietnam at that time, it is evident that there was a widely shared belief that it was impossible for the Viet Minh to succeed because of the superiority of the Americans. Some of this had to do with the technological and economic superiority of the United States.

Figure 3.4 Revolutionary Soldier Who Fought During the 1940s. Photograph by author, 2010

But I suspect this assuredness was also colonial in nature, in that the Americans were considered a superior race/civilization. This assumption led them to suppose that defeat was impossible and to conclude afterwards that the US-backed RVN government was not defeated but rather had been let down or abandoned by the United States. Their thinking was that if the United States had really tried, given its putative superiority, it could have won. In this way, then, these feelings of anger and betrayal were, at least in part, anchored in a colonial set of assumptions and sensibilities about US supremacy.

The military defeat of the Republic of Vietnam and its ally, the United States, resulted in incredible hardship for those who sided against the Democratic Republic of Vietnam. Not surprisingly there was dread of what would happen in the immediate aftermath of a military defeat. Yet what is so striking about some of the accounts of this moment was how their fears and anxieties were coupled with a profound sense of pride. Duong Elliot describes this moment based on the recollections of one of her family members:

> At this point, Nam could not sort out his emotions. On the one hand, he feared and disliked communism and mourned the passing of a society and a system that he knew and found tolerable—and in many ways even pleasant—although at times terribly corrupt. On the other hand, he also admired the victors out of a nationalistic pride. These were Vietnamese, like him, who had managed to defeat the most powerful nation on earth. He took personal satisfaction in their victory. It was as if, by winning, they had washed away his own hurt. He remembered the blue eyes of the American staring at him through the door of the helicopter; he had made no effort to pull him onboard and save him. Maybe the American was paralyzed by the horrifying sight, or perhaps he was afraid that he would be pulled to his own death. But Nam believed that the American was simply indifferent to his plight. He felt betrayed. The US had let down not only South Vietnam but also him personally. He was bitter, angry, and resentful. Through the communist victory, he felt that he had somehow exacted a measure of revenge. In the grip of these conflicting emotions, Nam went out to watch the arrival of troops from North Vietnam. They looked like they were in their mid-teens, with sallow complexion of people who had spent months in the jungle. . . . Looking at this column of children, Nam's neighbors could not believe their eyes. Some said, "they're so young, and yet they managed to defeat the South." Nam, too, stared in disbelief. The sight of armed children marching as victors into Saigon would remain stamped in his memory.[39]

It is interesting that the soldiers were remembered as children. It is possible that they had witnessed a column of teenagers, but I think that their identification as children was more symbolic than factual. It is clear that the onlookers were in shock that the Americans had been beaten and this disbelief, the incredible absurdity of this rout from a colonial perspective, communicated by the metaphor of children beating adults. I mentioned above how many Vietnamese, like Nam, felt "bitter, angry, and resentful" towards the United States. Outside a belief in US/Western/white supremacy, this intensity and kind of feelings seem misplaced. The United States spent more than a decade, billions of dollars, and tens of thousands of lives fighting a war that was, at least with the benefit of hindsight, not theirs. Feelings of sadness, disappointment, and discouragement would seem to fit the situation, but not the intense emotions of rage and revenge. At some level Nam, like many other Vietnamese, believed in the power of the blue-eyed American to save him *if he chose*; a scenario that only makes sense if one believes in the innate superiority of the United States, whiteness, and the West. It was this web of assumptions and their dislodgement that fueled this paradoxical set of emotions, which included rage toward one's allies and delight in defeat. After all, "Vietnamese, like him, had managed to defeat the most powerful nation on earth. . . . It was as if by winning, they had washed away his own hurt."[40]

Summarizing the focal argument of this section, I believe that the military victories over the French and the United States (and later, in the 1970s, the Khmer and Chinese) were key anti-colonial moments militarily, politically, socially, and *culturally*. These military achievements helped to burnish a positive valuation of Vietnameseness. Any sense of inferiority—no matter how subtle or insidious—was weakened if not washed away by these successes. In a generation the Vietnamese went from thinking of themselves as an inferior nation/race to beating two North Atlantic superpowers and their archrival, the Chinese. The discursive and symbolic effects of these triumphs helped to solidify, among other things, an editing mien toward modernization.

Emulation

The derivative or emulative epistemology of modernization "is based on the sense that 'our' modernity is the one that is simultaneously happening elsewhere."[41] This ubiquitous modernity, Koichi Iwabuchi argues, built upon a "yearning for a way of life and ideas of a dominant country, seems to be over."[42] At least in the case of Japan, Vietnam, and perhaps the whole of East Asia, this assessment resonates. The North Atlantic gaze, which long dominated the material and discursive construction of non-Western modernities, is past or at least profoundly diminished. In contemporary Vietnam, as detailed above, the North Atlantic no longer plays the role of the modern other to be aped. Instead modernization is conceptualized largely as a process of domestication and indigenization of Western modernities rather than imitation.

Some have attributed the shift toward an editing stance to the changing face of the global order. In particular, it reflects "a relative decline of the main actor, the United States" so that there is no longer an "absolute societal model to follow."[43] But history teaches us that this editing posture—at least in the case of Vietnam—predated by several decades the end of the so-called American Century. It is also telling that most scholars reaching this conclusion have been conducting research in East Asia and not Latin America, where the pull of the North Atlantic as a referent for modernity may be melting—but if so, then at a much slower pace.

Euclides da Cunha's *Rebellion in the Backlands*, published in 1902 and deemed by some the bible of Brazilian nationality, offers an excellent glimpse into the

Latin American imaginary of modernization. One aim of da Cunha's epic tale was to critique the military repression of the messianic, populist uprising that took place in 1897 in Canudos, a village in the arid backlands (*sertao*) of Northeastern Brazil. More importantly, however, da Cunha challenged the assumption, common at least among the elite, that these sectors of society were innately backward. Da Cunha concurred that the residents of the *sertao* were primitive, but took issue with the idea that they were incorrigibly so. To his mind it was a question of nurture rather than nature. Neglect by the more civilized sectors of society and the geography the *sertanejos* (residents of this backcountry) inhabited were to blame for their backwardness. Identifying himself with the coastal populations and thus the putatively more advanced or modern sectors of Brazil, as opposed to the backlands where the uprising took place, he wrote:

> Caught up in the sweep of modern ideas, we abruptly mounted the ladder, leaving behind us in their centuries-old semidarkness a third of our people in the heart of our country. Deluded by a civilization which came to us second hand; rejecting, blind copyists that we were, all that was best in the organic codes of other nations, and shunning, in our revolutionary zeal, the slightest compromise with the exigencies of our own national interests, we merely succeeded in deepening the contrast between our mode of life and that of our rude native sons, who were more alien to us in this land of ours than were the immigrants who came from Europe. For it was not an ocean which separated us from them but three whole centuries.[44]

Da Cunha perceptively observed that the littoral Brazilians, which primarily meant the professional, political, and planter classes of predominant European descent who were concentrated along the Atlantic seaboard, were "blind copyists" of North Atlantic ideals. Moreover, he noted that the elite saw themselves as more akin to Europeans than to their fellow countrymen of different nations—i.e., nonwhites. The chasm between themselves and these "rude native sons" was imagined by da Cunha as vast, larger than the Atlantic Ocean, at least "three whole centuries" wide. Da Cunha does not formally make the case for integrating these populations and their culture into the fabric of the nation as peers or partners on equal footing. Instead he argues that they were to be incorporated as inferiors who should be brought out of the darkness by mounting the modern ladder of Western civilization, which the coastal Brazilians were believed to have already ascended. It is important to add that there was a tension, if not contradiction, in da Cunha's text. In a way, he subverted his stated message about the inferiority of the non-elites by portraying them as the heroes in his story. This implicit celebration of the *povo*, the *sertanejos*, is an impulse that was more explicitly embraced and elaborated upon by the Brazilian modernists just a few decades later. These intellectuals, as I discuss below, attempted to build on this inkling and fashion the *popular*, *mestizo* sectors as the authentic Brazilians to be celebrated rather than reviled.[45]

Neo-Colonialism

The comparison of Vietnam and Brazil helps us to better appreciate how political and cultural colonialism are not as neatly coupled as is sometimes assumed. At the height of French colonialism Vietnam was, at least in certain respects, less colonial than Brazil—the editing posture being evidence of this. Brazil, on the other hand, was politically independent for more than a century before Vietnam. Yet, considering its understandings of nation, civilization, modernity, and race, Brazil is best described as a neo-colonial society.

Historical studies of the Brazilian elite in the early twentieth century have exhaustively documented their desire to imitate the North Atlantic societies, especially the aristocratic and bourgeois classes. Examples include: the baroque opera house built in Manaus, shipments of laundry to Paris to be cleaned, the sporting of English styles (such as wool suits, despite the tropical climate), *ausbildungs* (education) trips to Europe to confirm one's social status, and urban renewal projects that attempted, "in the tropical port capital [of Rio], along its sandy beaches and jungled hills, [to remake] Paris, with its theatres, boulevards, bois, women and restaurants—an incongruous vision, with all the details coffee could buy."[46]

Jeffrey Needell described this *belle epoque* period as being dominated by a desire among elites to become European and discard local traditions. He writes:

> [n]either the French nor the English looked on the other as a source of their civilization; they assimilated the others' culture to strong traditions they maintained as superior. The Brazilians, however, had no sense of such a superior cultural tradition; they tended to see themselves as backward. Thus, one Paulista planter, though staunchly proud of Brazil, looked to Parisian high society as a school of manners, where one might acquire "the good customs and those that we ought to introduce into our country."[47]

Similarly, Monica Velloso observed:

> The apotheosis of the Parisian model of civilization was the concomitant loss of prestige of our traditions. . . . More than ever, popular culture was viewed negatively to the degree that it did not fit the values of modernity. In stylish salons, in cafes, and at literary lectures any reference to things native became the height of poor taste.[48]

Contemporary ethnographies of the upper- and middle-classes have found that little has changed. The United States has replaced France as the referent of modernity, but otherwise the same logic holds. The North Atlantic continues to be viewed as the source of civilization to be aped and consumed. Moreover, things native are not valued and easily abandoned with little compunction. One case in point is the replacement of debutante parties with sojourns to Disney World.

> Like the trips to Europe in previous eras by elites with daughters who had just finished school or with sons about to enter a profession, Disney marks a turning point. It has become a highly desired rite among upper-middle-class Brazilian (and in general Latin American) teens, a quasi requisite for social validation. Like the debutante ball, the trip to Disney could be viewed as a teenage rite of passage.[49]

Maureen O'Dougherty has argued that one of the primary motives for these trips to Disney World is that they symbolically convey an aura of modernity to the traveler. That is, by journeying to and spending time in a place that signifies modernity, one's credentials as a first-world, modern person are burnished. This symbolic logic also undergirds some of the desire for North Atlantic consumer goods, such as vacuum cleaners. These commodities are often coveted for their totemic rather than utilitarian value. They are not employed as labor-saving devices. Evidence of this being that domestic servants are not even allowed, according to O'Dougherty, to touch the vacuums. Instead such commodities are a means of making modernity intimate. Like travel to Orlando, Florida, these items are sought-after for their ability to confer modernity upon the holder.[50]

The final scene of Sergio Bianchi's film *Chronically Unfeasible* deftly captures this fetishization of the North Atlantic as well as some of its pitfalls.[51] After detailing the myriad of social problems riddling contemporary Brazil—racism, poverty, violence, environmental destruction, and moral relativism—the middle-class protagonists pathetically cling to their desire to one day visit the first world. Rather than being mobilized to confront the societal challenges that are cannibalizing their society and their lives, through wired-shut, broken jaws, they mumble a barely audible toast to New York.

At this juncture, it should be evident how modernization is differently conceptualized in Brazil and Vietnam. In Brazil, unlike Vietnam, there is no angst regarding traditions that need to be protected from the forces of modernity. There are no concerns with becoming too Western or too North Atlantic. Indeed the primary worry is with not being first world enough. In Brazil, no one frets aloud about how modernities need to be assimilated to valued customs. There is no remorse about the loss of things native. Instead it is assumed that modernity is actualized by approximating the North Atlantic biologically, institutionally, and culturally. In *The Mystery of Samba* Hermano Vianna succinctly summed up this imitative impulse and its impact on development practice:

> In a peculiar and interesting way, the entire history of Brazilian national consciousness has been based on—and has derived energy from—the diagnosis of our "backwardness" in relation to the world's "civilized" countries. Many proposals have been made to "develop" Brazil, to make it more like the so-called first world.[52]

Thus, in sharp contrast to Vietnam, most Brazilians believe that socio-economic progress is had by making their society over in the image of the West.

Mestizo Nationalism

There have been many unsuccessful challenges to the Brazilian penchant for positioning the North Atlantic "as the social universe we would like to be."[53] The most famous among them was conceived by the Brazilian modernists of the 1920s and 30s. One of the leaders of this movement "to 'valorize' the Brazil that defied European models" was the sociologist Gilberto Freyre. A student of Franz Boas at Columbia University, "he declared official Brazil a 'phony and ridiculous' Europhile version that 'hid' the real Brazil."[54]

The real Brazil, in the opinion of the modernists, was the culture of the non-elite, mixed-race *povo* who made up the vast majority of the country. As part of their project to de-colonize Brazil, these social scientists and artists appreciated that the valorization of Brazilian culture required an embrace, rather than negation, of blackness. One of their first sorties in this direction was the celebration of samba, the music of the *favelas* of Rio de Janeiro. In a 1926 newspaper article titled "On the Valorization of Things Black," Freyre writes:

> Yesterday, along with some friends—Prudente and Sergio—I spent an evening-that-almost-reached-morning listening to Pixinguinha, a mulato, playing some of his carnival music accompanied by Donga, another mulato, on the guitar and by a (really black) black fellow, Patricio, singing. A wonderful, Carioca-style Brazilian night.
>
> As we listened, the three of us could feel the great Brazil that is growing half-hidden by the phony and ridiculous official Brazil where mulatos emulate Greeks . . . and *caboclos* [mixed-race persons of salient indigenous descent] try to appear Europeans and North Americans; everyone looking stupidly at things Brazilian . . . through the pince-nez of a Frenchified doctor of laws.[55]

Freyre would go on to develop these ideas further in the canonical *The Masters and the Slaves* (1933). In this book, Freyre made clear that the valorization of things black would not entail attempts to value black people by, for example, addressing social inequalities—such unpleasantries, he likely calculated, would not be appealing to his Frenchified audiences. Instead, to entice the "phony Brazil" to take more interest in things Brazilian, he applauded limited aspects of black and indigenous cultures. The end effect was to give a more appealing hue to the racially hybrid nature of Brazilian society. Or in the words of Hermano Vianna:

> Freyre's great feat was to provide a positive theoretical color for *mestiço* culture, defining "things Brazilian" as a combination—partly harmonious, partly conflictive—of African, Portuguese, and indigenous traits, the product of a historical encounter between "the big house and the slave quarters."[56]

What was most extraordinary about Freyre's intervention was that it actually took hold of official Brazil. In 1930, the professional classes, urban proletariat, military, and manufacturing elite backed a revolution against the landed oligarchy that had controlled Brazil for centuries. Searching for a way to distinguish and legitimate this new regime, Getulio Vargas (President of Brazil between 1930 and 1945, and from 1951 until his suicide in 1954) and his so-called *Estado Novo* (New State) regime espoused the celebration of mestizo-ness. Consequently, a few of the cultural products of the *povo*, which had been ignored or scorned by previous generations of elites and intellectuals, such as *feijoada* (a popular bean dish) and *samba* (a musical style developed in the *favelas* of Rio de Janeiro), were embraced as the icons of nation. Perhaps most importantly, Brazilians adopted, as a foundational narrative of nation, the idea that they were a mixed-race society—a fact to take pride in and celebrate.

This, then, raises the question of why mestizo nationalism failed to topple Brazil's imitative tendency or what Freyre described as the reflex to "Gulp right down . . . the detritus that comes to us from the United States and Europe!"[57] The answer rests largely with the racially inflected elitism detailed in Chapter 2. As long as the *povo* were viewed as an indolent, immoral, racially inferior, subhuman class, then it was probably inevitable that this bigotry and hostility toward the people would undermine any potential anti-colonial impact of mestizo nationalism. Even in Freyre's own texts, his valuation of select aspects of black and indigenous cultures was still racist. Whites gave all the prized institutions such as democracy, markets, and Christianity; Afro-Brazilians contributed dance and music; and native Brazilians a few foods and words to the Portuguese language.[58] I believe, however, these sorts of stereotypes and inaccuracies would have been rectified eventually had not mestizo nationalism become a tool for stifling anti-racism. As Brazilians accepted Brazilianness qua mestizo as praiseworthy given, the corollary that took root was that Brazil was a racial democracy. In the global context of Nazi Germany and a Jim Crow United States, it is understandable why mestizo nationalism assumed this meaning. But unfortunately, as Brazilianness was equated with nonracism it became taboo to even discuss, let alone critique, racism. To state or imply racial hierarchy existed was to effectively call into question the central narrative of nation. The ultimate effect was to thwart most anti-racist initiatives.

I first encountered this dynamic when I began conducting research on race in rural Brazil in 1992. Despite the fact that everyone on TV was white, the political and economic elite were white, most status-associated spaces—such as private clubs—were white only, and crudely racist comments circulated unchecked (e.g., "Bananas are the favorite food of blacks."), I was routinely questioned about how I had secured a grant to research what they viewed as a non-issue in Brazil. In order to make sure that I had fully understood that Brazil was a racial democracy, they would instruct, "Brazilians love the mix." This, for them, demonstrated beyond any reasonable doubt that Brazil was not racist. Any subsequent attempts by me to return to the theme of racism were met with a combination of dismay, defensiveness, and condescension. If I insisted on questioning them further about racism, the conversation would abruptly end. At that moment, I felt that I was labeled either an ignorant foreigner or an imperialist trying to inappropriately impose a US perspective on Brazil.

Ironically, then, Freyre's and the other modernists' attempts to curb Brazilians' adulation of North Atlantic civilisations only served to harden these emulative tendencies. By helping to birth a narrative of a mestizo, non-racist nation, discussions of racism were quashed and white supremacy was allowed to smolder and become further inflamed. This, in turn meant that a deep disdain for "most things native" continued largely unabated. Subsequently, most Brazilians continued "to look stupidly at things Brazilian" and concomitantly pine for the "white" societies of the north.

Lessons

As I discussed at the beginning of this chapter, there is a growing consensus that economic institutions, which are adapted to and build upon local strengths and resources, are more effective in advancing economic growth. Many of the proposed recommendations for fostering institutional tailoring in the development literature focus on institutional deglobalization or political democratization. These hypotheses, however, fail to explain the differences in institutional monocropping in Vietnam and Brazil. Vietnam is a globalized economy and is less democratic than Brazil but its economic institutions are more indigenized. The alternative thesis advanced in this chapter identifies the epistemology of modernization as the key independent variable. In Brazil, as we have seen, there is a racially inflected neofeudal social order that results in a devaluation of domestic culture and sycophantic relationship to the North Atlantic. These factors culminate in emulative modernization initiatives or what some Brazilians have described as an inability to create "things of our own that spring from the depths of our life and history."[59] In contrast I showed how imitation is regarded as an inappropriate method of modernizing in Vietnam. Traditions should be respected and preserved as much as possible, as Vietnam modernizes and develops its economy.

Thus, the juxtaposition of Brazil and Vietnam teaches how certain sociocultural variables can mediate the degree of institutional monocropping. Because of the particular understandings of modernity, tradition, and their preferred relationship, as detailed above, Brazilians are more prone to interpret failure as a shortcoming with Brazilian society rather than an issue with the imported formula they are attempting to adopt. The Vietnamese, on other hand, have a different epistemology and therefore draw different conclusions. Their impulse is not to fault local factors but rather to chalk up the ineffectiveness of foreign-inspired development models and practices to their lack of fit or inappropriateness for the Vietnamese context. Thereupon, should Vietnamese policymakers fail to respect or accept the established patterns of Vietnamese society, they run the risk of levels of political pushback that Gary Hamilton considered insurmountable in the case of Taiwan.[60] This is because the Vietnamese, and I suspect the Taiwanese as well, have a powerful discursive tool at their disposal, which they can and have invoked successfully to influence development policies. If foreign-inspired economic initiatives become too out of step with Vietnamese society, as most institutional monocropping endeavors inevitably are, then the Vietnamese people can modify or rein them in by asserting that these policies are an affront to Vietnamese traditions. In such instances, Vietnamese officials, elected or not, often have little choice but to change course given the symbolic valence of tradition. No similar sensibilities or discursive tools exist in Brazil.

We see, then, why I maintain that the epistemology of modernization—rather than global institutional constraints or weak democratic institutions—is why Brazilian policymakers have been less apt to respect the established socio-cultural patterns and economic momentum that exist within their society. In general, the Europeanized elite view the *povo* as backward deviations from a North Atlantic ideal of progress and not as peoples who bring assets to the development project. Complicating matters further, this is not simply the vantage of the elite but also one shared by large sectors of the general population (see Chapters 2 and 5). Ergo, the Brazilian public is less apt to pressure policymakers to indigenize development policies and projects. Moreover, even in those instances when certain sectors mobilize in defense of domestic patterns, they are disadvantaged by a common sense that positions such efforts as anti-modern. The lesson for development professionals is that in such a context, a political democracy may be helpful but it is no remedy for institutional monocropping. What is required, at least in societies like Brazil, is a direct and sustained attack on the racism that undergirds emulative development practices.

Notes

1 Schwarz, *Misplaced Ideas*, 1.
2 Bello, *Deglobalization*, 115.
3 In order to rebuild and stabilize the world's economy following WWII, the major industrial states established the so-called Bretton Woods system of monetary management. Part of this system included the creation of the International Monetary Fund (IMF) and the International Bank for Reconstruction and Development (IBRD), which today is part of the World Bank.
4 Bello, *Deglobalization*, 115.
5 Babb, *Managing Mexico*, 18.
6 Evans, "Development as Institutional Change," 3.
7 Rodrik, *One Economics, Many Recipes*; Evans, "Development as Institutional Change"; Fung and Wright, eds., *Deepening Democracy*; and Khagram, *Dams and Development*.
8 For an excellent discussion on this topic, representing different positions on the degree of space available to contemporary policymakers to create alternative models of capitalism, see *Putting Development First* (Kevin Gallagher (Ed.)).
9 Chang, "The East Asian Model of Economic Policy," 226.
10 Ibid.
11 Evans, "Development as Institutional Change," 35.
12 Rodrik, *One Economics, Many Recipes*.

13 Fung and Wright (Eds.), *Deepening Democracy.*
14 Evans, "Development as Institutional Change," 35.
15 Scott, *Seeing Like a State*, 357.
16 Hamilton, "Culture and Organization in Taiwan's Market Economy," 71.
17 Taylor, "Two Theories of Modernity."
18 Vietnam formally joined the WTO in 2007.
19 Thuy, a thirty-five-year-old administrative assistant, Hanoi, 2006.
20 Ha, a twenty-six-year-old internet technology developer, Hanoi, 2007.
21 Ong, *Flexible Citizenship.*
22 Taylor, *Fragments of the Present*, 192.
23 Nguyen, *The Unwanted.*
24 Taylor, *Fragments of the Present*, 150.
25 Taylor, "Framing the National Spirit," 128–129 (my emphasis).
26 Dinh, fifty-two-year-old taxi driver, Ho Chi Minh City, 2010.
27 Iwabuchi, *Recentering Globalization.*
28 Thirty-three-year-old food vendor, Hanoi, 2010.
29 Jamieson, *Understanding Vietnam*, 141.
30 Ibid., 146.
31 Ibid.
32 Marr, *Vietnamese Tradition on Trial.*
33 Ibid.
34 Ibid.
35 Jamieson, *Understanding Vietnam*, 173.
36 Elliott, *The Sacred Willow*, 103–104.
37 Ibid., 237.
38 Ibid.
39 Ibid., 409.
40 Ibid., 408.
41 Iwabuchi, *Recentering Globalization*, 45.
42 Ibid.
43 Ibid., 41–42.
44 Da Cunha, *Rebellion in the Backlands*, 161.
45 I would like to thank Charles Bergquist for his insightful observations about this tension in da Cunha's writings.
46 Needell, *A Tropical Belle Époque*, 166.
47 Ibid.
48 Velloso, *A cultura das ruas no Rio de Janeiro (1900–1930)* (Street culture in Rio de Janeiro (1900–1930)).
49 O'Dougherty, *Consumption Intensified*, 98.
50 Ibid., 122.
51 *Cronicamente inviavel* (Chronically unfeasible). Directed by Sergio Bianchi. Brazil, 2000.
52 Vianna, *The Mystery of Samba*, 116.
53 Barbosa, "The Brazilian Jeitinho," 47.
54 Vianna, *The Mystery of Samba*, 9.
55 Ibid.
56 Ibid.
57 Ibid., 61.
58 Freyre, *The Masters and the Slaves.*
59 Schwarz, *Misplaced Ideas*, 10
60 Hamilton, "Culture and Organization in Taiwan's Market Economy," 71.

Bibliography

Babb, Sarah L. *Managing Mexico: Economists from Nationalism to Neoliberalism.* Princeton, NJ: Princeton University Press, 2001.

Barbosa, Lívia Neves de H. "The Brazilian Jeitinho: An Exercise in National Identity" In *The Brazilian Puzzle*, David J. Hess and Roberto A. DaMatta (Eds.), 35–48. New York: Columbia University, 1995.

Bello, Walden F. *Deglobalization: Ideas for a New World Economy*. Dhaka/London: University Press/Zed Books, 2004.

Chang, Ha-Joon. 2002. "The East Asian Model of Economic Policy." In *Models of Capitalism: Lessons from Latin America*, Evelyn Huber (Ed.), 197–236. University Park, PA: The Pennsylvania State University Press.

Coates, Ta-Nehisi. *Between the World and Me*. New York: Spiegel and Grau, 2015.

Cronicamente inviavel (Chronically unfeasible). Directed by Sergio Bianchi. Brazil, 2000.

Cunha, Euclides da, Translated by Samuel Putnam. *Rebellion in the Backlands*. Chicago, IL: The University of Chicago Press, 1944.

Elliott, Duong Van Mai. *The Sacred Willow: Four Generations in the Life of a Vietnamese Family*. Oxford: Oxford University Press, 2000.

Evans, Peter B. "Development as Institutional Change: The Pitfalls of Monocropping and the Potentials of Deliberation." *Studies in Comparative International Development* 38, no. 4 (2004), 30–52.

Freyre, Gilberto. *The Masters and the Slaves: A Study in the Development of Brazilian Civilization*. Translation by Samuel Putnam. Berkeley, CA: University of California Press, 1986.

Fung, Archon, and Erik Olin Wright (Eds.). *Deepening Democracy: Institutional Innovations in Empowered Participatory Governance (The Real Utopias Project)*. London: Verso, 2003.

Gallagher, Kevin P. (Ed.). Putting Development: The Importance of Policy Space in the WTO and the International Financial Institutions. New York: Zed Books, 2005.

Hamilton, Gary. "Culture and Organization in Taiwan's Market Economy." In *Market Cultures: Society and Morality in the New Asian Capitalisms*, Robert W. Hefner (Ed.), 41–77. Boulder, CO: Westview Press, 1998.

Iwabuchi, Koichi. *Recentering Globalization: Popular Culture and Japanese Transnationalism*. Durham, NC: Duke University Press, 2002.

Jamieson, Neil L. *Understanding Vietnam*. Berkeley, CA: University of California Press, 1995.

Khagram, Sanjeev. *Dams and Development: Transnational Struggles for Water and Power*. Ithaca, NY: Cornell University Press, 2004.

Marr, David G. *Vietnamese Tradition on Trial, 1920–1945*. Berkeley, CA: University of California Press, 1984.

Needell, Jeffrey D. *A Tropical Belle Époque: Elite Culture and Society in Turn-of-the-Century Rio de Janeiro*. 1st ed. Cambridge: Cambridge University Press, 2010.

Nguyen, Kien. *The Unwanted: A Memoir of Childhood*. New York: Back Bay Books, 2002.

O'Dougherty, Maureen. *Consumption Intensified: The Politics of Middle-Class Daily Life in Brazil*. Durham, NC: Duke University Press, 2002.

Ong, Aihwa. *Flexible Citizenship: The Cultural Logics of Transnationality*. Durham, NC: Duke University Press, 1999.

Rodrik, Dani. *One Economics, Many Recipes: Globalization, Institutions, and Economic Growth*. Princeton, NJ: Princeton University Press, 2008.

Schwarz, Roberto. *Misplaced Ideas: Essays on Brazilian Culture*. London: Verso, 1992.

Scott, James C. *Seeing Like a State: How Certain Schemes to Improve the Human Condition Have Failed*. New Haven, CT: Yale University Press, 1998.

Taylor, Charles. "Two Theories of Modernity." In *Alternative Modernities*, Dilip Gaonkar (Ed.), 172–196. Durham, NC: Duke University Press, 2001.

Taylor, Nora A. "Framing the National Spirt: Viewing and Reviewing Painting under the Revolution." In *The Country of Memory: Remaking the Past in Late Socialist Vietnam*, Hue-Tam Ho Tai (Ed.), 109–134. Berkeley, CA: University of California Press, 2001.

Taylor, Philip. *Fragments of the Present: Searching for Modernity in Vietnam's South*. Honolulu, HI: University of Hawai'i Press, 2000.

Velloso, Monica. *A cultura das ruas no Rio de Janeiro (1900–1930): Mediagoes, linguagens e espago* (Street culture in Rio de Janeiro (1900–1930): Meditations, languages, and space). Rio de Janeiro: FCRB, 2004.

Vianna, Hermano. *The Mystery of Samba: Popular Music and National Identity in Brazil*. Chapel Hill, NC: The University of North Carolina Press, 1999.

4 Corruption and the Commons

This is not the land of know-how but of know-who.

Roberto DaMatta (b. 1936)[1]

To this point I have shown how invaluable interpretive economics can be for development studies. In Chapter 2, I used it to fill in an explanatory black box regarding one of the more significant development variables: human capital. With a trained eye on culture, the discourses of class, poverty, and the countryside emerged as the likely forces behind the political support that drives levels of investment in capacity-building. More specifically, I argued that the racially inflected elitism in Brazil lends itself to a mean-spirited othering of the *povo* that makes it extremely difficult to generate a willingness, especially among the elite and middle classes, to invest adequately in transportation, communication, health care, education, and sewage treatment. In Vietnam, in contract, I concluded that investment in human capital is more robust and equitable because the general public is viewed more favorably than in Brazil.

With respect to institutional monocropping, in the previous chapter we learned how theories that privilege modes of governmentality, in particular levels of democracy, are inadequate in the cases of Vietnam and Brazil. Democratic institutions are much shallower in Vietnam than in Brazil and yet efforts to tailor capitalism to local particularities are more prevalent in Vietnam, as is true throughout East Asia. Interpretive economics allowed me to expose very distinctive epistemologies of modernization. The Vietnamese with whom I spoke felt that tradition had to be respected and therefore development initiatives should be edited, as much as possible, to protect valued aspects of Vietnamese culture. In Brazil there is no such similar concern with tradition. Consequently, modernization is understood as an emulative process, which results, I surmised, in a higher propensity for institutional monocropping than in Vietnam.

Undoubtedly these theoretical inroads represent some of the lowest-hanging fruit for interpretive economists because scholars working on human capital and institutional monocropping have largely ignored culture. The same, however, cannot be said for the focus of this chapter: solidarity, trust, social cohesion, or what development scholars like to call social capital. This is one of the few arenas in development studies where scholars have given culture more serious consideration. The great advantage of this is that rather than having to build theories from scratch, as was the case in the previous two chapters, I am able to use the juxtaposition of Vietnam and Brazil to focus more on testing, nuancing, and refining the existing explanatory models of social capital in development studies.

One of the more original contributions I make to the social capital literature is identifying the significance of honor codes. Building on the insights from Kwame Appiah's research on moral revolutions, I illustrate how honor codes are not aligned with legal and ethical codes in Brazil. In Vietnam they are, and I theorize that this is a chief reason why there are much higher levels of social capital in Vietnam. What this means for development practitioners in Brazil, I maintain, is that unless or until honor codes are reworked and better harmonized with ethical and legal codes, patronage and other related forms of corruption are likely to continue irrespective of any institutional reforms, and levels of social capital will, in turn, remain low.

Societal versus Government Corruption

My comparative investigation of social capital begins with one of its most notorious foes: corruption. As foreshadowed in previous chapters, most Vietnamese with whom I spoke identified government harassment for a payoff (*tham nhong*), embezzlement (*tham o*), and bribery (*hoi lo*) as the number one set of problems facing their country. Almost everyone recounted the everyday payments required to secure a building permit, get a passport, avoid a traffic ticket, or increase the chances of one's child receiving a decent education. Most informants complained bitterly about the need to pay doctors, who no longer even bothered to code bribes as gifts but demanded them directly up front in order to get timely medical attention even in cases of emergency. Unethical land grabs, the buying and selling of government positions, and other unsavory deeds by government bureaucrats were the hot topics of *bia hoi* (draft beer) conversations. In one of these discussions, a thirty-something, motorbike taxi driver from Hung Yen, Tho, told me that if one did not have a well-placed relative in the military, then the only way to make a career in the armed forces was through a payment. He then explained how his brother-in-law had to pay his superiors 4,000 USD or 8,000,000 VND in 2012 to be promoted from private and secure a job in the army; otherwise he would have been forced to leave the military and return to farming. All fumed about the major corruption trials that were intermittently detailed in the media in which extreme levels of graft within state-owned enterprises and the banking system were exposed. One of the more recent scandals included the conviction of Vu Quoc Hao, the former general director of Agribank Financial Leasing Co., who was sentenced to death in 2012 for embezzling 531 billion VND (25 million USD) of state property—this in a country where the vast majority earn less than 150 USD a month.

Admittedly, my initial reaction to the topic of corruption in Vietnam was a bit blasé. In the aftermath of years of ethnographic research in Brazil, I felt, somewhat jadedly, that I had heard it all before. In Brazil, the so-called *mensalao*, or "big monthly payment" by political parties to congressional representatives for legislative votes, was exposed as routine in 2005. More recently, Operation *Lava Jato* (Car Wash) uncovered how at least 3.5 billion USD had been funneled from Petrobras, the state-controlled oil company, into the coffers of political parties and the offshore bank accounts of Petrobras executives. In yet another high profile scandal, when federal investigators decided to temporarily freeze builders involved in kickback schemes to politicians in 2015, construction almost came to a complete standstill in Brazil. Various other kinds of corruption are the constant subject of muckraking journalism and everyday conversations. For example, residents of Babilonia complained incessantly about the police taking bribes to influence arrests, collaborating with gangs in drug trafficking, and moonlighting as assassins of the homeless.[2]

In any event, I eventually overcame my early disinterest with corruption in Vietnam enough to recognize an important distinction between Vietnamese and Brazilian corruption stories. In Vietnam complaints were largely targeted at the state and the CPV that controls it. In Brazil, in contrast, corruption was seen as universal. Those with whom I spoke viewed politicians and the state as the tip of an unscrupulous societal iceberg because it was believed that almost everyone was gaming the system. Brazilians considered society as a whole—CEOs, NGOs, the middle classes, unions, and even the poor—to be unethical. Perhaps most tellingly, the *jeitinho*—the ability to break or bend the rules or use personal resources to get things done—was heralded as a central facet of the Brazilian national character.[3]

The perceived omnipresence of corruption in Brazil surfaced as well in Maureen O'Dougherty's ethnography of the middle class in Sao Paulo. Her respondents attacked both "Brazilian *society* and state for being corrupt and/or bent on exploiting rather than working productively."[4] As one of O'Dougherty's interviewees commented:

> The country is like this: the president robs, his assistant robs, everyone robs, everyone wants to get into government. Why? For love of country? No! It is very hard to be genuine in a country like this, in a country in which the people are always suspicious about something. You can't be nice to anyone because if you are, this person is going to think you want to get something out of it, you see, that you want to take advantage of something, that there is something behind it. . . . Here in Brazil, to be honest is to be a fool, to be honest is to be naïve. Imagine a guy who worked on the budget committee and didn't steal money! He would be famous for being stupid [and] naïve."[5]

Survey researchers have found that most Brazilians share this person's opinion and do not trust or have little confidence in their fellow citizens. In response to the question on the World Values Survey, "Can most people be trusted?" A mere 9.4 percent of Brazilians said yes. This is one of the lowest rankings of any country in the world. In contrast, 52.1 percent of Vietnamese answered affirmatively.

Or to the question "One cannot be too careful," 90.6 percent of respondents in Brazil agreed, compared to 47.9 percent in Vietnam.[6]

Such suspicions and lack of trust are mirrored in the urban physical landscapes. Houses and apartment complexes are constructed in fortress-like fashion. The bars, glass-studded high walls, guard dogs, doormen, barbed wire, and security systems are pervasive and conspicuous. These measures are not based on misperceptions or unfounded fears but are largely warranted, given the levels of crime. Pitched gun battles between rival gangs or between the gangs and police are routine in most major cities. Rates of assaults, muggings, robberies, and homicides are higher than in many war zones.

When I hosted the Undersecretary for Public Security for the state of Rio de Janeiro, Julianna Barroso, in Seattle in 2012, she told me that she had a colleague who had been offered a job in Iraq. Initially Undersecretary Barroso urged her colleague not to accept the position because of the well-publicized violence there—due to the US invasion and on-going civil war. But then she was told—to her astonishment—that when comparing the indicators of major crimes, including murder, Rio de Janeiro was a much more dangerous place. In 2012 there were 4041 homicides in the state of Rio de Janeiro and 1209 homicides within the city of Rio de Janeiro. This put the homicide rate in the city of Rio de Janeiro at twenty-four homicides per 100,000 citizens—in Iraq it was 8 per 100,000.[7] And Rio de Janeiro continues to be rated "critical" for crime by the US State Department—a rating it has held for over twenty-five years—because of the murder rate combined with the high and rising levels of crimes in the categories of robbery, rape, fraud, and residential thefts. Such problems are, of course, not isolated to Rio de Janeiro. For example, the Brazilian newspaper *Globo* published the findings of a 2011 survey of Brazilian city-dwellers by the National Confederation of Industry. In "A Portrait of Brazilian Society: Public Security," it was reported that just within the past year, 79 percent said they had witnessed or experienced some type of crime and 8 percent had witnessed a homicide.[8]

This Hobbesian world is well captured in contemporary Brazilian cinema. *Central Station*[9] portrays urban Brazil—which is where 80 percent of Brazilians live—as a space of immorality: retired teachers take advantage of illiterate Brazilians and even consider selling children for body parts so that they can upgrade their televisions. In *What is it worth?*[10] social do-gooders are characterized as embezzlers, profiteers, and tax-cheats who are willing to resort to murdering pregnant women to hide their misdeeds. The most prestigious person in one Rio suburb, in *Man of the Year*,[11] is the one who carries out extra-judicial assassinations of drug addicts, gangsters, and the homeless.

The contrast with Vietnam is unambiguous. Almost everyone I interviewed in Vietnam saw state malfeasance as the exception to the rule. Private enterprises were seen as requiring workers to work hard but were not dismissed as corrupt. Successful entrepreneurs were, as we have seen, lionized as creative visionaries rather than reviled for their cronyism. Muggings and graffiti were rare, gun battles were nonexistent, and security measures did not dominate cityscapes. Moreover, the individual who could take advantage of the system, discover a *jeitinho* or call

Table 4.1 Number of Major Crimes in Brazil and Vietnam

Major Crimes per 100,000	*Brazil*	*Vietnam*
Homicides (2013/2011)	21.8	1.8
Rapes (2013/2003)	24	1.64
Burglaries (2013/2011)	119.80	1.48

Sources: World Bank Data (2016); World Bank Report No 36525 (2016), United Nations Office on Drugs and Crime (2015); CIA The Fact Finder (2015).

in a favor, was not celebrated or held up as emblematic of the Vietnamese people. In sum, I found that the general public was not considered saintly but overall was regarded as consisting of decent, hardworking people who played by the rules; if they got ahead, it was not because they had cheated or had an unfair advantage but rather because they were smarter, luckier, or more industrious.[12] It was the political leaders, civil servants, and party officials that were regarded by those with whom I spoke as scoundrels—not society writ large.

Let me caution the reader that I am not trying to paint too rosy a picture of the situation in Vietnam—just a relatively better one. Almost half of the Vietnamese polled in the World Values Survey, for example, said one could not trust most people.[13] In one interview, Han, a sixty-eight-year-old retired civil servant, expressed this perspective to me in 2014 when she said:

> Now you see Chinese herbicides in all the food we consume, or you buy some pho and you don't see how they make it. Maybe it was very dirty . . . maybe they used old broth. These days you can only trust family, friends, and acquaintances in Vietnam.[14]

What is interesting is that even for such societal critics there was the insinuation that widespread malfeasance was atypical, not part of the traditional Vietnamese character, but rather something that had only recently emerged (note the temporal locations of "now" and "these days"). A return to the good and honest nature of Vietnamese people was, thus, implied to be within reach should certain unspecified changes take place. In Brazil, in contrast, corruption was essentialized as part of the ineffaceable fabric of the Brazilian character. At least among those I interviewed, it was not seen as something new and therefore correctable but rather a long-standing, indelible feature of the Brazilian people.

Social Capital

A consideration of trust, reputation, and norms brings us directly into debates that extend back at least two centuries. Over this period of time a number of social theorists—such as Emile Durkheim, Alexis de Tocqueville, and Adam Smith—have argued that political and economic development hinge upon what has been variously termed by theorists over the centuries as social cohesion, trust, civility, brotherhood, and most recently, social capital. These social scientists and philosophers have long understood that polities and economies are dysfunctional if people act primarily according to self-interest and in dishonest ways. Without a healthy commons, in which trust, concern for others, civility, and a generalized reciprocity are nurtured within a given society or organization, things fall apart.

One scholar who helped to rejuvenate attention to social capital was Francis Fukuyama. Fukuyama argued in *Trust: The Social Virtues and the Creation of Prosperity* that key differences in political economies across the world reflected differences in a society's underlying social capital.[15] He pointed out that the orthodox categorization of the United States and Japan as polar opposites, in terms of their political economies, was paradoxical given that both countries led the world in economic performance. However, this paradox could be resolved, he reasoned, once theorists recognized that the two nations had the common characteristics of high social capital—in particular high trust between strangers.[16]

In his review of the social capital literature, Paul Whiteley seconded Fukuyama's take on the economic importance of social capital. He, too, agreed that it "was more essential for development than human capital. . . . It also has about the same impact on economic growth as the 'catch-up' variable (countries that start behind tend to catch up), though somewhat less importance than investment in physical capital."[17] He concluded:

> It is clear that social capital is an important factor in explaining cross-national variations in economic growth. When the variable is incorporated into a modified neo-classical model, it is a highly significant predictor of growth in a diverse set of countries, and in the presence of various control variables. . . . It cannot be ignored in any adequate model of economic growth.[18]

Robert Putnam is the person most credited with putting social capital back on the map of development studies in recent decades. In his seminal book, *Making Democracy Work*, Putnam argued that social capital was key to the different qualities of the polities and economies in northern and southern Italy.[19] Much like the classical theorists of the nineteenth century, he maintained that the efficiency of society was enhanced where there were higher levels of trust, norms of reciprocity, and networks of civil engagement. In short, he made the case for the centrality of social capital for economic and political development. But perhaps his biggest contribution to this current of development studies was the attention he brought to non-governmental institutions. This is because Putnam, working in the institutionalist tradition, attributed the different levels of social capital to the quantity and quality of voluntary associations. Trust, reciprocity, and civility were seen by Putnam as an outgrowth of organizations and in particular non-governmental ones.

One major problem for Putnam's hypothesis of the links between voluntary associations and social capital is empirical reality. Most case studies have not found what his theory predicted. Vietnam and Brazil are excellent examples of this.

Brazil has much higher levels of voluntary associations and participation than Vietnam and yet, as we have learned, social capital is greater in Vietnam. According to the World Values Survey, 25.3 percent of Brazilians said they had been active in an organization and 74.7 percent said they were currently involved in an organization.[20] In Vietnam, 71.2 percent said they had never been involved in an organization.[21] While 9.8 percent of Vietnamese said they had been at one time involved as a volunteer and the remaining 19.1 percent said they were currently involved in an organization.[22] Despite these rates of membership and participation in voluntary organizations, the general state of social capital is much healthier in Vietnam than in Brazil. As outlined above, the traits of a community lacking civility—what Putnam defined as "defection, distrust, shirking, exploitation, isolation, disorder and stagnation"—are much more on display in Brazil.

Favors

If the different levels of social capital cannot be attributed to institutional density, then what is behind the varying degrees of social capital? Clearly the social inequalities outlined in Chapter 2 are very important. A society that is highly unequal and adversarial is, for obvious reasons, less likely to be characterized by trust, civility, and reciprocity. Alexis de Tocqueville, appreciated this in the United States almost two hundred years ago:

> Among the novel objects that attracted my attention during my stay in the US, nothing struck me more forcibly than the general equality of condition among the people. . . . I soon perceived that the influence of this fact extends far beyond the political character and the laws of the country, and that it has no less effect on civil society than on the government; it creates opinions, gives birth to new sentiments, founds novel customs, and modifies whatever it does not produce. The more I advanced in the study of American society, the more I perceived that this equality of condition is the fundamental fact from which all others seem to be derived and the central point at which all my observations constantly terminated.[23]

The failure to deal with inequality has been a focal point of a number of critics of Putnam, especially as he has applied his ideas to the United States. The problem, they argue, is not that North Americans are "bowling alone,"[24] the title of Putnam's sequel book, but rather that CEOs now make on average well over 400 times what their workers make. In 1980 it was "just" forty-four times more.[25] In effect, then, the impressive increases in US productivity in the past half century have largely gone to widening the economic divide rather than raising the standard of living of the general public. This, rather than the drop in voluntary associations, is believed to be largely responsible for the weakening of social capital in the United States over this same period of time. If these critics are correct, it suggests one more reason why the discourses outlined in Chapter 2, which divide and fragment Brazilians, are so detrimental to economic growth. The construction of the *povo* as inferior, immoral, and responsible for their marginalization would not only seem to adversely affect human but also social capital.

Area studies experts often focus on a different explanation for corruption and the concomitant low levels of social capital in Brazil and throughout Latin America. They blame what Brazilianists commonly term "favors." The practice of favors is regarded as something that runs deep in the socio-cultural sinews of Brazil or as one expert put it, "under a thousand forms and names, [favors has] formed and flavoured the whole of national life."[26] Some of the other names include clientelism, nepotism, and patronage, but they all essentially mean advancement and gain via rule-bending practices based on personal relationships and loyalties rather than merit, credentials, or the formal processes of an institution. Thus, for instance, one does not vote based on whom one believes to be the best candidate or on their political platform but rather on whether the candidate gives them a job, roofing materials, or protects them from other powerbrokers. Government contracts are not doled out based on the quality of work or the price of the bid but rather on social contacts and the promise of kickbacks. Jobs are given to those who are connected or loyal rather than an individual's skill set, hard work, or professional experience. Laws are selectively enforced contingent on social rank and networks.

Brazilian historians have often attributed favors to an outgrowth of Iberian feudal traditions that were animated by the particularities of conquest, colonialism and slavery. This was how the elite historically brokered careers, allegiances, and power. "The emperor," for example,

> engendered loyalty through patronage and promotions; similarly, he punished disloyalty by withholding patronage. Promotions to senior officer ranks continued to be heavily influenced by ascribed rather than achieved status. Geographic origin, wealth, and familial connections often counted more than professional abilities, experience or education.[27]

In the context of the conquest in Brazil, patron–client relationships became a central mechanism for expanding and controlling vast tracts of land at great distances and with relatively primitive transportation infrastructure and communication technologies. Local elites were given a large degree of autonomy and sometimes even ersatz nobility titles, such as Colonel or Baron, in exchange for keeping local populations in check.

The poor, too, have long been complicit in the practice of favors. For slaves and the tenant farmers of African and indigenous descent, patronage provided one of the few means available to mitigate poverty and the extreme disparities of power and status. Given their plight as poor, illiterate, and physically vulnerable, assistance could usually only be had for the promise of future services and loyalty. One interviewee, Lira, a sixty-five-year-old artist and founder of the Workers' Party in the Jequitinhonha Valley in Minas Gerais (whose story is detailed in the next chapter), offers insight into how favors continue to play out among the poor in parts of contemporary Brazil.[28]

> What still is a challenge is the system of favors. A rich person doesn't owe anyone anything. They owe no favors. But the poor. . . . It isn't so positive yet on this front. There's still lots of people who need favors. To go to the doctor, for example. If you have money you just get in a plane and fly to see a doctor in Belo Horizonte. It's different for poor people, especially for those who live in small places. So it's not so easy yet. There have been improvements, but the improvements are small. This dynamic of favors is horrible. People become dependent on those with power. It's horrible. This system of favors and obligations leaves one imprisoned. It is because of the poverty. A person with money conquers everything. They don't need favors. It was always like that in politics. Oh, I got this from X, and now I have to vote for them. This doesn't change overnight. I saw this working with the Workers' Party. It's not easy working with base communities . . . people want a direct quid pro quo for their vote. They want food, a job, etc. The people are like this. If the candidate says, "I'm going to give your daughter a job," then they will vote for him. Imagine the day when everyone has the consciousness to do what he or she believes they should do and support who would ensure this change.[29]

It is obvious from Lira's comments that the practice of favors helps to reproduce and sustain a very unequal social order. A poor person does not dare challenge those with power because she or he wants to be able to ask for a favor when it is needed. Contrary, then, to what Marcel Mauss found in the more egalitarian, indigenous societies of the Pacific Northwest and Polynesia, these "gift" exchanges reinforce the benefactor's authority as well as the client's dependency and "littleness," rather than serving as a social leveling mechanism.[30] Finally, and most relevant for our understanding of corruption, favors inevitably entail the perversion of the rule. There are the formal procedures and processes, which the unprotected must obey. And then there are the options and opportunities for those who are connected. With a patron one secures a modicum of status and respect. One can go to the front of the line, break the law, cut through red tape, and get a child her medicine. It is this set of practices that makes a mockery of the liberal emphasis on *formal* rights, procedures, and equality, encapsulated in the Brazilian saying: "To our friends everything, to our enemies the law!" In sum, it is fair to say that Roberto Schwarz's observations about nineteenth-century Brazil still largely apply:

> Favor was present everywhere, combining itself with more or less ease to administration, politics, industry, commerce, the life of the city, the court, and so on. Even professions, such as medicine, or forms of skilled labor, such as printing, which in Europe were on the whole free of favor, were among us governed by it. As the professional depended on favor to exercise his profession, so the small proprietor depended on it for the security of his property, and the public servant for his position. Favor was our quasi-universal social mediation.[31]

These norms, sensibilities, and habits of the heart help to illustrate why corruption continues despite the adoption of various institutional "best practices" in Brazil. Time and time again, liberal democracy, transparent budgetary practices, independent judiciaries, and meritocracy-based government bureaucracies have proven no match for the machinations of patronage and favors. This should not be taken to mean that institutional reforms are quixotic or ill-advised but rather that alone they are often insufficient. Socio-cultural change is usually required as well. One task, then, for development scholars working in places like Brazil is to identify what specific changes are needed to curb or end the practice of favors. On this crucial economic matter, unlike the issues of human capital and institutional monocropping, development scholars offer culturally informed explanations. The problem, however, is that their theories make no sense once Vietnam, rather than the West, is the referent.

Personalism

With the North Atlantic, and in particular the United States, as a comparator, Brazilian clientism appears to be a by-product of what Brazilianists David Hess and Roberto DaMatta call personalism. By personalism they mean that one is identified with and judged more on social standing, family background, and social networks than her or his accomplishments and misdeeds. They argue that it is this higher degree of personalism—where "personal loyalties" tend to figure more centrally than "individualistic principles" as in the "modern West—that is at the root of favors. Conversely, formal processes and procedures are theorized as being less distorted and violated in the United States because "one's identity as an individual rather than a person" has "the upper hand."[32]

With Vietnam, rather than the West, as the site of comparison such a conclusion becomes less persuasive. In Vietnam, as in much of the world, there has been a steady move away from personalism toward what David Halpern describes as a "widespread increase in the value placed on independence of thought and personal autonomy, while the value placed on obedience to authority has fallen."[33] Most Vietnamese with whom I spoke said that, in contrast to their parents' generation, they wanted their children to forge their own path in life, speak their mind, and select their spouses instead of having arranged marriages. Nonetheless, family and friendship networks continue to be potent institutions, which heavily shape and influence identities and agency. Children and spouses are expected to sacrifice their desires and aspirations for the sake of the family to a degree that is not the norm in Brazil or the United States. This is what many Vietnamese interviewed meant by the supremacy of family values in Asia when compared to the West. It is not that they assume that family is unimportant in the West but rather that the duties it entails are less onerous there. Parents are viewed as much less likely to ride out an unhappy relationship, stick with an unrewarding job, or make other sorts of personal sacrifices for their children's benefit. Conversely, filial piety is believed to be much less demanding in the West. Children are not seen as likely to defer to their parents' wishes, or sacrifice their personal happiness and aspirations for the welfare of the family.

A few observations that help to illustrate the particularities of personalism in Vietnam include government sanctions and punishments. In the aftermath of the American War it was not only those who sided with the Republic of Vietnam that were punished but also their family members. In the newly unified Vietnam, individuals were barred by the government from certain occupations or attending university, not because of anything they had personally done but because of the sins of their parents and grandparents. I am not aware of any similar policy or law in Brazil in which individuals are formally punished or sanctioned based on their familial affiliation. A further example of personalism in Vietnam is "the cult of the ancestors [which] is practiced by the quasi totality of Vietnamese families regardless of their wealth, social class, and political or religious creed."[34] (See Figure 4.1.) Everyone I interviewed said they practiced ancestral worship, and all homes had an altar for their deceased relatives. These spirits are seen as key to the well-being of the living and are routinely respected and honored through everyday prayer, the Lunar New Year holiday, Tet,[35] and the celebration of death anniversaries. One further illustration of personalism is the disappointments of Vietnamese Americans—or at least the ones I know—with how their children and grandchildren fail to abide by familial duties and expectations that they would have been held to in Vietnam. I believe it telling that I have never heard Brazilian expatriates complain about this. They may miss the food, the weather, or the social openness in Brazil but they do not mention concerns about their children not observing their proper roles as sons, daughters, or grandchildren.

Despite the levels of personalism in Vietnam that match and probably exceed those in Brazil, I did not find a culture of favors to be more prevalent in Vietnam than in Brazil. To be sure patronage exists, but it does not dominate the machinations of institutions and formal procedures as in Brazil. This should not be taken to mean or suggest that government corruption is less common but only that clientelistic forms of corruption are less prevalent in Vietnam. As noted above, to acquire a building permit, to see a doctor, to get a child a good education, to resolve a traffic violation, to get a business license—all often require a bribe. Unlike Brazil, however, this sort of malfeasance is largely impersonal. A Vietnamese citizen simply pays the informal fee, usually dressed up as a gift, but largely irrespective of one's identity, social location, or relationships. Of course a well-placed friend or family member can be hugely advantageous but unless the traffic cop is one's uncle or the doctor is one's sister, most fraud boils down to a straightforward, monetary transaction rather than a favor rooted in personalism.

Contrast this transactional, impersonal mode of corruption in Vietnam with the one commonly cited in the academic literature on Brazil. An individual parks her car inappropriately and receives a parking infraction. Her response is then to confront the ticketing officer: "Do you know who you are talking to? I'm a friend of so-and-so, who is a friend of so-and-so, who is your boss."[36] One plausible outcome is that the police officer is later obliged to apologize and risks being fired. DaMatta and Hess write, "The result is that in Brazil the 'Do you know who you are talking to?' operates as a ritual of inversion that transforms an egalitarian, individualistic situation into a hierarchical, personalistic one."[37] In Vietnam an offender is not apt to utter such a defense and if she or he did it would likely prove ineffective. Moreover, it is inconceivable that the ticketing officer would be reprimanded or sacked for properly citing someone. The typical response, as noted above, is to simply pay the "fine" to the ticketing officer in order to avoid having to pay a higher, formal penalty and becoming enmeshed in government red tape.

Figure 4.1 A Family Altar. Photograph by author, 2010

With Vietnam as the referent, the hypothesis of a causal relationship between personalism and favors becomes dubious at best. If favors were the direct consequence of an underdeveloped individualism, then one would expect to find higher (rather than lower) levels of patronage in Vietnam, where one's identity as an individual has even less of a pull than in Brazil. Given this finding, it would be unwise to recommend or encourage policy interventions aimed broadly at reducing personalism or increasing individualism as a remedy for patronage in the hopes of improving social capital in Brazil. Indeed, there is a high risk that such a course of action, especially one targeted too broadly at eliminating all kinds of personalism or advancing all forms of individualism, could have very deleterious effects on trust, civility, and social solidarity. As I detail later in the chapter, the weakness of certain kinds of communitarian identities—such as nation—can adversely impact social capital. Moreover, not all forms of individualism, such as the more materialistic and narcissistic modes that have increased in the United States in recent decades, are correlated with higher levels of social capital. Such a positive relationship has only been found in places that have experienced a rise in what Bo Rothstein calls "solidaristic individualism." In countries like Sweden, for instance, he found that "people seem to be finding a way of expressing their growing individuality within a lifestyle that maintains and enhances the connections between them."[38]

Part of the solution for reducing patronage and bolstering social capital in Brazil may entail combating poverty. As Lira pointed out above, economic dependency leaves the poor few options but to engage in favors. Therefore, the more materially independent people become, the easier it will likely be to root out such practices. Ultimately, however, it is safe to assume that it will take more than poverty reduction to diminish patronage, given that these habits and norms are not isolated to the interactions between the haves and have-nots. Recall that the *mensalao* (big monthly payment) involved transactions exclusively among the political elite, and the poor were not participants in the Petrobras scandal. These intra-elite forms of clientelism indicate that the practice of favors is not a simple by-product of socio-economic marginalization. And in the case of Brazil, as I illustrate below, it is the semiotics of patronage, in particular the honor that it brings, that is primarily to blame.

Honor Codes

In visiting major cities in Vietnam, a Seattleite such as myself cannot help but be struck by the different transit culture. There is the incessant, robotic-like use of horns that create a hypnotic hum. The traffic is so thick and constant that pedestrians cannot cross the street by waiting for an opening but instead must slowly enter the flow with the faith that the steady swarm of motorbikes and other vehicles will adjust. Several intersections have no traffic lights or signs. Instead scores of motorists converge, slowly merge, and resurface largely unscathed on the other side of the junction. As exotic as all of this is for someone from a city in which pedestrians risk a ticket if they do not wait for the "walk" signal before crossing the street, it seems to be a serious nuisance to the Vietnamese I interviewed. Navigating the hordes of motorbikes to commute to and from work and run one's daily errands was considered an onerous, tiresome, and a dangerous chore. In fact, most identified this, along with corruption, as two of the foremost societal challenges or concerns.

If complaints about corruption in Vietnam were at first mundane to me, then these grievances about traffic struck me as quaint. In major Brazilian cities, traffic is also terrible. Most commute several hours a day in overcrowded, unairconditioned buses. Even for the privileged in Rio de Janeiro, the thirty-mile trek to the airport in their cars or taxis can often prove to be a five-hour saga. Yet crime and violence pose a much more serious problem for Brazilians. When one is constantly worried about their children being killed by a stray bullet or being robbed at gunpoint, transportation woes tend to fall more in the category of hassles and annoyances rather than a major societal problem.

Fortunately I have never personally been the victim of a crime in either Brazil or Vietnam, but I take many more precautions when in Brazil. I dress down (t-shirt, shorts, and flip flops), avoid wearing jewelry, and disguise my more expensive possessions (smart phone, camera, laptop) in plastic bags if I must carry them in public. In Vietnam I can be open with such accessories with little concern that someone will take them from me at knife or gunpoint. In Brazil almost everyone I know or have interviewed has had a personal encounter with the kinds of crime and violence that would be unimaginable in Vietnam. For example, one interviewee, Caio, a forty-year-old photographer who lives in the *favela*, Babilonia, explained how one evening, in 2010, he and his family of three young children were asleep when heavily armed men forced their way into his home. Fourteen gang members, with AK47s, were being pursued by BOPE (a special police unit called *Batalhao de Operacoes Policias Especias*) and decided to hide in their house until they could safely flee. If the BOPE had found them, their house would have been caught in the crossfire. Thus Caio and his family had little option but to abandon their house and to make sure that their children never mentioned what had happened for fear of a revenge killing. The gangsters occupied their house for three weeks and then left a note of gratitude in second-grade level Portuguese upon leaving.

In the early 1980s the rate of violent crime in Brazil was no higher than in most major US cities. This began to change as Brazil underwent democratization. Given the racially inflected elitism discussed in Chapter 2, many Brazilians were unsettled by the enfranchisement of the popular sectors. According to Teresa Caldeira, Brazilians reacted to these changes via the circulation of crime narratives, which criminalized the poor among other things.[39] Much like terrorists have been discursively constructed in the United States post September 11, 2001, criminals were and are imagined by most Brazilians as evil incarnate—and evil, it is decided, can only be curtailed through violence rather than respect for habeas corpus, due process, and basic human rights. This has legitimated and fueled vigilante justice by the police, and the predictable result has been an upsurge in violence. As the authorities became cavalier with violence and the law, so too did more and more civilians.

Figure 4.2 A Babilonia Family. Photograph by Nando Neves, 2014

Torture and killings are illegal and considered unethical in Brazil. Unlike Vietnam, capital punishment is unconstitutional. This may help to explain why the police are reluctant to *publicly* assassinate suspected criminals. This has not always been the case in Brazil. Public floggings, torture, and executions were once great spectacle, at least until the early twentieth century. Some of the main squares reveal this history with names such as the *pelourinho* (pillory or whipping post). In contemporary Brazil, however, even kidnappers who are threatening the lives of their victims are not publicly killed if it can be avoided. This happened, for example, with the homeless man who held hostage passengers on a bus in Rio de Janeiro in 2000.[40] Police snipers had a clear shot but chose not to pull the trigger, even when they believed he was about to kill his hostages. However, once they had him safely in custody and away from the public eye, it was widely assumed that the police would beat him to death and this is precisely what happened.

The moral and legal codes—with respect to violent crimes—are remarkably similar between Vietnam and Brazil. One shall not kill or steal is an edict that is beyond debate and reinforced by the state, religion, families, the media, and schools. Comparing the two societies, however, it would appear that Vietnam wins the public education campaign for encouraging good behavior. T. R. Reid concluded that this was one of the reasons that crime was so much lower in East Asia when compared to the United States:

> Just about anywhere you go in China, Japan, Korea, Singapore, Malaysia, Indonesia, Taiwan, Thailand, etc. you find moral instruction right before your

> eyes—often in letters (or characters) ten feet tall. Acting on what appears to be a pan-Asian conviction that there can't be too much of a good thing, these countries are constantly preaching values, morality, and good citizenship to their citizens in the form of slogans, posters, billboards, advertisements and TV commercials.[41]

In Vietnam such teachings are also abundant. Banners and billboards encouraging patriotism, civility, and ethical conduct are on virtually every street corner. However, I could not help but feel that such reminders were likely of little consequence. My impression was that these messages were often tuned out much like the government's morning news that is blared at dawn through loudspeakers in various neighborhoods, or the Marxist-Leninist philosophy taught in schools that no one I interviewed could discuss with any level of proficiency.

What I believe to be more significant or impactful than the comparative degree to which moral codes were reiterated and reinforced was the relationship between honor and ethics. In Brazil, a common and cutting way of criticizing someone is not to charge her or him with being unethical but rather to accuse the person of having no concern with face or self-respect, to be "without shame" (*sem vergonha*). Some have argued that honor matters even more in Vietnam, and have labeled this "exaggerated concern for face saving" as a negative trait.[42] Although I do not see this anxiety as deleterious, I too found a consistent, almost obsessive, worry about protecting, guarding, and building ones' reputation in Vietnam. However, what I believe to be a more significant distinction between Vietnam and Brazil, at least with respect to social capital, is not the relative degree to which honor matters but rather the degree to which honor and ethics overlap.

In *The Honor Code*, Kwame Appiah observed that honor, moral, and legal codes do not always match. In fact, the lesson he drew from the study of many historic moral revolutions—such as the abolition of slavery and the ending of footbinding—was that change happened only when certain practices or institutions became shameful. People often began doing what was right not because it was suddenly deemed unethical or illegal but because it became dishonorable to do otherwise. Dueling in Europe, for example, was long considered immoral and illegal before the practice ended. It only ceased, according to Appiah, once it came to lack honor.[43]

In Brazil, there is little esteem to be taken by working hard and playing by the rules. This just indicates how lowly, unimaginative, and unconnected one is. The individual who deserves respect is the person who is able to break or bend the rules in order to accomplish certain ends. This indicates creativity, cleverness, as well as an individual's social rank. This should, then, help to clarify the woman's response to a parking ticket detailed earlier. Outside this symbolic universe her actions would be considered both malicious and ridiculous. In Brazil, however, an individual's status is enmeshed with whether she or he must obey the rules. Consequently, the ticket was an affront to her reputation and social standing. It suggested that she was a little person—an individual without connections, honor, and therefore someone who must obey the law.

Honor codes are articulated very differently in Vietnam. I never witnessed the celebration of the rule breaker. Instead what brought honor and respect was praying to family ancestors, prioritizing the family, working hard, being humble, and emphasizing righteousness over materialism—these were the characteristics that were almost universally revered and respected by the people I interviewed. Moreover, gaming the system was not a badge of honor, a coveted symbol of status, or rationalized as excusable because "everyone does it." Instead most forms of corruption, unethical behavior, and crime carried the stigma of shame, if and when discovered. A fifty-year-old art dealer, Cam, described it this way:

> With friends and acquaintances it's important to maintain as good a relationship as possible in case you need their help. It's important to nurture these relationships. Businesses are a little different but even there trust matters a great deal. Once you build up a good relationship, then you can be trusted. If you do something bad, something unethical, then everyone would shame you. I know that personally I worry about my reputation. I would be afraid if people around me started seeing me as not a good person. I would lose their trust. I would lose face in my community.[44]

A recent corruption scandal, involving a Brazilian tax inspector, Luis Alexandre Cardoso de Magalhaes, and his ex-wife Vanessa Alcantara, helps illuminate how different Brazil can be in this regard. In exchange for allowing construction companies to evade more than $200 million in taxes, they admitted to receiving

> boxes of Cuban cigars, which cost about $500 each, $2260 [worth of] bottles of Vega Sicilia Unico. . . a Porsche Cayenne, speedboat jaunts to tropical islands, and all-night soirees with high-end escorts. . . . Ms. Alcantara said she and Mr. Magalhaes . . . would count the money in her living room, on occasion finding more than $180,000 on their hands.[45]

Rather than this scandal resulting in shame, Ms. Alacantra "is mulling a venture into politics" with the "slogan, 'Being a thief is easy; I'll be honest amid the thieves.'"[46] As noted above, similar kinds of graft occur in Vietnam, but once uncovered, the honor codes do not permit such misdeeds to be a springboard into politics, as they can be in Brazil. Instead, the culprit would lose face, be shunned by friends and acquaintances, taint her or his family, and have serious difficulties in rebuilding a career, let alone a political one.

This raises the question of why there is such a difference between Brazil and Vietnam in the degree of overlap between honor and ethics. I believe much of it has to do with the fact that status in Brazil has historically been ascribed rather than achieved. The "Portuguese elite brought to their colonies ideals that attributed esteem to those who possessed 'pure blood' that granted prestige, opportunities, and legal privileges to those with a traceable noble lineage."[47] These traditions were only hardened and deepened by race-based modes of colonialism and slavery.

This legacy is evident today in that the elite and middle classes seem to view themselves as honorable exclusively because of their social ranking, rather than based, say, on their good behavior or a laudable accomplishment. An important symbol of this social standing and repute, as was true in the past, is whether or not one is expected to follow the rules and obey the law. Indeed "the inability to protect oneself from impersonal authority" has been a basic indicator of "a lack of status" in Brazil for centuries.[48] In other words, the package of standing and honor is demonstrated by the ability to skirt formal processes and call upon patron–client ties to avoid the law. This is why for Brazilians, unlike people in Vietnam, there is little or no shame associated with breaking the law, bending the rules, or gaming the system. What this means for development practitioners is that unless or until honor codes are revamped and brought in line with certain ethical and legal codes in Brazil, the practice of favors is apt to continue, and levels of social capital will, in turn, remain low.

Religion and Resistance

If the elite is essentialized as honorable, then the opposite holds true for the *povo* in Brazil. The marginalized majority of Brazilians, who reside in the periphery of cities, *favelas*, and the countryside, are presumed undignified because of their positioning as members of a backward, racially inferior class. This is one reason why it is so common for poor Brazilians to note that she or he is a garbage collector or domestic servant, and then quickly add "but at least I am not a drug trafficker or a prostitute." Others make less occupation-specific comments and say things such as, "I'm poor, but I'm honest." Tellingly, I never heard a dentist, lawyer, banker, accountant, or some other middle-class professional in Brazil announce their occupation and then immediately insert "but at least I'm not an adulterer or embezzler." None of them ever said, "I'm rich, but I'm honest." Given the epistemology of honor, there is no need to make such a qualifying statement. As members of the civilized, upstanding gentry of society, their honor is a given. They are presumed to be dignified even when their actions suggest otherwise; whereas the working class are supposed, as if by nature, to be uncouth, immoral indigents and therefore of disrepute.

In the 1960s, Paulo Freire recognized that the *povo*'s internalization of this construction of themselves as a tainted people without dignity undergirded poverty and social inequalities in Brazil. To counter this self-hatred he pioneered a teaching method, the so-called pedagogy of the oppressed.[49] Freire believed that as the poverty-stricken came to critically understand the oppressive structural conditions in which they lived—through dialogue, reason, and sustained reflection—they would eventually shed their sense of shame and littleness. In the next chapter I detail a successful use of Freire's method in advancing economic development, but at this stage I wish to discuss what I found to be a different mode of resistance among ordinary Brazilians to their stigmatization: living an ethical life. When the impoverished assert they are poor but also honest, they are effectively calling into question both their positioning as undignified as well as the epistemology of honor in Brazil. That is, they are rejecting an ascribed basis of esteem and contending, instead, that prestige is a by-product of good conduct rather than social standing. This discursive move opens up the possibility for them to be honorable—at least in their own eyes—so long as they live a moral life. The thinking goes something like this, "I'm not a dishonorable person because I'm poor. Indeed I'm a person of respect because of my ethical behavior."

The challenge, of course, is that to live a righteous life is no easy feat in a society in which corruption is rife, elitism extreme, the playing field unequal, and education and legitimate job opportunities limited. Temptation for deviating from the straight and narrow is everywhere, especially given that it is the hustler rather than the rule follower that is celebrated and valued in the broader society. One of the exceptions to this is many of the faith-based communities in Brazil. Within these spheres a moral life is often prized, nurtured, and supported. Offering an arena where a virtuous life is encouraged and valued, increases the odds that congregants will resist temptation and live an honest life. Over the years, many *crentes* ("believers," as Evangelical Christians in Brazil are called) have confided in me that they originally converted to Protestantism—a faith that 30 percent of Brazilians now claim—for pragmatic reasons such as helping them to stop drinking and womanizing. The academic literature on Evangelical Christianity in Latin America has also recognized these motives.[50] Obviously overdrinking and womanizing can lead to an unhealthy lifestyle and dysfunctional relationships and thus there is a great deal to be gained in terms of social and physical well-being by curbing such practices. However, what is less commonly appreciated

Figure 4.3 Evangelical Christians, Babilonia. Photograph by Nando Neves, 2010

is the cultural politics involved. By helping the *povo* to be incorruptible, these religious organizations afford ordinary Brazilians a unique chance to stake claim to a sense of dignity in a society in which they are assumed to have none.

This thesis about the symbolic appeal of evangelical Christianity aside, it is indisputable that most religious communities in Brazil contribute to the building of social capital by creating and sustaining social spaces in which honor codes are brought in line with ethics. In this way, I contend, they foster trust, civility, and cohesiveness that are, as noted above, in very short supply in Brazilian society. Interestingly many Brazilian academics and social activists have ignored or looked unfavorably upon the socio-political impact of religion, especially its evangelical and messianic forms. This is probably because these religious organizations and movements are evaluated exclusively on the level of the doctrinaire and thus are, from a secular-rationalist perspective, pushers of falsehoods that only serve as escapist or reactionary detractions from a critical evaluation and contestation of an unethical, unequal, and unjust socio-economic order. But what such a reading of these religions misses is their vital role in both empowering the *povo* to combat their ill repute as well as enhancing social capital by building arenas where honor and ethics overlap.

The Commons

The great Brazilian filmmaker, Glauber Rocha, made it clear in several of his films, such as *Black God, White Devil* (1964), that he believed that both messianic Christianity and social banditry were ineffectual responses by the poor to their marginalization. On this first score, I disagree with Rocha. As discussed in the previous section, Evangelical and messianic religions' response to social hierarchy is at least partially constructive in that it allows the poor to challenge their positioning as undignified as well as contributes to the building of social capital in a society in which it is in short supply. However, on the matter of social banditry and its contemporary iteration, gangs, I concur with Rocha. Becoming a gangster may be an understandable response to extreme levels of disenfranchisement, but ultimately it is an ineffectual and self-destructive reaction that only compounds the problems that the poor face.

Unlike the media-infused perceptions in Brazil, peripheral communities are not teeming with gangsters. Nonetheless, gangs are undoubtedly a potent organization and a sad fact of life in many poor communities in Brazil. The tale of a thirty-something tour guide in Salvador, Bahia offers a window into the corrosive impact of gangs. Upon leaving the Sao Francisco church in Salvador in 2014, and reflecting upon how little things had changed socially since the early colonial days in which the poor were excluded from the church, he explained how only he and one other classmate had not been killed or incarcerated of the 27 boys in their high school cohort. The others were the victims of gang related crime and violence. He added that it was unwise for poor people to travel more than one kilometer in any direction in Salvador because of the likelihood of being killed—a person from another community is automatically marked as an enemy gang affiliate regardless of whether she or he participates in a gang.

It is commonly assumed that gang membership is driven by economic necessity, but most studies have found that it is largely the product of a social and existential vacuum.[51] Boys and young men, in particular, are drawn to these criminal organizations because they offer them a sense of belonging, meaning, and respect—something largely lacking in communities that have been abandoned by the state and dismissed as spaces of inferior, undignified peoples. Any potential upsides to gangs—such as offering purpose and community to adolescents and young adults—are clearly offset by their downsides. A gang's primary *raison d'etre* is crime and violence. A member's livelihood and reputation within the group is dependent upon drug trading, theft, violence, and even murder. The few times I spoke with gang members in communities like Babilonia, it was clear that they did not see such behavior as ethical or legal, but rationalized it as a necessary evil. Moreover, and most germane to the question of social capital, members could glean prestige from such misdeeds. As one resident of a *favela* in Rio de Janeiro, Vigario Geral, noted in the documentary film *Favela Rising*, "The guys join the gangs because they want to be respected. And the girls chase the guys that have machine guns. They, too, want to be respected."[52]

Some scholars have theorized that violent crime is more a symptom than a cause of anemic social capital, but I think that the relationship is multidirectional. As the comments by a US expatriate living in Tokyo underscore, absent a fear of violent crime and assault, trust of others (a basic ingredient of social capital) finds much more fertile terrain:

> Although we were living in the heart of one of the largest cities in the world, we learned to live without fear. Or perhaps I should say that, over time, we forgot to be afraid. We forgot to worry about what might happen if a strange person started walking behind us on an unknown street after dark. We forgot to keep a constant eye on our luggage when we set it down in the airport or bus station. When we went bike riding, we forgot to carry that big, heavy Kryptonite lock we always used back home. We acquired a basic confidence that the members of our family, even the smallest ones, could go anywhere in a massive city without worrying about crime. And this made a fundamental difference in the way we led our lives.[53]

Too often, in Brazil, the approach to dealing with crime has been a draconian formula of militarized police tactics and extra-judicial violence—an approach sanctioned and fueled by race-inflected elitism as well as discourses which construe criminals as evil incarnate.[54] Most of East Asia, in contrast, has achieved incredibly low levels of violent crime without police-state tactics. Per-capita ratios of police to citizens are much lower and punishments tend to be less severe than in the United States or Brazil. Instead of isolating the criminal from society, "a convict is sent back to his neighborhood, family, and job so that the social pressure to fit in and pain of being shamed before the group will lead him to go straight."[55] Along these lines, Confucius long ago advised:

> Guide them with edicts, keep them in line with punishment, and people may stay out of trouble but will not have a sense of shame. But if you guide them by your own virtue, and keep them in line with acts of decency, they will develop a sense of shame and control themselves.[56]

For such an approach to be effective, however, honor codes must be firmly in line with ethics and the law. And, as I have described, outside of a few arenas, such as certain religious communities, this alignment does not exist within much of Brazilian society. Even worse, in certain settings, such as within gangs or among the well-off, esteem often comes from violating ethical codes, bending the rules, and breaking the law.

At this juncture, it should be evident that working to limit or undermine certain communitarian identities, such as gangs, would surely help to boost trust and civility immensely by reducing crime, violence, and the valorization of illicit behavior. Nonetheless, it would be a grave mistake to deduce from this that *all forms* of personalism should be replaced with individualism, as some Brazilianists and neo-modernizationists have recommended.[57] For starters, a person who does not have a healthy socio-emotional attachment to other people or the broader society will obviously not be motivated by social pressures to conform to the laws, norms, and expectations of a community. It is more likely to result in an atomized and fragmented society where people tend to be excessively narcissistic and narrowly pursue perceived self-interests with little regard for others. Thus, development policies ought not to be crudely aimed at weakening and supplanting solidarities. In fact, many kinds of personalism should be nurtured or scaled up. One challenge, then, for development theorists and practitioners is to identify which specific social ties and identifications are beneficial and offer concrete recommendations for building these solidarities.

An example of a favorable affiliation, as already discussed, is found in the various religious organizations, such as some of the Evangelical churches, the Catholic Church, and various Afro- and Indigenous religions like Umbanda and Candomble that help to align honor with ethics, and allow the have-nots to stake out a sense of dignity and self-worth. Afro-Reggae is a secular association that has had a similar impact in certain neighborhoods in Rio de Janeiro. This grassroots organization has fought alienation, violence, and gangs by creating alternative social spheres, in which adolescents and young adults derive meaning, love, and respect through the celebration and performance of the Afro-Brazilian culture of the *favela* as well as earning an honest living, denouncing crime and violence, and giving up drugs and alcohol. In various communities, these organizations and solidarities have proven a powerful antidote to gangs.[58] In Vigario Geral, a neighborhood of 40,000 residents, gang membership and violence dropped precipitously after Afro-Reggae was established. Not coincidentally, trust, civility, and social cohesion swelled.[59]

Although these sorts of meso-level, horizontal affinities can be beneficial for generating social capital in neighborhoods and among the wider public, in general bolstering large scale, vertical ties has proven more effective in countering alienation, disaffection, and distrust in society. That is, collaboration, reciprocity, trust, and ultimately, economic well-being often spring from a robust fraternity, camaraderie, and cohesiveness that extend across class, religion, and sectarian divides. In Brazil such attachments to the commons have been weak historically. One reason for this may be that the public arena, or "street," has been culturally constructed as immoral. According to Brazilianists like Roberto DaMatta, "Brazilians associate the house with honor, order, marriage, safety, family, and private power while the street implies disgrace, chaos, illegitimacy, danger, vagrancy, and vulnerability to the vagrancies of impersonal public authority."[60]

Not surprisingly, then, researchers have discovered little concern for the commons, even in elite, homogenous settings. In one upper middle-class housing development, for instance, Teresa Caldeira found residents used common areas exclusively according to personal convenience. General rules and respect for other people's rights were ignored. Thus, even in settings where social distinctions were leveled, "a public life ruled by democratic principles, public responsibility, and civility" failed to emerge.[61] Perhaps not surprisingly, as Calderia elaborates below, Brazilian developers do not attempt to market housing developments, even upscale ones, as sites of community.

> In the United States "community" is a common designation of condominiums of various types. In São Paulo developers do not think of themselves as "community builders," and ads do not present closed condominiums as a new type of communitarian life, but only as a place of residence for homogenous social groups. In other words, ads do not insist on a community of shared values and interests, do not try to create any special sense of belonging to a community, and do not appeal to the importance of a space that can facilitate face-to-face interaction. For Brazilian developers and their clients, the advantages of social homogeneity do not imply the desirability of a local sociability.[62]

Until the anti-colonial movement and revolution in the mid-twentieth century, Vietnam was also characterized by having an anemic commons outside of the family or village. On this point, Alexander Woodside writes:

> A solidarity deficit is usually seen in the West as a modern problem, attributable to a rights-oriented liberal individualism whose preoccupation was to loosen feudal bonds in early modern Europe. But the examinations-based bureaucracies of the Mandarinates, and the distance of bureaucratic planners from local needs, had also weakened vertical ties between rulers and ruled in them, and generated a solidarity deficit earlier in history.[63]

When the referent is moved from the West, what stands out in Vietnam are not the weak vertical ties of the past but rather how the public sphere was never imagined as site of impurity or in opposition to the familial-private sphere as in Brazil. In pre-colonial times, affinities were understood as ever-weakening concentric circles of commitment: family, village, and lastly, the kingdom. Subjects prioritized family but they did not shun the kingdom or consider it a realm of profanity. It simply held the lowest level of allegiance.

For a brief moment, during the high socialist period, the Communist Party of Vietnam attempted to frame familial and national solidarities in more adversarial, if not mutually exclusive terms. In an effort to counter the long-standing solidary deficit noted by Woodside, the CPV attempted to forge stronger vertical ties through nation by usurping and displacing attachments to the family and village—the attack on family values for which many former allies of the Republic of Vietnam, as discussed in Chapter 3, bitterly critiqued the CPV. An illustration of this move was government efforts to stake claims to the memories of the fallen soldiers of the French and American wars. Mark Bradley writes:

> The Vietnamese state sought to own the memory of its war dead, an effort most starkly revealed in the official memorial services organized by local party cadres. Here a fallen soldier's sacrifice for the state and revolution, rather than this relationship to his lineage or village, served to exclusively define the meaning of his life and death.[64]

Beginning in the 1980s, various filmmakers and artists, perhaps most famously in Dang Nhat Minh's 1984 film, *When the Tenth Month Comes*, began to push back against the state's attempts to displace the family by monopolizing the significance and memory of the war dead. To their credit, these critics did not reproduce the CPV's framing of nation and family as an adversarial relationship. That is, they did not attempt to undermine or disparage the commons as a tactic for reclaiming and bolstering space for family attachments. Evidence of this was how Dang's film ends with an extended shot of the flag and the national anthem playing in the background. Clearly, national and family ties were conceptualized, at least by Dang, as complementary rather than adversarial—a conceptualization of solidarities that has much deeper roots in Vietnam than the one the CPV attempted to promote in the twentieth century.

Nation

For much of the nineteenth and twentieth centuries, intellectuals and revolutionaries throughout the world posited weak communitarian identities as one of the major barriers to economic and social progress. Specifically, a vibrant sense of nation, which could engender powerful collective action and temper free-rider or sectarian impulses, was considered essential for decolonization, modernization, and economic development. An eclectic array of liberal, fascist, social democratic, and socialist modernizers agreed that absent a robust commons anchored in nation it would be nearly impossible to successfully confront and tackle the challenges of the modern era.

On this theme of nation, the distinctions between Vietnam and Brazil could not be starker. In Vietnam, revolutionary nationalism emerged with gusto in the mid-twentieth century and is credited with being one of the primary reasons why the Vietnamese people were able to pull off two of the greatest military upsets in modern history.[65] And in contemporary Vietnam, nation continues to have a vitality and appeal that one does not typically find, in my experience, in the United States, Western Europe, or Brazil.

In interviews on this topic, I would often become the interviewee. As a way to politely point out how ridiculous they found my "Are-you-proud-to-be-Vietnamese?" query, interviewees would turn the question back on me and ask whether I was proud to be an American. In a rambling response, I would discuss how there were aspects about which I was proud and many other things that I found abhorrent and then cap it off with how I identified in more cosmopolitan than national terms. Usually before I got to the cosmopolitan part of my answer, the interviewee-turned-interviewer would look puzzled because for them, as I eventually came to understand, to be proud of and loyal to one's nation was viewed as something God-given or bone-deep. It was analogous, perhaps, to asking someone whether she or he was proud of her or his children. To respond that one was equally committed to and proud of all children throughout the world—rather than saying that yes, of course, my kids come first—makes no sense.

In Brazil, national identities have been comparatively weaker than Vietnam in the past century. Clearly, at moments or in certain contexts, Brazilians have a strong attachment to nation, but in general these vertical ties have been more erratic and much shallower than in Vietnam. One of the best cinematic representations of these more feeble national sentiments appears in *Carindiru*—a film about an infamous prison massacre in Sao Paulo in 1992. In one scene, the prisoners begin their day in the prison yard with the playing of the national anthem as a tattered national flag is raised. A few prisoners come to a respectful attention, but most are completely disinterested and indifferent. Except for a few outliers, nation seems to have virtually no emotional appeal—an attitude that I took to be a commentary about the state of nation in Brazil more broadly.

Among area studies experts, pessimism about communitarian identities runs high. The observations of Hermano Vianna offer a case in point. Note how he wonders whether solidarity is even possible anymore in the world's "peripheral economies"[66]:

> The nationalist project has now seen better days. Not only cultural nationalism but also economic nationalism, too, has been eclipsed in Brazil. The 1950s developmentalism of Brazilian president Juscelino Kubitschek offered its own emblem of national unity and modern identity: Brasilia. But the new capital city, middle-aged at the close of the twentieth century, never became a widely recognized national symbol, and despite the efforts of successive developmentalist governments, Brazil has not "won its place in the First World." World Capitalism itself clearly works against nationalist projects in

> late twentieth century Brazil. We live in a society that has become globalized and fragmented to an extreme, creating a dilemma for Brazilians and other inhabitants of the world's peripheral economies. . . . Is there a chance, anymore, for a first-person-plural we in the story that Brazilians once so liked to tell themselves about themselves?[67]

Vibrant national identities in Vietnam and pessimism about even the possibility of a "first-person-plural we" in Brazil represent a dramatic reversal of fates in the regions. For instance, in *Imagined Communities* Benedict Anderson documented how national identities first emerged in Latin America in the eighteenth and nineteenth centuries whereas during this same period vertical ties were very dim in Vietnam—as noted above, this had been one the biggest challenges that the Mandarins faced in East Asia for centuries. As late as the 1930s, at the height of French colonialism, many Vietnamese intellectuals and anti-colonial activists, reminiscent of Latin American intellectuals today, had serious doubts as to whether nation was even possible.[68]

Most Latin Americanists, like Vianna above, blame global capitalism and its cultural analog, post-modernity, for the weakness of collective, macro-level identities. The basic, neo-Marxist idea is that capitalist-driven globalization has penetrated societies to such an extent that it has rendered collective solidarities untenable. In its wake all that remain are alienated, fragmented individuals who can barely muster a coherent story of self, let alone rally around a unifying narrative of society. In writing about Mexico City, Nestor Canclini offers another good example of this perspective:

> Large cities torn by erratic growth and multicultural conflicts are the sites where we can best observe the decline of metanarratives, of utopias that projected an ascendant and cohesive human development throughout time. . . . To narrate is to know that it is no longer possible to have the experience of order that the flâneur expected to find in his strolls through the city at the beginning of the century. Nowadays the city is like a video clip, an effervescent montage of discontinuous images. . . . I end by asking myself if we will be able to narrate the city again?[69]

I return to the theme of multiculturalism in the next section, so let it suffice to remark here that Vietnam, and the rest of East Asia for that matter, demonstrates that global capitalism and post-modernity are not to blame for the decline of collective solidarities in Latin America. Vietnam is just as interpolated by "World Capitalism" as Mexico or Brazil. It is a member of the WTO and heavily dependent on global trade. Its citizens are eager consumers of Hollywood films and Korean popular music, connected socially and financially with overseas Vietnamese, passionate followers of English Premier League soccer, recipients of millions of tourists each year, and send their children to study abroad at very high rates.[70] Yet *no one* disputes the salience and vibrancy of nation in Vietnam.

In Chapter 1, I discussed how a number of East Asian and comparative development studies scholars have theorized this strength of nation in East Asia as one of the factors behind the economic success in the region. Chalmers Johnson was an originator of this hypothesis. In *MITI and the Japanese Miracle*, which was first published in 1982, he argued that development qua revolutionary nationalist project was why the developmental state had worked so well in Japan and the rest of East Asia.

> The successful capitalist developmental states have been quasi-revolutionary regimes, in which whatever legitimacy their rulers possessed did not come from external sanctification or some formal rules whereby they gained office but from the overarching social projects their societies endorsed and they carried out. . . . This one overriding objective—economic development—was present among the Japanese people after the war, among the Korean people after Syngman Rhee, among the Chinese exiles and Taiwanese after Chiang Kai-shek acknowledged that he was not going home again, among the Singaporeans after the Malayan Emergency and their expulsion from Malaysia, among the residents of Hong Kong after they fled communism, and among Chinese city dwellers after the Cultural Revolution.[71]

I would add Vietnam to this list. The people whom I met were keenly focused on developing their economy and framed this project as not what comes after the revolution but rather its next logical step. Development was considered by almost everyone that I interviewed the natural, if not inevitable, culmination of a national project of liberation and modernization that had begun with the anti-colonial struggle in the early twentieth century. Comments by Hai, a fifty-three-year-old yogurt shop owner, were typical: "First we defeated the Chinese, then the French and then the Americans. Now we need only develop the economy—surely this will be difficult but nothing compared to the wars we fought and won."[72] Similar, then, with how Johnson described other East Asian societies, the Vietnamese think of development as an overriding, quasi-revolutionary national project. Indeed this is one reason why many observers of Vietnam have argued that the government's legitimacy hinges less on democratization or human rights issues than on whether it can deliver on what many Vietnamese consider the final phase of the revolutionary nationalism: economic development.

In brief, Vietnam and the rest of East Asia teach that a robust inter-class identification with nation is possible in the present era of global capitalism. Given the importance of such vertical ties for social capital and economic growth, the question that we, as development scholars, need to answer is how similar allegiances to the commons could be realized in places like Brazil. The objective should not be to recreate "development-as-a-revolutionary-nationalist project" in Latin America—this would, of course, be unrealistic given the historical and societal particularities of the region—but rather produce some, if not all, of its functional equivalents. For instance, how might one of its most salutary attributes—strong collective solidarities—be manufactured in Brazil? It is to this task that I now turn.

Race to Development

As mentioned in the previous section, Latin Americanists have tended to theorize neoliberal capitalism and multiculturalism as the central foes of nation. The heavily globalized societies and economies of East Asia undercut this first thesis of a "fragmented-global-capitalist modernity," but what about multiculturalism? The argument here is reminiscent of T. J. Pempel who, recall from Chapter 1, blamed the social heterogeneity in Latin America for the lower levels of social fraternity in the region—but without explaining what specifically about diversity was the issue. Latin Americanists, like Vianna and Canclini cited above, often attempt to fill in this theoretical gap with the thesis that multiculturalism, in particular the social movements that valorize black and indigenous identities and cultures, is fragmenting and undermining the commons. "The blocos afros," Vianna laments, "turn away from nationalism to redefine their vision of the world, but they turn in a new direction, toward 'the third world' and toward 'negritude' ".[73] In this section I outline why I believe racism, not multiculturalism, is the central impediment to nation and that therefore the focus of development practitioners should be on anti-racism rather than attacking multiculturalism as a means of remedying the social solidarity deficit in Brazil.

In the early twentieth century, as discussed in Chapter 3, scientific racism prevailed throughout the Atlantic. Almost all social scientists in the region presumed that humankind was divided up into four or five different subspecies or races, and that this "biological" lineage determined culture.[74] Therefore a great civilization needed, these experts agreed, the right race qua biology.[75] Different societies devised different mechanisms to achieve this outcome. In the United States, municipalities, states, congress, and the courts crafted segregation and anti-miscegenation laws ostensibly to protect the "white" race from contamination. In Brazil, as throughout Latin America, whiteness was to be achieved through race mixing. During the early part of the twentieth century, the preeminent Brazilian intellectuals of the time theorized that after two or three generations of racial mixing the non-white elements would be washed away and in this way Brazil would become white and finally join the ranks of the civilized. And so racial mixing was encouraged as a means of achieving whiteness—and with it, modernity. With the rise of mestizo nationalism in the 1930s, as discussed in Chapter 2, the semiotics of racial mixing or *mesticagem* was refashioned by intellectuals, artists, and policymakers. Racial mixing continued to be encouraged and celebrated, but not as a tool to bleach away non-whiteness. Instead of trying to negate or eliminate blackness, racial mixing was guided by an effort to valorize limited aspects of black culture. To a degree, this happened. Samba, *feijoada*, carnival, and other cultural practices associated with blackness were celebrated and featured as the icons of nation. In the global context of apartheid in the United States and South Africa, European colonialism, and Nazism in Germany, Brazil as the land that "loved the mix" led to the rise of the racial democracy ideology. This narrative captured the imagination of those at home and abroad, which is why UNESCO funded research on race in Brazil after WWII. It was believed that racism was less acute in Brazil and therefore it was hoped that anti-racist lessons could be gleaned from Brazil to help other societies in the world to become less racist.

The problem is that the socio-economic reality in Brazil fell further and further out of step with the rest of the world. Rather than the celebration of the mestizo incentivizing anti-racist initiatives and movements, it ended up snuffing them out because talking about racism was interpreted by most Brazilians as calling into question the bedrock narrative of nation. As the rest of the world made varying degrees of anti-racist progress (e.g., scientific racism was discredited, European colonialism imploded, and apartheid ended in South Africa and the United States), little changed in Brazil. In contemporary Brazil black domestic servants continue to service middle class and elite white households using segregated entrances and service elevators. Crude stereotypes of black inferiority and Indian savagery circulate unchecked in the media, schools, and everyday chatter.[76] An almost all-white political and economic elite still rules Brazil.[77] Most nonwhites are relegated by institutional and quotidian racism to de facto ghettos where basic social services are unavailable.[78] And still the majority of people continue to assert that racism has little or no impact on them. As Helena, a twenty-year-old black tutor in Contagem, a suburb of Belo Horizonte, explained to me:

> If I were to rank my problems from one to twenty, with one being the worst of all my problems, racism would be number eighteen or nineteen. Racism just isn't something I'm greatly concerned about. I have bigger problems, such as putting food on the table, getting into a university, or getting a decent job.[79]

This is a common response in contemporary Brazil, even among nonwhite Brazilians who are overwhelmingly concentrated in the poorer sectors of society.[80] The *povo* tend to see race and class as separate issues (rather than intertwined) and theorize social inequalities as anchored in class alone. Consequently they often fail to appreciate how one's capacity to get a job or put food on the table is enmeshed with race. Few understand how racism shapes the labor market, social welfare regimes, taxation policies, housing and land rights, educational opportunities, and so forth, which make meeting even basic economic needs extremely precarious for most Brazilians. In short, the majority of Brazilians, including most poor people of color, do not believe that race underpins economic and social inequalities.[81]

Breaking the silence around racism and building peoples' racial literacy would help to not only reduce social inequalities and imitative modernization projects, as discussed in Chapters 2 and 3, but also build social capital by giving substance and resonance back to Brazil's central narrative of nation, the racial democracy. In this way it would strengthen communitarian identities, solidarity, and economic growth. But, as has been noted, developmental entities and experts devote almost no attention or resources to, say, preparing primary and secondary school teachers in how to educate children to better recognize racism and challenge its quotidian

Figure 4.4 Anti-racist Activist in Salvador, Bahia. Photograph by Erivan Morias, 2014

and institutional manifestations. For instance, the NGOs that are attempting to advance anti-racist pedagogy in Brazilian schools, such as the ones studied by Jose Antonio Bacelar da Silva in Salvador, Bahia, receive little or no development support.[82] Or what about nurturing and expanding the counterpublics where racial literacy is more advanced? Indigenous or *quilombo* communities[83], for example, have been found to be less colorblind in their outlook and their members more consistently active in contesting racism by bringing into being alternative, nonracist symbolic orders in which whiteness is not hyper valued as the good, the beautiful, the desired, or the deserving.[84] Rather than attempt to ally with and nurture these people and their interpretive worlds, most Latin American intellectuals and pundits, as we have seen, scold them for fragmenting nation. And, not coincidently, the only development monies that these communities typically see are the ones aimed at destroying them—the Belo Monte Dam in the Xingu being just the latest iteration of this kind of anti-development initiative being carried out, ironically, in the name of economic growth.

Theoretical Developments

Let me close this chapter by summarizing some of the most significant contributions that this comparison has allowed me to make vis-à-vis social capital. First, I have lent more empirical support to those who question the significance of non-governmental organizations. In the cases of Brazil and Vietnam, voluntary associations were not found to be a significant variable. The fact that social capital is stronger in Vietnam, despite it having fewer nongovernmental organizations than in Brazil, should serve as further caution to development practitioners who imagine that the remedy for the solidarity and trust deficits is through voluntary associations á la *Bowling Alone*. Although this finding will come as little surprise to many scholars of social capital, the stature of Putnam's ideas among US opinion makers makes it important to reiterate and highlight this point.

Second, this comparison underscores the deeply corrosive impact that social inequalities have on economic growth. The causal relationship between social equality and social capital is something that scholars have recognized for almost 200 years, beginning with Alexis de Tocqueville in the nineteenth century. And yet, shamefully, large segments of the development establishment continue to ignore or minimize this well-documented fact. It is astonishing how much attention has been placed on, for example, advancing "good institutions," even though there is no evidence that this makes any positive difference,[85] whereas social inequalities receive at best rhetorical mention or a few token policy measures despite overwhelming and irrefutable evidence of how hugely important reducing socio-economic inequities is for economic growth.

Third, security emerged as an important independent variable. Much like the question of equality, it has long been appreciated that violence and the lack of security are economically damaging. Nonetheless, police reform and anti-gang efforts have not been taken up with much vigor in Brazil. One of the few exceptions to this are Pacifying Police Units (UPPs) that have been advanced in at least fifteen neighborhoods in the city of Rio de Janeiro. Even though these modest attempts at police reform—tempering militarized policing methods, paying police officers a somewhat higher salary, increasing day-to-day policing presence in poor neighborhoods—have proven successful in reducing violent deaths in a handful of communities, including Babilonia, the political will to move away from militarized policing toward community policing remains weak and seems unlikely to prevail.[86] Interclass protests emerged around the mega-projects in Brazil in the build up to the World Cup and Olympics but no similar movements and cross-class coalitions have surfaced to tackle police reform and the war-like level of violence that is endemic in poor neighborhoods.

This inattention to policing and human rights is most noticeable to me when I am invited to speak about Vietnam or Brazil. Human rights violations are much more routine and egregious in Brazil than in Vietnam, as measured by most conventional metrics such as police killings and torture, inhumane prison conditions, unfair trials, and so on. Despite these empirical realities, the audience and interviewers almost always raise questions about human rights violations when the topic is Vietnam and this rarely comes up when Brazil is the focus. There are undoubtedly many reasons for this oversight: residue of the Cold War discourses, anxieties surrounding the rise of Asia, and historically specific understandings of terrorism in the post-9/11 era. However, regardless of the reasons, this chapter underscores how such an omission is an error that needs to be corrected by development scholars and practitioners if economic growth is desired in countries like Brazil.

In addition to challenging, confirming, and nuancing a number of existing theories of social capital, I have also made a few original contributions to the social capital literature. To my knowledge, no one has hypothesized a causal relationship between honor codes and social capital. This finding could offer potentially rich, new directions for development practice—lending support, for example, to organizations, activists, educators, religious leaders, and social movements that are working hard to bring honor in line with ethics and the law.

This chapter also offers a way to move beyond the fatalism that dominates area and comparative development studies on the question of solidarity deficits and nation. First, contrary to what various Latin American analysts have concluded, Vietnam and the rest of East Asia demonstrate that "a first person plural 'we' " is possible in the era of global capitalism. Second, despite what many comparative development scholars imply with their theories of East Asian exceptionalism, I have shown how vibrant nation-based communitarian identities are achievable in Brazil absent socio-political revolutions or efforts to create more socially homogenous societies. Throughout most of Latin America, the central discourse of nation hinges on the idea of racial democracy or non-racism. The problem, as in Brazil, is that racism is ubiquitous and deeply entrenched and thus there is a massive disconnect between reality and narrative. The obvious and realizable development remedy, then, is to advance anti-racist initiatives in order to give currency to the central story of nation and in the process bolster social capital that, as countless development scholars argue, is one of the essential ingredients of economic growth. I now turn to a case study of a municipality in the rural backlands of Brazil, which offers concrete evidence of how such an outcome is reachable and practicable in contemporary Brazil.

Notes

1 DaMatta, "Is Brazil Hopelessly Corrupt?" 296.
2 See, for example, Ribeiro Jr., *A privataria tucana* (The Brazilian Social Democracy Party's privatization scam).
3 Barbosa, "The Brazilian *Jeitinho*: An Exercise in National Identity."
4 O'Dougherty, *Consumption Intensified*, 168. Emphasis mine.
5 Ibid., 182–183.
6 World Values Survey. www.wvsevsdb.com/wvs/WVSAnalizeQuestion.jsp. Accessed December 20, 2015.
7 United States Department of State Bureau of Diplomatic Security, "Brazil 2013 Crime and Safety Report: Rio de Janeiro" www.osac.gov/pages/ContentReportDetails.aspx?cid=13966; and United Nations Office Drugs and Crime, www.unodc.org/#state:1. Accessed April 4, 2014
8 Michener, "Crime Rates in Brazil—Grim Stats," *Observing Brazil: A Blog about Brazil, Its Politics and Political Culture* (blog), October 2011 www.observingbrazil.com/2011/10/20/crime-rates-in-brazil-grim-stats. Accessed December 12, 2015.
9 *Central do Brasil* (Central Station), directed by Walter Salles, 1998.
10 *Quanto Vale ou E Por Quilo?* (What is it Worth?), directed by Sergio Bianchi, 2005.
11 *O Homem do Ano* (Man of the Year), directed by Jose Fonseca, 2005.
12 Even luck, it is interesting to note, was considered manageable. If one eats certain foods or performs certain rituals, one was assumed to have control over fate.

13 World Values Survey www.wvsevsdb.com/wvs/WVSAnalizeQuestion.jsp. Accessed November 10, 2015.
14 Han, forty-five-year-old café owner, Hanoi, 2013.
15 Fukuyama, *Trust.*
16 Ibid.
17 Whiteley, *Economic Growth and Social Capital* as in cited in Halpern, *Social Capital*, 59.
18 Whiteley, *Economic Growth and Social Capital*, 18.
19 Putnam, Leonardi, and Nonetti, *Making Democracy Work.*
20 World Values Survey. www.wvsevsdb.com/wvs/WVSAnalizeQuestion.jsp. Accessed November 10, 2015.
21 Ibid.
22 Ibid.
23 de Tocqueville, *Democracy in America*, 3.
24 Putnam, *Bowling Alone.*
25 Weir, *Class in America*, 120.
26 Schwarz, *Misplaced Ideas*, 22.
27 Wilcken, *Empire Adrift*, 27.
28 *O Partido dos Trabalhadores* (Workers' Party) was banned by the military dictatorship (until 1982) and then quickly developed into the main left-of-center party in Brazil by the 1990s. As some of my interviewees noted, it represented one of the only organizational channels available to the people to express their hopes and desires in the 1980s and 90s. Predictably, it was viewed as a threat by those who did not want to see changes to the political status quo. Thus, the original organizers of the Workers' Party, especially at the grassroots level, faced a great deal of push back, including assassinations, by the local elite and their henchmen.
29 Lira, sixty-five-year-old artist, Aracuai, Minas Gerais, 2011.
30 Mauss, *The Gift.*
31 Schwarz, *Misplaced Ideas*, 22.
32 Hess and DaMatta (Eds.), *The Brazilian Puzzle*, 7.
33 Halpern, *Social Capital*, 275.
34 Ngoc, *Wandering Through Vietnamese Culture*, 91.
35 The Vietnamese Lunar New Year, which is called Tet, is the most important holiday of the year. People take off several days of work to celebrate, among other things, their birthdays and pay respect to their deceased ancestors.
36 Hess and DaMatta (Eds.), *The Brazilian Puzzle*, 9.
37 Ibid.
38 Halpern, *Social Capital*, 223.
39 Caldeira, *City of Walls.*
40 *Bus 174*, directed by Jose Pedilha and Felipe Lacerda.
41 Reid, *Confucius Lives Next Door*, 166–167.
42 Ngoc, *Wandering Through Vietnamese Culture*, 500.
43 Appiah, *The Honor Code.*
44 Cong, fifty-year-old art dealer, Hanoi, 2010.
45 Romero, "Brazil is Entranced by a Tale of Love, Taxes and Bribery," *New York Times*, November 27, 2013, A6.
46 Ibid.
47 Wilcken, *Empire Adrift*, 8.
48 Ibid., 18.
49 Freire, *Pedagogy of the Oppressed.*
50 See Brusco, *The Reformation of Machismo*
51 See Neate and Platt, *Culture is our Weapon*; and Gates and West, *The Future of the Race.*

52 *Favela Rising.*
53 Reid, *Confucius Lives Next Door*, 20.
54 Caldeira, *City of Walls.*
55 Ibid., 26.
56 Ibid., 172.
57 Hess and DaMatta (Eds.), *The Brazilian Puzzle.*
58 Neate and Platt, *Culture is our Weapon.*
59 Ibid.
60 Hess and DaMatta (Eds.), *The Brazilian Puzzle.*
61 Caldeira, *City of Walls*, 275.
62 Ibid., 275.
63 Woodside, *Lost Modernities*, 70.
64 Bradley, "Contests of Memory," 199.
65 Examples include scholars as diverse as Pelley, *Postcolonial Vietnam*; Ninh, *A World Transformed*; Gainsborough, *Vietnam*; Laderman, *Tours of Vietnam*; and Truitt, *Dreaming of Money in Ho Chi Minh City.*
66 Vianna, *The Mystery of Samba*, 117.
67 Ibid., 116–117.
68 Woodside, *Lost Modernities.*
69 Canclini, *Consumers and Citizens*, 84–85.
70 Nguyen-Vo, *The Ironies of Freedom*; and Erik Harms, *Saigon's Edge.*
71 Johnson, "The Developmental State," 52–53.
72 Hai, fifty-three-year-old shop keeper, Hanoi, Vietnam 2007.
73 Vianna, *The Mystery of Samba*, 101.
74 Skidmore, *Black into White.*
75 Ibid.
76 Simpson, *Xuxa*; Telles, *Race in Another America*; Warren, *Racial Revolutions.*
77 Sheriff, *Dreaming Equality*; Hanchard, *Orpheus and Power*; Telles, *Race in Another America*; Twine, *Racism in a Racial Democracy.*
78 Holston, *Insurgent Citizenship.*
79 Helena, twenty-two-year-old tutor, Contagem, Minas Gerais, Brazil, 1995.
80 Twine, *Racism in a Racial Democracy*; and Sheriff, *Dreaming Equality.*
81 Telles, *Race in Another America*; Hanchard, *Orpheus and Power*; Twine, *Racism in a Racial Democracy*; and Warren, *Racial Revolutions.*
82 da Silva, "Dialogism as Anti-Racist Education," 319–336.
83 Quilombo historically meant a maroon or run-away slave community. Today its meaning has expanded to also include a community of African-descent slaves who have a distinct identity and culture.
84 French, *Legalizing Identities*; Arruti, *Mocambo*; and Warren, *Racial Revolutions.*
85 Sundaram and Chowdhury (Eds.), *Is Good Governance Good for Development?*
86 Santos, *Women's Police Stations.*

Bibliography

Anderson, Benedict. *Imagined Communities: Reflections on the Origin and Spread of Nationalism*. New York: Verso, 1983.

Appiah, Kwame Anthony. *The Honor Code: How Moral Revolutions Happen.* New York: W. W. Norton & Company, 2010.

Arruti, Jose Mauricio. *Mocambo: Antropolgia e historia do processo de formacao quilombola* (Mocambo: The anthology and the history of the formation of the quilombola community). Sao Paulo, Brazil: Edusc, 2006.

Barbosa, Livia Neves de H. "The Brazilian *Jeitinho*: An Exercise in National Identity." In *The Brazilian Puzzle: Culture on the Borderlands of the Western World*, David J. Hess, and Roberto DaMatta (Eds.), 35–48. New York: Columbia University Press, 1995.
Bradley, Mark Phillip. "Contests of Memory." In *The Country of Memory*, Hue-Tam Ho Tai (Ed.), 196–226. Berkeley, CA: University of California Press, 2001.
Brusco, Elizabeth E. *The Reformation of Machismo: Evangelical Conversion and Gender in Colombia*. Austin, TX: University of Texas Press, 1995.
Bus 174. Directed by Jose Pedilha and Felipe Lacerda. São Paulo: Zazen Produções. Brazil, 2003.
Caldeira, Teresa Pires do Rio. *City of Walls: Crime, Segregation, and Citizenship in São Paulo*. Berkeley, CA: University of California Press, 2000.
Canclini, Nestor Garcia. *Consumers and Citizens: Globalization and Multicultural Conflicts*. Cultural Studies of the Americas, Vol. 6. Minneapolis, MN: University of Minnesota Press, 2001.
Central do Brasil (Central Station). Directed by Walter Salles, Brazil, 1998.
Central Intelligence Agency. *The World Factbook*. www.cia.gov/library/publications/the-world-fact-book. Accessed July 26, 2015.
DaMatta, Roberto. "Is Brazil Hopelessly Corrupt? In *The Brazil Reader: History, Culture, Politics*, Robert M. Levine, and John J. Crocitti (Eds.), 295–301. Durham, NC: Duke University Press, 1999.
da Silva, Jose Antonio Bacelar. "Dialogism as Anti-Racist Education: Engaging with Competing Racial Ideologies in Brazil." *Anthropology and Education Quarterly* 45, no. 4 (2014): 319–336.
de Tocqueville, Alexis. *Democracy in America: Volume 1*. New York: Vintage, 1990.
Favela Rising. Directed by Jeff Zimbalist and Matt Mochary. HBO, 2005.
Freire, Paulo. *Pedagogy of the Oppressed*. New York: The Continuum Press, 1993 (1970).
French, Jan Hoffman. *Legalizing Identities: Becoming Black or Indian in Brazil's Northeast*. Chapel Hill, NC: University of North Carolina Press, 2009.
Fukuyama, Francis. *Trust: The Social Virtues and the Creation of Prosperity*. New York: Free Press, 1995.
Gainsborough, Martin. *Vietnam: Rethinking the State*. Chiang Mai, Thailand: Zed-Silkworm Books, 2010.
Gates, Henry Louis Jr., and Cornel West. *The Future of the Race*. New York: Vintage Press, 1996.
Halpern, David. *Social Capital*. Cambridge, MA: Polity, 2005.
Hanchard, Michael. *Orpheus and Power: The Movimento Negro of Rio de Janeiro and Sao Paulo Brazil*. Princeton, NJ: Princeton University Press, 1991.
Harms, Erik. *Saigon's Edge: On the Margins of Ho Chi Minh City*. Minneapolis, MN: University of Minnesota Press, 2011.
Hess, David J., and Roberto DaMatta (Eds.). *The Brazilian Puzzle: Culture on the Borderlands of the Western World*. New York: Columbia University Press, 1995.
Holston, James. *Insurgent Citizenship: Disjunctions of Democracy and Modernity in Brazil*. Princeton, NJ: Princeton University Press, 2008.
Johnson, Chalmers A. "The Developmental State: Odyssey of a Concept." In *The Developmental State*, Meredith Woo-Cumings (Ed.), 32–60. Ithaca, NY: Cornell University Press, 1999.
Laderman, Scott. 2009. *Tours of Vietnam: War, Travel Guides, and Memory*. Durham: NC: Duke University Press.

Mauss, Marcel, Translation by Halls, W.D. *The Gift: The Form and Reason for Exchange in Archaic Societies*. New York: W. W. Norton, 2000.

Michener, Greg. "Crime Rates in Brazil—Grim Stats." *Observing Brazil: A Blog about Brazil, its Politics and Political Culture* (blog). October 2011. www.osac.gov/pages/ContentReportDetails.aspx?cid=13966; and United Nation Office Drugs and Crime, www.unodc.org/#state:1. Accessed April 4, 2014.

Neate, Patrick, and Damian Platt. *Culture is our Weapon: Making Music and Changing Lives in Rio de Janeiro*. New York: Penguin Books, 2010.

Ngoc, Huu. *Wandering Through Vietnamese Culture*. Hanoi: The Gioi Publishers, 2008.

Nguyen-Vo, Thu-Huong. *The Ironies of Freedom: Sex, Culture, and Neoliberal Governance in Vietnam: Critical Dialogues in Southeast Asian Studies*. Seattle, WA: University of Washington Press, 2008.

Ninh, Kim N. B. *A World Transformed: The Politics of Culture in Revolutionary Vietnam, 1945–1965*. Ann Arbor, MI: University of Michigan Press, 2002.

O'Dougherty, Maureen. *Consumption Intensified: The Politics of Middle-Class Daily Life in Brazil*. Durham, NC: Duke University Press, 2002.

O Homem do Ano (Man of the year). Directed by Jose Fonseca. Conspiricao Filmes. Brazil, 2003.

Pelley, Patricia M. *Postcolonial Vietnam: New Histories of the National Past*. Durham, NC: Duke University Press, 2002.

Quanto Vale ou E Por Quilo? (What is it Worth?). Directed by Sergio Bianchi. Agravo Producoes. Brasil, 2005.

Putnam, Robert D. *Bowling Alone: The Collapse and Revival of American Community*. New York: Simon & Schuster, 2000.

Putnam, Robert D., Robert Leonardi, and Raffaella Y. Nonetti. *Making Democracy Work: Civic Traditions in Modern Italy*. Princeton, NJ: Princeton University Press, 1993.

Reid, T. R. *Confucius Lives Next Door: What Living in the East Teaches Us About Living in the West*. Reprint. New York: Random House, 2000.

Ribeiro, Amaury, Jr. *A privataria tucana* (The Brazilian Social Democracy Party's privatization scam). Sao Paulo: Geracao Editorial, 2011.

Romero, Simon. "Brazil is Entranced by a Tale of Love, Taxes and Bribery." *New York Times*, November 27, 2013: A6.

Santos, Cecilia. *Women's Police Stations: Gender, Violence, and Justice in Sao Paulo, Brazil*. London: Palgrave Macmillan, 2005.

Schwarz, Roberto. *Misplaced Ideas: Essays on Brazilian Culture*. New York: Verso Press, 1992.

Sheriff, Robin E. *Dreaming Equality: Color, Race, and Racism in Brazil*. New Brunswick, NJ: Rutgers University Press, 2001.

Simpson, Amelia. *Xuxa: Mega-Marketing of Gender, Race, and Modernity*. Philadelphia, PA: Temple University Press, 1993.

Skidmore, Thomas E. *Black into White: Race and Nationality in Brazilian Thought*. Durham, NC: Duke University Press, 1993.

Sundaram, Jomo Kwame, and Anis Chowdhury (Eds.). *Is Good Governance Good for Development?* New York: Bloomsbury Academic, 2012.

Telles, Edward. *Race in Another America: The Significance of Skin Color in Brazil*. Princeton, NJ: Princeton University Press, 2004.

Truitt, Allison J. *Dreaming of Money in Ho Chi Minh City*. Seattle, WA: University of Washington Press, 2013.

Twine, Francine Winddance. *Racism in a Racial Democracy: The Maintenance of White*

Supremacy in Brazil. New Brunswick, NJ: Rutgers University Press, 1997.

United Nations Office on Drugs and Crime. https://data.unodc.org/?lf=1&lng=en. Accessed July 28, 2015.

United States Department of State Bureau of Diplomatic Security. "Brazil 2013 Crime and Safety Report: Rio de Janeiro." www.osac.gov/pages/ContentReportDetails.aspx?cid=13966. Accessed April 4, 2014.

Vianna, Hermano. *The Mystery of Samba: Popular Music and National Identity in Brazil*. Chapel Hill, NC: University of North Carolina Press, 1999.

Warren, Jonathan. *Racial Revolutions: Antiracism and Indian Resurgence in Brazil*. Durham, NC: Duke University Press, 2001.

Weir, Robert E. *Class in America: An Encyclopedia (Volume 1: A-G)*. Westport, CT: Greenwood Press. 2007.

Whiteley, Paul. *Economic Growth and Social Capital*. Sheffield, UK: Political Economy Research Center, 1997.

Wilcken, Patrick. *Empire Adrift: The Portuguese Court in Rio De Janeiro, 1808–1821*. London: Bloomsbury, 2005.

Woodside, Alexander. *Lost Modernities: China, Vietnam, Korea, and the Hazards of World History*. Cambridge, MA: Harvard University Press, 2006.

World Bank. *Brazil—Crime, violence and economic development in Brazil: elements for effective public policy*. Washington, DC: World Bank, 2006. http://documents.worldbank.org/curated/en/2006/06/7742317/brazil-crime-violence-economic-development-brazil-elements-effective-public-policy. Accessed July 12, 2015.

World Bank. *Data: Intentional Homocides per 100,000*. http://data.worldbank.org/indicator/VC.IHR.PSRC.P5. Accessed March 2016.

World Values Survey. www.wvsevsdb.com/wvs/WVSAnalizeQuestion.jsp. Accessed March 2016.

5 Development Lore

> The first step is to help the people to value that which they already have.
>
> Francisciscus Henricus van der Poel (b. 1944)[1]

Given how little scholarly attention has been given to cultures of development, undoubtedly future research projects will be required—ones which I hope this book inspires—to confirm, nuance, complicate, and add to the various claims I have made about Vietnamese and Brazilian cultures and their links to economic growth. Even if pundits take issue with my description about how the poor are imagined in Vietnam or my theorization of the relationship between social capital and honor codes, I hope that the bigger picture is not lost in such disputes and discussions. All along my primary goal has been to convince development scholars and practitioners that economies are culturally constituted and that therefore it is a mistake to continue to ignore or minimize the centrality of norms, values, discourses, and symbols to economies and their well-being.

In Chapter 1 I speculated how a source of resistance to accepting the cultural nature of markets may be the fear that taking seriously this premise could lead to a radical upending of the canons around which researchers and practitioners have built and staked their professional lives. I believe that I have demonstrated how such concerns, should they exist, are overblown. Bringing culture to economics certainly complicates matters, but it does not negate the good work done by development scholars so much as offer many of the missing ingredients required to determine how certain factors come to be and why they matter. Recall that I did not show or argue that social capital, monocropping institutions, or human capital—the focal point of a great deal of development scholarship—are irrelevant or inconsequential. Instead I used interpretive economics to explain how these development variables emerge and why they vary in different societies.

This does not preclude the possibility that certain assumptions or pet theories could be unsettled or overturned. For instance, there seems to be an emerging consensus among development scholars that neoliberalism was bad macroeconomic policy in Latin America. It is true, as noted above, that most if not all Latin American countries that adopted market fundamentalism posted insipid growth rates. But if we take culture into account, we might reach different conclusions about the wisdom of minimizing the role of government. If the neoliberal reforms had taken place in conjunction with attempts to reduce poverty and social inequalities, might the outcome have been very different? It is possible that attempts to shrink the role of the state, reduce tariffs and taxes, or wean domestic manufacturers from subsidies and protections may not have been the issue but rather the race-based elitism that heavily shaped neoliberalism (as well as developmentalism in the mid-twentieth century). Or as Amartya Sen succinctly put it in *Development as Freedom,* "financial conservatism should be the nightmare of the militarist, not the school teacher or the hospital nurse."[2] Thus the wrong macroeconomic lessons may have been drawn because of the failure to take into account the socio-cultural. My goal here is not to resuscitate or defend neoliberalism, but rather to point out that a consideration of culture may indeed muddy if not upset a number of development theories to which many (including me!) are politically and professionally attached. But ultimately I believe that its overall impact will be to enrich and advance conventional wisdom—as was done in the previous chapters—rather than topple or bring down schools of thought and mainstream development practice as some may fear.

Likely a bigger impediment to interrogating the cultural side of development—than the worry that it may displace conventional theories and methods—is a concern with feasibility. That is, the important and inevitable question arises in the context of interpretive economics as to whether development cultural work is doable, or merely an impractical, ivory tower, pie-in-the-sky endeavor. I can easily imagine that for many, if not most, development practitioners, it is hard even to envision what this sort of work would look like in practice. Building a bridge, updating accounting and budgeting procedures, reforming the financial or judicial systems, encouraging democratic elections, and solidifying property rights probably all seem much more legible and achievable than reforming honor codes, challenging colonial epistemologies, transforming conceptions of the poor, or advancing racial literacy. Much of this reflects, no doubt, the training and expertise of those who tend to be involved in development. Schooled as engineers, physicians, diplomats, accountants, teachers, entrepreneurs, military advisors, or public administrators, most development practitioners often have little to no formal training in semiotics, identity formations, or discourse analysis. Not surprisingly, then, the kind of development cultural work advocated by this study would seem odd and perhaps daunting.

To help allay some of these understandable concerns, I present in this chapter a detailed case study of successful development cultural work in Brazil. Among other things, this should help to concretize and demystify these practices. The cultural change that religious leaders, artists, and educators have brought about in the Jequitinhonha Valley of Minas Gerais in the past forty years shows how cultural work is no more difficult or less viable than conventional development work. Moreover, and more importantly, it can be a much more effective and cost-efficient approach to development.

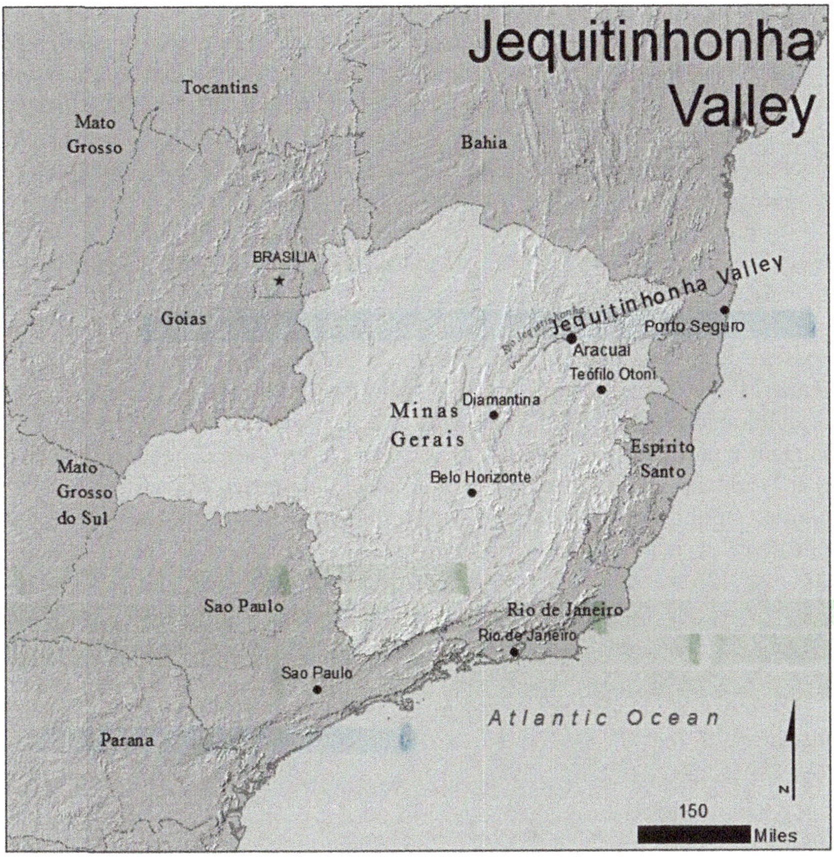

Map 5.1 Map of Jequitinhonha Valley

The Valley of Misery

One of my Brazilian research sites for the past twenty years has been the Jequitinhonha Valley in northeastern Minas Gerais. In the 1960s the Jequitinhonha Valley was considered by UNESCO to be one of the poorest regions in the world and was widely referred to by Brazilians as the Valley of Misery. At that time, there were no telephones, running water or sidewalks. The majority of the population lacked formal education; most people were illiterate. Severe health problems such as *chagas* disease (American trypanosomiasis) were commonplace. Even basic health care was unavailable. Older residents recounted to me in interviews in 2009 that it was not unusual as late as the 1970s to see people dying on buses while en route to seek medical care.

The reasons for this immense poverty were centuries in the making. With the invasion of Portugal by the French during the Napoleonic Wars, the Crown fled to Brazil in 1808, where the king set up his court in Rio de Janeiro. The first act of King John VI upon his arrival in Brazil was to declare a "just war" on the indigenous peoples who controlled large sections of the Mucuri, Doce, and Jequitinhonha Rivers Valleys in eastern Minas Gerais. The objective was twofold: colonization and ethnic cleansing. Large slaveholders from bordering regions, who coveted these lands, brutally conquered the outnumbered and outgunned indigenous people.[3] The king rewarded these mercenaries with land, indigenous slaves (primarily the orphaned children who survived these massacres), and the pseudo nobility title of colonel. Many of the "colonels" brought slaves, primarily of African descent, with them, who eventually mixed socially, culturally, and biologically with the indigenous survivors of this conquest.[4]

The resulting social order was a racially modulated feudalism. The colonels "possessed economic and political power over the local government and over the means of law enforcement. . . . They maintained monopolistic control over agricultural production and commerce and controlled the best lands. They maintained power even through unlawful means."[5] The general population, on the other hand, was landless, extremely poor, and at the mercy of their patrons, the colonels. If the peasants were not slaves, they lived on the peripheries of plantations as tenant farmers or existed as sharecroppers in slave-like conditions. Moreover these peasants were cast as racial subalterns. Physical features, histories, or cultural practices associated with indigenousness or blackness were hyper stigmatized. Indigeneity and Africanness, the dominant ancestries of these subalterns, became a racial stain and source of shame.

This social-political order began to unravel in the 1990s when the people elected one of the so-called little people, Maria do Carmo Ferreira da Silva (or

Figure 5.1 Rural House in Jequitinhonha Valley in the 1960s. Photograph by Frei Chico, 1969

Caca) as mayor of Aracuai—a city in the heart of the Jequitinhonha Valley. In the land of the colonels, it is no exaggeration to call the election of a petite black woman from the Workers' Party a revolutionary change.

Caca's electoral victory signaled an end to a political system, as the seventy-three-year-old cobbler Luiz described, "that favored just one sector and the other side had nothing. One only saw the rich getting richer because they were able to use public power to buy more land and plantations and this came to an end."[6] As part of this change, Caca's administration instituted a number of changes such as participatory budgeting and budget transparency. To this end, councils, made up of local experts and interested citizens, were set up by Caca's administration to oversee various government ministries. The councils set priorities and helped to ensure that public monies were used appropriately. In the past, one individual or family dominated all the ministries of government with little or no transparency or oversight. The establishment of these councils helped to reduce corruption dramatically, and consequently, basic infrastructure improved and most public services, such as health care, were delivered more efficiently, cost-effectively and widely. The inclusion of the *povo* in the governing process also helped to burnish, at least according to the local scholar and activist Geralda Soares, a different idea of citizenship:

> Before one just elected a person and put him there like a saint. It was like selecting a saint, put him there on the altar and then simply believe that he'll make miracles. Now it's different. We feel more responsible for life here. Things have become more collective. We see that a state by itself doesn't work. [Without sustained engagement] you end up doing the same foolishness.[7]

Figure 5.2 Mayor Caca. Photograph by Geralda Soares, 1995

In addition to fostering participatory democracy and greater civic engagement, the electoral defeat of the colonels ushered in an explosion of civil society. Mayor Caca created a municipal Ministry of Culture that supported various artisan associations, choirs, theater troupes, art festivals, cinemas, and salon-like venues. Several wings of the anti-racist movement, which included a small, urban, black organization (Quigem), a *quilombo* (Bau),[8] and three indigenous communities (Pankararu, Pataxo, and Arana) were no longer viewed with disdain by the political authorities. Their leaders were invited to meet periodically with the mayor as well as formally represent their communities at various ceremonial events hosted by the municipal government. Moreover, they were also given small grants to establish, among other things, cultural centers.

Caca's administration also recruited NGOs in other parts of the country, such as the Popular Center of Culture and Development (Centro Popular de Cultura e Desenvolvimento or CPCD), to expand its operations to the region. In Aracuai CPCD created among other things, two successful afterschool programs for poor children and adolescents. The K–8 program, *Ser Crianca* (To Be a Child), offers a play-based curriculum that is anchored in the culture and history of the *povo*. The primary goals are to provide a positive learning experience and teach children how to collaborate, develop a concern for others, and constructively deal with emotions and differences through respectful group dialogue in which participants are seated in a circle. This methodology of the *roda* (wheel) as it is called, teaches students ethics and skills that Brazilians often do not acquire in the public schools. The *Fabriqueta* (The Little Factory), which is a kind of artisanal-based trade school, allows teenagers to learn administrative and social skills as well as develop technical expertise in furniture making, painting, ironwork, and clothing design. One of the impacts of these innovative education ventures, according to Andrea Fonseca, the twenty-five-year-old director of the *Fabriqueta*, has been to create a positive association with the culture of the valley. In her words:

> Through the choirs, *Ser Crianca*, and other CPCD initiatives like the *Fabriqueta*, people are becoming proud of their culture. People are increasingly recognizing the valley . . . they are getting to know it through its music and art. Through this valorization, we are becoming proud.[9]

Table 5.1 Human Development (HD) Index by Municipality in Jequitinhonha Valley

Municipality	*Population*	*1991*	*2000*	*2010*
Almenara	38,775	382	529	642
Aracuai	36,013	338	516	663
Capelinha	34,803	355	490	653
Pedra Azul	23,839	364	516	627

Note: HD is a measurement of well-being based on a combination of education, health care, and income.

Source: Atlas do Desenvolvimento Humano No Brazil (Atlas of Human Development in Brazil), accessed January 9, 2015. www.atlasbrasil.org.br/2013.

In the next section I detail and analyze the linkages between the valorization of culture and self-esteem. At this point, however, I wish to first take stock of the tremendous civic, governmental, social, and economic transformations that have occurred since the election of Caca. Government institutions have become more democratic and less corrupt, and civil society has ballooned dramatically.

Social inequalities have also lessened. Poverty has been reduced from 66 percent in 1991 to 30 percent of the population in 2010.[10] Infant mortality has declined from 41.19 per 100,00 births in 1991 to 16.5 in 2010.[11] Almost all homes now have running water, electricity, and garbage collection (75 percent, 99 percent, and 95 percent, respectively, in 2010, as compared to 38 percent, 56 percent, and 24 percent in 1991).[12] Most city streets have been paved, and all sewage is treated (something that most major Brazilian cities cannot claim). Finally, the local hospital, Sao Vincente de Paulo, has been expanded and transformed into a regional leader in health care.

Per the predictions of development scholars (see Chapter 2) these investments in capacity-building have resulted in higher levels of prosperity. Within a context of regional development—something for which Aracuai's political and civic leaders deserve at least some credit, given the city's pivotal role in the Jequitinhonha Valley—Aracuai has improved the most (see Table 5.1). Its human development index, which is a combined metric of per capita income, education level, and life expectancy, moved from being the lowest of the major municipalities in the Valley at 0.338 in 1991 to the highest at 0.663 by 2010. None of this is meant to suggest that significant economic challenges do not remain in Aracuai and the broader region, but it is hard to dispute the extraordinary progress that has been made and that the municipality is on a much more solid footing for sustained economic growth.

It would be easy to interpret this development success story as offering clear-cut support for an institutionalist thesis of economic growth: development was had through democratization (a process that began in Brazil in late 1970s and culminated with universal suffrage in 1988), which led, in turn, to a number of positive reforms in government bureaucracies and helped to open up space for a flourishing civil society that, in a kind of virtuous cycle, further solidified the inroads that electoral democracy initiated. Such a narrative could easily be imposed on the events in Aracuai and used to confirm the need to focus development efforts on elaborating participatory democracy, budgetary transparency, and non-voluntary associations in other parts of Brazil. The problem with this reading—at least in the case of Aracuai—is that it is incomplete. It overlooks an essential ingredient: the cultural work that made these political, social, and economic happenings possible and ultimately effective. Participatory democracy, budgetary transparency, and civil society did not mechanistically emerge from this electoral victory in 1995. Moreover, the election of Caca did not happen as the automatic outcome of democratization that began in Brazil in the 1980s. Her election was (and continues to be) the exception to the rule in the Jequitinhonha Valley and most other parts of rural Brazil and especially in those regions historically controlled by the so-called colonels. This was why Lula, as the leader of the Workers'

Party at the time, choose to visit her inauguration over other PT candidates that were elected to municipal positions in 1994. To tell the full lore of development in the Jequitinhonha Valley, one has to look back at least as far as 1969, the year that a Dutch friar arrived in Aracuai.

Freire's Disciples

To avoid potential deportation by the military dictatorship, Franciscus Henricus van der Poel (aka Frei Chico) requested to be assigned to a remote region of Brazil when he concluded his seminary studies in Rio de Janeiro in late 1968. In the backlands of Brazil, he thought he would be less noticed and thus less likely to be expelled. The Church authorities granted his request and he was sent to Aracuai—the seat of the parish in the Jequitinhonha Valley. At the time, liberation theology influenced the thinking of many in the Catholic Church, including approximately half the bishops in Brazil.[13] Frei Chico was no exception. He went to Aracuai with the conviction that it was his and the church's responsibility to prioritize and side with the poor.

Liberation theology had a number of political and philosophical affinities with Marxism. This often came, as noted above, with elitist baggage, in that the *povo*'s true identity and their recipe for liberation was pre-determined. The poor were to identify as "workers" or "peasants" and advance their liberation and society's modernization by unionizing, challenging and limiting the national bourgeoisie's authority, breaking with global capitalism, and distancing themselves from their "feudal traditions."[14] This latter prescription led to a positioning of popular culture, be it religious or otherwise, as a backward impediment to progress. In this way, more critical views within the church dovetailed with the general elitism in Brazilian society (see Chapter 2). It also echoed a long-held perspective within the Brazilian church, which largely looked with suspicion on popular religious practices. The second Vatican had been a challenge to this worldview, but besides the laity being taught in their native language, little had changed in Aracuai by 1969.

Frei Chico notes a pivotal moment that led him to question his attitude about the culture of the *povo*. A celebration during Holy Week prompted him to see and confront the inadequacies of his assumptions. He performed a mass on Good Friday, enjoyed a beer afterward, and went to sleep content with a day's good work, only to be awakened in the middle of the night. Following the sounds, he returned to the church to find it alive with people.

> Initially I thought what ugly singing. People shouting. Spitting rum. Attacking one another. I thought it was ugly. Then I decided I'll wait until they stop and encourage them to go to bed. While waiting, I listened closely to the music they were singing. It echoed the music of love that one heard on the radio and I began to see that they had a faith or love that I didn't have. There were prostitutes singing with such force, such conviction, that it left one speechless with emotion. And so I began to see the other side. I became very emotional. I went up front, as planned, after the music had stopped and I said the opposite of what I was originally going to say. I said "This is very beautiful. You can

> sing as long as you want and next year I want to stay the whole evening with you." That for me wasn't theory. It was a moment when you see something and make a decision. The next day people told me that when I entered the church the people thought I was going to prohibit it because the priest at the time prohibited it.[15]

This experience generated a crisis in Frei Chico's thinking. A self-identified socialist and liberation theologian, Frei Chico was confronted with his biases against popular culture.

> Socialism, in my opinion, got weak because it never valued the religion, the culture, the vision of the poor. Liberation theology had the same defect. . . . I was certain that what I had seen did not fit these concepts. So I decided to abandon my ideas, my baggage, to leave them behind. I perceived I needed the courage to abandon beautiful theories.[16]

Like many of his contemporaries, who were also reaching similar conclusions about the shortcomings of socialism and liberation theology, Frei Chico turned to the ideas of Paulo Freire.

> Money is not basic to helping the poor. It certainly helps but it is not the most important thing. The first step is to help the people to value that which they already have. This I learned from Paulo Freire. Value their history, culture, ideas, leaders, their faith . . . give value to what they have. When this happens a person is going to have self-esteem.[17]

Even though Brazil banned Paulo Freire's writings during the military dictatorship, which extended from 1964 until the mid-1980s, smuggled copies of his groundbreaking text, *Pedagogy of the Oppressed* (1968), served as a key point of reference for intellectuals, educators, and activists concerned with combating poverty and improving the livelihoods of ordinary Brazilians. Working with sugar cane workers in the northeast of Brazil in the early 1960s, a region similar to that of the Jequitinhonha Valley, Freire developed a method for enabling poor communities to transform themselves from objects, "those who are known and acted upon," to subjects, "those who know and act."[18] He contended that power was largely reproduced through subjectivities rather than force. And activists who were dismissive of the culture, values, perspective, and identities of the poor—the prevalent attitude of the Catholic Church, leftist activists, and conservative modernizers at the time—ultimately changed nothing. Despite their good intentions of wanting to improve the lives of the poor, little is altered because they effectively attempt to substitute one paternal order for another.

Paulo Freire focused his so-called pedagogy of the oppressed on literacy, in part because literacy was a necessary requirement to be able to vote. Many of his disciples, however, advanced his methodology through different means. Frei Chico, for one, focused on excavating, nurturing, and celebrating popular culture. Rather than using literacy campaigns as a tool for transforming subjectivities and advancing the lives of the poor, Frei Chico emphasized the culture of the people and most especially popular religion as a tool for helping the people to value what they already had.

One of the first concrete steps taken in this direction began in the shower. As there are no ceilings in most homes in the Jequitinhonha Valley, sound carries readily from one room to the next. While bathing, Ms. Fila, the cook for the parochial house where Frei Chico lived, would sing while preparing meals. She caroled the songs that the people commonly sang while carrying out their daily chores. Listening to them as he bathed, he was moved by their beauty. These songs ultimately inspired him to establish Os Trovadores do Vale (The Troubadours of the Valley), a choir that performed the melodies of the people of the valley.

The original members of the choir, encumbered as they were with a kind of internalized "littleness," were initially reluctant to perform these songs. Peoples' feelings of inferiority and inadequacy were reflected and intertwined with how they saw their own culture. According to Frei Chico they would say, "Ah no, this is not beautiful, no, we are not going to sing this, no." Ms. Fila herself considered them *bobagem* (foolishness). Frei Chico added "they wanted to perform the tunes that they heard on the radio. They were embarrassed and ashamed of their own culture." And when the choir eventually appeared on TV, the director of the bank and hospital, the colonels and their descendants, or what the people in the Valley refer to as *os grandes* (the big ones), "reacted badly." They interpreted these performances as yet another way of signifying the Jequitinhonha Valley's lack of modernity, its backwardness. According to Frei Chico, there was the general mentality that "local culture didn't have any value." However as this cultural movement grew and more outsiders affirmed their traditions, "the people," recalls Frei Chico, "began to believe and have confidence in their culture and themselves."[19]

Figure 5.3 Troubadours of the Valley. Photograph by Geralda Soares, 1985

The Ethnographers

Perhaps the most influential person to be affected by the Freireian-inspired embrace of popular culture was Maria Lira Marques. A woman of African and indigenous descent, Lira was born in Aracuai in 1945 and was raised by her mother, a launderwoman. At the invitation of a friend, she attended one of the first rehearsals for the Troubadours of the Valley.

> At the first choir rehearsal that I attended, I saw myself in everything that was happening. They sang the *cantos de roda* [the wheel songs], the *batuques* [African-influenced drumming music], and other kinds of songs that we sung at home. My mother would sing them when she was ironing clothes, and working around the house. . . . So these were songs that I knew intimately. I just didn't understand that they had value. That day I came running back home. I was so happy. I said, "Mom, there at the church . . . you should see . . . everything that they sing are songs that you know. . . ." And she said to me "You look like a wild cow!" Everytime that she recalled that moment, she would say, "You arrived just like a wild cow!"[20]

Lira explained that she was so excited because for the first time in her life her culture—the music of her mother and her neighbors—was being celebrated and affirmed. Perhaps most importantly this was taking place within the church, an institution of high regard in the Jequitinhonha Valley. In any event, she said this simple act of validation "changed [her] sensibilities." Almost immediately, Lira became insatiably curious about popular culture. She would pester her mother and others to sing as many songs as they knew. As she recalls, Frei Chico perceived this awakened passion and invited her to participate in the choir as both a performer and researcher.

> I would meet with people, and . . . I would ask them "What is the lullaby that you know? The work songs?" They would pass them along to me without really being aware of the value that these songs had. Sometimes they were even ashamed to teach them to me. But I would challenge them. I'd say: "The priest sings this. We are singing this. This has value!" After I challenged them and showed them the importance and value of these songs, they would give me more [songs]. I would then copy them down. After I had filled my notebook, I then started going around with a tape recorder and I would ask them to "Sing this, sing that" and they would sing it all. This wasn't difficult for me, as I'm one of the people. This was all very easy for me. Eventually I started to invite Frei Chico to come along with me. . . . He would go with me to meet the people and visit them in their homes. In this way the research grew and at one point he said, "Oh, Lira, you really know what it is that we are doing." After this moment he began to give me books to read. . . . He gave me texts of folklorists like Camera Cascudo and Renato de Almeida. And . . . in this fashion, the research took shape. After we had done this for several years, we selected what we found to be the most beautiful songs and recorded

> them. This became our first album, which is called *Ainda bem que eu cheguei* [It's Good that I Arrived].[21]

Together, Lira and Frei Chico became a formidable research team. They shared a sense of calling with respect to popular culture and its documentation. Moreover, they complemented one another exceptionally well. Frei Chico had formal training, knowledge of and access to libraries and other research materials, and a social status that came with being a friar, white, European, and male. Lira, as she notes, brought an insider's perspective. This afforded them an access to popular culture that would have been difficult, if not impossible, for Frei Chico to ever achieve by himself. Also Lira, according to Frei Chico, brought to the table a different awareness.

> Lira is very different than me. When we would pass a place with homeless children, she would cry. She is touched by such inequalities. I'm thinking of my nephews, she'd say. Or when we would pass an MST [*Movimento dos Trabalhadores Rurais Sem Terra* or the Movement of the Landless Rural Workers] encampment, she would get very emotional. I also think these disparities are wrong, but she reacts differently than me to these realities. This favored our relationship immensely.[22]

Importantly Frei Chico was able to avoid much of the elitism and paternalism that so often emerges in relationships when the power imbalance is so stilted. They had to become equals. Not equals in the sense of being equivalently situated vis-à-vis the myriad axes of power but equals in terms of respect and reciprocation. Frei Chico put it this way:

> We discovered that we were friends. To be friends you have to be equals. It wasn't simply a story of Lira helping me, but me also helping Lira. So it was a process. . . . For example, I would pick out anthropology books and ask her to read them. She'd mark the whole book up. I'd think, why did she think that this part was so interesting? Maria Lira Marques, black woman, from the Jequitinhonha Valley, seven years of schooling . . . and I'd think, "Why the hell didn't I see that?!"[23]

Thus, rather than fashioning himself as the teacher, the expert, who was there to help the poor whom he pitied, he understood that he, too, was a student who had as much, if not more, to gain. This posture was evidenced repeatedly. In reflecting back on the ceremony that he stumbled upon late at night during Holy Week, he told me that he learned about faith from the people there. These were individuals who were much less fortunate than himself and yet he came to see that they had a much deeper faith in God than he had. Or note his advice about collaboration with the *povo*:

> The plans that the *povo* have to improve this country . . . they will be revised, rethought. I can't say what will happen; what those plans should be. It's the people who must decide. They must choose the path forward. One has to have patience. One cannot intervene and say "Now you're going to do this!"[24]

These are not the words of someone who sees the people as unenlightened objects who must be shepherded in a prearranged direction. As Frei Chico notes, the path forward is open and not for him to decide. It was this perspective that helped him and Lira to become comrades and, as I elaborate below, effective development agents.

After several years of research, Lira and Frei Chico had documented seemingly every aspect of popular culture: culinary traditions, burial rituals, oral histories, knowledge about the fauna and wildlife, iron and leather work, construction and agricultural techniques, and methods of childrearing. Their obsession with the quotidian had produced copious volumes of recordings and field notes that had to be organized in some fashion. It was Lira who recognized and pushed for a deeper consideration of popular religion, which eventually became the analytical framework for ordering their data.

> I woke up a curiosity in Frei Chico. . . . Without asking him, I began collecting . . . prayers. The prayers against one's enemy, to get rid of a snake in the bush, for rain. . . . This all scared him. But he didn't tell me at that time. . . . He only told me this many years later. If he had told me his fears at that time, it would have embarrassed me. I was very timid. So he didn't tell me for fear I would stop. He read what I collected and began reflecting. He began to see their value and wanted to understand more. What protects these people are their prayers. For someone who has resources, they go immediately to the doctor. However for someone who doesn't have money . . . they seek out those resources that they have in order to defend themselves, right? And so it was an immense work, documenting the wisdom of the people. We even went to the cemetery, collecting the sayings that are written on peoples' gravestones. For example, "Little with God is a lot, a lot without God is nothing." Sometimes as a child we wouldn't have enough to eat. My mother would say, "My daughter, little with God is a lot, a lot without God is nothing." She was trying to give meaning to our hunger. She was saying that we should be content in the little that we have because in the future we won't be hungry. . . . This speaks a lot about faith, right? . . . And so we began to see how everything is linked. The homemade teas, the charms and the prayers, everything is linked together. This [insight] gave birth to the dictionary on popular religion.[25]

Together, through their inductive examination of their detailed ethnographic work, they began to see how "religious life is not separate from the life of the people, it is entwined with it."[26] And this understanding ultimately led Frei Chico to organize the 240 cassette tapes of recordings, 2000 slides, and 5000 pages of ethnographic notes as an encyclopedia on popular religion in Brazil. This 1150-page book, titled *The Dictionary of Popular Religion* (2013), which took forty years to complete and is, according to Frei Chico, the first encyclopedia about popular religion in the world. But their most impressive accomplishment, according to the anthropologist Sebastiao Rocha and head of CPCD, was "they allowed people to begin to recognize their identities . . . to affirm and begin to valorize themselves. To move from self-loathing to having high self-esteem in their music, race, etc."[27]

The Subjects of History

The power of the colonels was sustained partially through the use of patronage and *jaguncos* (hired assassins). Yet, as Antonio Gramsci long ago observed, the biggest barrier to social change is rarely force or other material constraints but rather people's identities and common sense. It is no coincidence, then, that as the burgeoning cultural movement altered popular sensibilities, the political status quo became unsettled as well.

In the late 1970s the democratization movement within Brazil began gaining traction. It was advanced, in part, by a 1979 amnesty law, which allowed intellectuals and activists in exile to return to Brazil. Democratization was also bolstered by a rejuvenated labor movement, that scored a number of victories in the industrial ABC region of Sao Paulo in the late 1970s.[28] These confluences led to the establishment of an anti-Leninist and non-corporatist Workers' Party (PT) during this same period of time. Luiz Inacio Lula da Silva, who had led the metal and auto workers in their successful strikes in Sao Paulo, quickly emerged as its leader. Eventually, in 2002, this former shoeshine boy from northeastern Brazil, with little formal education, would become president of the republic.

It was during the early part of the transition period toward democracy, after the PT was granted legal status by the military regime in 1982, that Lira set out to establish a local branch of the PT in the Jequitinhonha Valley. She became the first president of the PT in Aracuai because, according to her, "nobody else wanted to be president."[29] Working behind the scenes, she orchestrated, managed, and carried out the labor-intensive and often tedious work of administration, grassroots organizing, producing an underground newspaper *O Portador* (The Carrier), and "conscientizing" the people.[30]

She was, of course, ideally situated to build the Workers' Party. As an ethnographer, she was already meeting regularly with hundreds of people to record their kernels of wisdom. This combined with the fact that she was from the community allowed her to move seamlessly among the *povo*. Perhaps better than anyone else, she intimately knew their troubles, philosophies, art, and patois. She was also very unassuming. She herself admits that she is not a gifted public speaker. Such demeanor and public discretion combined with her appearance and background as a short, black woman, who sang songs with a church choir and documented what many people, perhaps most especially the political and economic elite, considered insignificant folk culture, led her to be underestimated as a serious political threat. Finally, she brought a different awareness, one less marked by patronage and a negative self-imagery and more by an understanding of one's agency. This was thanks, at least in part, to her involvement with Frei Chico and the larger cultural movement they had helped to birth.

The initial group of party members consisted exclusively of the little ones. Indeed Lira was very concerned that one of the big ones would try to enter the party.

Figure 5.4 Maria Lira Marques. Photograph by Frei Chico, 1979

> I was afraid that maybe someone wealthy, maybe a doctor, would want to enter [the party]. I wanted to restrict the party due to my fear that they would try to take the party out of our hands. They have the power to do this. The people who were participating in the party were all very poor . . . very poor and many of them were illiterate. *Os grandes* with their sweet talk . . . with the formal education and credentials that they have . . . I was so afraid of them taking over the party. I didn't believe that they would enter for the good of the party. I was always worried that they would take the party away from us.[31]

During the first election in which the PT ran a candidate, they lost. After a few more years of grassroots work and the deepening of the cultural movement discussed above, the party was able to elect one of their candidates, Manuel Pinheiro, to the city council. Lira remembers that the big ones did everything that they could to co-opt him.

> The second time we were able to elect Manuel but he suffered the wounds of Christ. He was the only member from the PT and the other council members were all from the opposition parties. . . . Every project that was brought up [by the PT] wasn't approved. Nothing was approved because he was only one person [on the city council]. And when the meetings ended, they would keep Manuel there, looking for a way of getting Manuel into the mayor's office to try to convince him to change his party affiliation. He suffered

> a great deal. He'd often arrive in my house so confused after those meetings. The pressure that they put on him to leave the party. . . . We counseled him, advised him not to leave. They tried to get him to change sides, they offered him money, but God helped us and he stayed with the party.[32]

A pivotal moment for the party happened when Lula, the national leader of the Workers' Party and presidential candidate at the time, decided to visit Aracuai. Permits were required and Lira, as the president of the PT, had to secure them.

> I ended up going to see the chief of police, with the vice-president of the PT. We arrived at the police station . . . and the chief said to me, "Well, Maria, Lula's coming here, right?" and I said, with a fear that I can't describe, "Yes, sir." And then he began to lecture us, "Maria, neither you nor Lula will change the situation in Brazil. Brazil will only get worse." We didn't say a word. Only he spoke. He lectured us about Russia, Japan, . . . and I just kept nodding my head."
>
> And then he asked me, "Maria, do you read the Bible?" and I said "Sometimes I read it." He said, "Ah, it is a strong book; my most powerful weapon." . . . And then he started to speak about the revolutionaries in the Bible and he started to insult the church [*descer o pau na igreja*]. He spoke badly about the church, priests, nuns, and then he said again that the most powerful weapon he had was the Bible. After this he lectured us about Getulio Vargas, Jango, Janio Quadros [all former Brazilian presidents]. He went on and on about them. It seemed like he wanted to bait us into saying something, but we didn't say a word. We kept our mouths shut as we had been trained. . . . I thought to myself, I'm not going to say anything . . . just let him make a fool out of himself. He continued, "Well, Maria, I am a very experienced man, and in the past the people ate beans and potatoes, but they ate them contentedly. Today they eat meat, rice and beans and they are unsatisfied." I stayed quiet. We kept silent.
>
> Then he asked, "What do you do, Maria?" And I said, "I'm an artisan." He wrote this down and asked for my parents' names. "You, sir, over there, what do you do?" And Mr. Paiado said, "Me, I used to live in the country, I worked as a tenant farmer and then I moved to the city. Today I work as a *biscate* [handyman]. As I'm old, I can't bear hard work anymore, I live from my work as a handyman. I clean people's backyards." After this, the police chief said "Well, Maria, now your names are going to the Secretary of Public Security." At this I became afraid but I didn't show it. I didn't say a word. I let him keep talking.
>
> And then finally he said, "Well, Maria, tomorrow you can come pick up the permit. You can come here to pick up the permit." This gave me such joy. I asked myself "Is this really going to happen?" And that was it. "God bless you, Maria," he said. I replied, "Amen, God bless you too." [laughs]. After that we left. When we got outside, I thanked God as it seemed like all the weight of the world had been lifted from my shoulders.[33]

This interaction demonstrates the relationship between consciousness and socio-political change. Lira's fears were at least partly fueled by the possibility of violence, incarceration, or other harsh sanctions, given that the authoritarian regime had tortured and killed thousands of its critics. No doubt too, the memories of physical retaliation were fresh in people's minds, especially in light of the recent history of slavery and the ongoing neoslave relationships, and so even their implicit threat must have struck fear in the hearts of most. Yet in my various conversations and formal interviews with Lira and other activists during this time, no one mentioned a killing, beating, or imprisonment. Thus this incident helps to highlight how what ultimately held people in check was an intimidation anchored in their subordinate status as the *povo*, an inferiority that had been internalized. That is, the power of the colonels rested on a culture in which individuals like Lira were made to feel small, unintelligent, unworthy, and undeserving. As long as Lira performed her role as the obsequious, docile subaltern, the chief was reassured. But had it not been a performance—had Lira seen herself as the descendant of inferior races, a member of an undignified community, then she would have never set foot in that office, let alone have organized a political party to challenge the authority of *os grandes*. His condescending, patronizing lecture would likely have awakened all her insecurities about being a little, insignificant person and led her to back down.

And so it was a cultural world, a symbolic order, upon which the social order was anchored. Consequently, as the cultural movement, built as it was in the affirmation of popular religion, began to undermine this interpretative order, as people began to move from self-loathing to seeing the value of their culture and themselves, colonelism became unhinged. Dostoevsky, the local artist and high school teacher quoted at the beginning of this book, described the links between culture and political change in the region like this: "I always believed that cultural workers like us artists are the great instruments of political and social change. . . . I believe that the government, how it changed, was largely due to the artists and the cultural movement in Aracuai."[34] In other words, had the artists, indigenous and *quilombo* activists, ethnographers, educators, and religious leaders not manufactured a successful cultural movement, then little would have changed in Aracuai even as people won the right to vote. Instead, the *povo* would likely have used their suffrage to elect agents, rather than opponents, of the neoslave order.

Culture Works

The case of Aracuai demonstrates that development cultural work is feasible. A handful of individuals, with little or no financial support, were able to affect a profound interpretative and symbolic shift by valuing an otherwise stigmatized people's culture. Their method was straightforward. It entailed establishing choirs, validating popular religion, rejuvenating cultural traditions such as the Festival of the Rosary, and documenting the quotidian lives of ordinary people. This is not to suggest that this approach is what is needed or would work elsewhere in the world, because, as discussed in Chapter 3, most development practice should be tailored to the context in question. My goal, instead, was to demonstrate that cultural work is doable and cost-efficient—especially when compared to the millions of dollars frequently spent on very questionable development initiatives such as dam and soccer stadium construction.

Of course some of the resistance to such development practice is political-economic—persons in power perceive such projects as a threat to their self-interests. Yet, this may not be as big of a factor as commonly assumed. For example, most of this cultural work in the Jequitinhonha Valley took place during a military dictatorship in a region that was notoriously conservative. Moreover, even after Pope John Paul II (1978–2005) had purged and replaced many of those in the church sympathetic to liberation theology, Frei Chico continued to enjoy the backing of the Catholic Church in Brazil. In my interviews with him, he underscored how the church consistently supported and prized his work. Church leaders encouraged him to write down his ideas and present his research. The church published two of his books in its press. He was given several years of sabbatical to pursue his research and writing. And the church never pressured him into becoming a priest, even though priests were in short supply.

With respect to the development establishment, it is hard to imagine that development practitioners or organizations would perceive this kind of work as a threat to their careers or professional interests. The central problem, I believe, is that they do not see culture as interwoven with economies, and therefore as relevant to development. As detailed throughout this book, popular religion, the subjectivities of the poor, discourses of class, and the semiotics of race are not considered economic matters by most development specialists. Development variables include tariffs, monetary policy, infrastructure, or the size and role of government; *not* identities, sensibilities, consciousness, or habitus. As a consequence, most development professionals are blind to the cultural work of people like Lira and Frei Chico.

Imagine for a moment if the development establishment were to recognize and legitimate these sorts of individuals, organizations, and movements. In my experience one of the far-reaching and most effective lines of attacks leveled against development initiatives and agents such as choirs, artists, popular festivals, indigenous communities, *quilombolas*, and critical pedagogues is to suggest that they are obstacles to progress, modernity, and development. Seen through the emulative epistemology of modernization, in which economic development and other facets of modernity are imagined to unfold via the elimination and replacement of traditional, indigenous, or native cultures with a modern, US, Western one (see Chapter 3), these initiatives, subcultures, and entities are routinely dismissed by both the general public and opinion makers as impediments to progress. What if, however, development scholars, economists, and institutions like the Brazilian Development Bank, World Bank, and International Monetary Fund were to use their authority and cachet to critique and discredit this line of thought? What if they were to publicly acknowledge these cultural workers as vital to economic growth? How much quicker might development occur if these development agents, which undoubtedly exist in hundreds of thousands of communities throughout the world, were given the legitimacy and funding they deserve as a vanguard of prosperity.

Notes

1 Frei Chico, sixty-nine-year-old friar, Aracuai, Minas Gerais, Brazil, 2009.
2 Sen, *Development as Freedom*, 145.
3 Most of the indigenous peoples were Botocudos, Coroados, Coropos, Puris, Maxakali, and Kamaka.
4 For a detailed account of this history see *Lembrancas da terra* (Memories of the land) edited by Ribeiro; and Langfur, *Forbidden Lands*.
5 Cohen, *Why Religion?*, 432.
6 Luiz Gonzaga, seventy-three-year-old retired cobbler, Aracuai, Minas Gerais, Brazil, 2009.
7 Geralda Soares, sixty-four-year-old Indigenous pedagogue, Aracuai, Minas Gerais, Brazil, 2009.
8 A *quilombo* originally meant a community of run-away slaves and their descendants. In the 1988 Brazilian Constitution, *quilombos* were granted the rights to their own land, schools, and cultural protection. Since 1988 the meaning of the term *quilombo* has expanded to include communities composed primarily of the descendants of African slaves who have some cultural distinctions from surrounding or adjacent communities. See Arruti, *Mocambo*; and Warren, *Racial Revolutions*.
9 Andrea Fonseca, twenty-five-year-old Fabriqueta director, Aracuai, Minas Gerais, Brazil, 2009.
10 Altas do Desenvolvimento Humano no Brasil (Atlas of Human Development in Brazil) www.atlasbrasil.org.br/2013. Accessed January 9, 2015.
11 Ibid.
12 Ibid.
13 Löwy, *The War of the Gods*.
14 Warren, *Racial Revolutions*, 155–156; and Wilkinson, *Silence on the Mountain*.
15 Frei Chico, sixty-nine-year-old friar, Aracuai, Minas Gerais, Brazil, 2009.
16 Ibid.
17 Ibid.
18 Freire, *Pedagogy of the Oppressed*, 20.
19 Frei Chico, sixty-nine-year-old friar, Aracuai, Minas Gerais, Brazil, 2009.
20 Maria Lira Marques, sixty-five-year-old artist, Aracuai, Minas Gerais, Brazil, 2009
21 Ibid.
22 Frei Chico, sixty-nine-year-old friar, Aracuai, Minas Gerais, Brazil, 2009.
23 Ibid.
24 Ibid.
25 Maria Lira Marques, sixty-five-year-old artist, Aracuai, Minas Gerais, Brazil, 2009.
26 Frei Chico, sixty-nine-year-old, Aracuai, Minas Gerais, Brazil, 2009.
27 Sebastiao Rocha, sixty-six-year-old director of CPCD, Aracuai, Minas Gerais, Brazil, 2009.
28 The term "ABC region" is an industrial region in the greater metropolitan area of Sao Paulo, Brazil. The name refers to three smaller cities south of Sao Paulo: Santo Andre, Sao Bernardo do Campo and Sao Caetano do Sul.
29 Maria Lira Marques, sixty-five-year-old artist, Aracuai, Minas Gerais, Brazil, 2009.
30 *Conscientizacao* is a term Freire borrowed from Frantz Fanon (*consciencier*) and popularized both in Brazil and abroad. Don Adams and Arlene Goldbard defines conscientization "as an ongoing process by which a learner moves toward critical consciousness. This process is the heart of liberatory education. It differs from 'consciousness raising'

in that the latter may involve transmission of preselected knowledge. Conscientization means breaking through prevailing mythologies to reach new levels of awareness—in particular, awareness of oppression, being an 'object' of others' will rather than a self-determining 'subject.' The process of conscientization involves identifying contradictions in experience through dialogue and becoming part of the process of changing the world." Adams and Goldbard, *Creative Community*, pp. 107–108.

31 Maria Lira Marques, sixty-five-year-old artist, Aracuai, Brazil, 2009.

32 Ibid.

33 Ibid.

34 Dosteoevsky da Silva, forty-five-year-old teacher and artist, Aracuai, Brazil, 2009.

Bibliography

Altas do Desenvolvimento Humano no Brasil (Atlas of Human Development in Brazil) www.atlasbrasil.org.br/2013. Accessed January 9, 2015.

Adams, Don, and Arlene Goldbard. *Creative Community: The Art of Cultural Development*. New York: The Rockefeller Foundation, 2001.

Arruti, M. A. *Mocambo*. Bauru, Brazil: Editora da Universidade do Sagrãdo Coraçao, 2006.

Cohen, Yehunda. *Why Religion*? Jerusalem: Priests' Publications, 2003.

Freire, Paulo. *Pedagogy of the Oppressed*. New York: Continuum, 1989.

Langfur, Hal. *Forbidden Lands: Colonial Identity, Frontier Violence, and the Persistence of Brazil's Eastern Indians, 1750–1830*. Palo Alto, CA: Stanford University Press, 2006.

Löwy, Michael. *The War of the Gods*. London: Verso, 1996.

Ribeiro, Eduardo. *Lembrancas da terra: Histórias do Mucuri e Jequitinhonha* (Memories of the land: Histories of the Mucuri and Jequitinhouha valleys). Belo Horizonte, Brazil: Centro do Documentacao Eloy Ferreira da Silva, 1996.

Sen, Amartya Kumar. *Development as Freedom*. Oxford: Oxford University Press, 2000.

Van der Poel, Franciscus Henricus. *Dicionario da religiosidade popular: Cultura e religiao no Brasil* (Dictionary of popular religion: Culture and Religion in Brazil). São Paulo: Nossa Cultura, 2013.

Warren, Jonathan. *Racial Revolutions*. Durham, NC: Duke University Press, 2001.

Wilkinson, Daniel. *Silence on the Mountain*. Boston, MA: Houghton Mifflin Company, 2002.

6 Trade Tips

> These are the preferences of the universe itself: verbs over nouns, actions over states, struggle over hope.
>
> Ta-Nehisi Coates (b. 1975)

In this comparative study of Vietnam and Brazil I have demonstrated the value that interpretive economics holds for development studies and practitioners. I have used it to make theoretical advances, identify fruitful directions for development policy, and render visible some of the cultural work that should be supported rather than ignored and disparaged. Nonetheless, a lone scholar or one book, no matter how persuasive, is not apt to prompt an analytical shift or bring together intellectual camps that are not typically in dialogue. This requires a collective effort, which can only be had by teaching and mentoring others in the practice of interpretive economics. It is with this goal in mind that I conclude with a list of recommendations and suggestions for development professionals (or aspiring ones), who wish to incorporate culture into their analyses and cultural work into their menu of practice.

In my experience methodological guidebooks are too rare in the social sciences and humanities. I am not sure exactly why this is because the ones that I am familiar with, such as C. Wright Mills's *Sociological Imagination*, Avery Gordon's *Ghostly Matters*, Howard Becker's *Tricks of the Trade*, and Kristin Luker's *Salsa Dancing into the Social Sciences*, have been incredibly illuminating and useful. I mention these texts not to suggest that this short chapter is on par with them in terms of depth or sophistication but only to highlight how such an endeavor can be of tremendous benefit. I think this is especially true in an emerging area or subdiscipline like interpretive economics in which there is very little scholarship to offer direction and few mentors available to train prospective practitioners.

Most, if not all, of the concepts and ideas outlined below were covered in the previous chapters. However, many of those teachings were situated within the nitty-gritty details of the Vietnamese and Brazilian case studies and so it is possible that at least a few of the more important, broader points may have been lost or become a bit fuzzy along the way. These tips, then, should not only serve as a guide for future scholars, students, and practitioners of interpretive economics but also offer a concise summary of many of the central ideas and arguments presented in this book.

Stay attuned to the cultural nature of markets.

I have found that keeping in mind the cultural nature of markets can be very challenging because this foundational premise of interpretive economics runs counter to most people's analytical instincts—including my own. For example, one day I was leaving my house and the neighbors were cutting down a beautiful tree in their backyard. There had been a windstorm a few days earlier and so I assumed that the tree had been structurally compromised and therefore the owners were felling their tree for fear of the damage it might cause. When I asked them what was going on, they said it was too dark in their backyard and they wanted more natural light. Thus it was aesthetics that killed the tree—not the motives of power, money, or physical safety—and yet my first thought, my reflex analysis, pivoted on a premise of instrumentalism.

It should not be too surprising that this is my mind's muscle memory—or anyone else's—given that this reflects the common sense of much of the world. Various scholars have attributed the ubiquity and hold of these assumptions to capitalism. One of its cultural legacies, the argument goes, has been to make economistic logics seem like the only reasonable or "rational" ones.[1] I am not sure how much blame capitalism deserves for the reach of this epistemology, but it is certainly true that instrumentalist assumptions are widespread.

About fifteen years ago, for instance, I was conducting research on indigenous resurgence in Brazil, and I was surprised how most non-Indians theorized shifting racial identities in purely utilitarian terms. Even though my study uncovered a complex web of material and cultural variables responsible for an increase in the number of Brazilians assuming indigenous identities, non-Indian Brazilians speculated, a la rational choice theory, that indigenous resurgence was a straightforward case of these newly identified Indians simply wanting more resources: land, health care, and various social services.

I frequently notice this analytical bias in the United States as well. When I poll students in large survey classes at the University of Washington about what they believe are the primary causes of pollution in the Puget Sound, they speculate that "property owners don't want to spend monies to improve their septic tanks," "local governments don't want to ante up tax monies to capture or filter storm waters better," or "big businesses resist tighter and more effective environmental regulations because it will impact their bottom line." Rarely is a non-instrumentalist thesis offered out of the 300-plus students, despite the fact that one of the primary drivers of pollution in the Puget Sound involves culturally driven practices. Let me explain. Weed-killers, like Roundup, used to maintain grass yards are some of the top sources of contamination. The need for grass yards is not about physical survival, moneymaking, or some biological imperative. The primary reason for these external landscapes is aesthetics. This is what many people in the Puget Sound consider attractive or the proper way to design and maintain outside spaces. And yet most students never mention this or any other similar cultural factor. Moreover, when they first learn of this, they consider it surprising, almost counter-intuitive. And yet if I were to conjure up a fictive utilitarian explanation along the lines of "water pollution is primarily caused by regional manufactures that pressure policymakers to allow them to dump untreated industrial waste into the waterways in order to make more money," no one would bat an eye.

These utilitarian predilections, combined with the instrumentalism of the social science disciplines that dominate the study of economies (see Chapter 1), mean that even converts to interpretative economics have to be diligent about reminding themselves about the significance of culture. I have learned that this is most especially true when it seems that culture is a minor or irrelevant factor. An example of this would be the following kind of taken-for-granted notion that I often hear in casual conversations and read in op-ed pages or academic journals: "The rich are against progressive taxes because it is not in their interests." It is at such moments when it seems like such a straightforward matter of economic interests piloting actions that interpretive economists need to be most scrupulous and begin asking: Which rich people and what percentage of them? Why are some rich people in favor of higher income taxes on upper income earners? Is this because they misread their interests? Or perhaps they calculate their interests differently, like the billionaire Nick Hanauer:

> The other side thinks that growth produces a thriving middle class. That's not true. That's wrong and backwards. A thriving middle class is the source of growth in a technological, capitalist economy. Investing in the middle class is the most pro-business thing you can do.[2]

The point here is that worldviews and interpretive frameworks are always present, influencing, among other things, how people calculate self and societal interests. And yet it is easy to allow our economistic folk wisdom to lull us into overlooking this dimension—something which even interpretive economists must be careful to avoid.

Mind that culture is (a) ever intertwined with the material; (b) a shifting, contested, heterogeneous object; and (c) includes dimensions beyond the doctrinaire.

The first truism of culture is that it is interconnected with the material, rather than one unidirectionally steering the other. That is, culture matters but it is not all that matters. It shapes and is shaped (but not determined) by physical violence, human biology, natural environments, economic interests, social orders, technologies, organizations, and physical landscapes. Consequently, culturalism is no more analytically correct or accurate than materialism.

Another set of features of culture is that it is eclectic, often contested, malleable, in flux, and interconnected with power. In other words, it is not hermetically sealed, homogenous, static, apolitical, or reducible to binary categories. To help understand and remember this, I recommend that one think about their family. At least in mine, members have a range of different assumptions and opinions. There are certain values, norms, and traditions that have staying power; whereas others fall out of fashion. Moreover, some ideas carry more credibility or institutional power, depending on who espouses them (my grandmother, distant cousin, or kid-sister). In a microcosm, a family and its dynamics capture much of how culture looks and works in the broader society. The particular values, assumptions, traditions, ideas, and politics differ, but these sorts of underlying traits are comparable.

Finally, the realm of explicit views and values (such as a belief in limited government, romantic love, or a sentient God) represents just one dimension of culture. Another important arena is habitus. According to Pierre Bourdieu, this embedded understanding includes the totality of learned habits, bodily skills, tastes, styles, and other non-discursive knowledge that might be said to "go without saying" for a specific group.[3] Thus habitus—such as how whenever I return from an extended stay in Brazil I cannot help but immediately notice peoples' eye color or when abroad I almost always recognize an American by the person's gait and body language—operates largely outside the realm of stated-beliefs. Much of the antipathy towards the poor in Brazil (the focus of Chapter 2) can also be described as visceral rather than ideological. Development interventions, then, have to be devised to transform not just anti-poor discourses but also this elitist habitus.

Another non-doctrinaire dimension of culture is the background understandings against which our beliefs are formulated. In *On Certainty*, Ludwig Wittgenstein offered this classic description of epistemology:

> I don't normally have a belief that the world didn't start only five minutes ago, but the whole way I inquire into things treats the world as being there since time out of mind. Similarly I don't usually have the belief that a huge pit hasn't been dug in front of my door, but treat the world that way as I emerge in the morning to go to work. In my ways of dealing with things is incorporated the background understanding that the world is stable and has been there a long time.[4]

Examples from this study would include my discussion of indigenizing and emulating takes on modernization. Few Brazilians or Vietnamese would likely declare how they hold certain assumptions about modernity, tradition, and their proper relationship (as few people go around professing their belief in a stable world), but these background assumptions are ever present and influence, as I argued in Chapter 3, why modernization projects tend to unfold differently in the two places.

Formal training in cultural studies—discourse analysis, rhetoric, identity formations, semiotics—is highly recommended.

It is important that the novice in this area not let the technical terms of cultural studies be too off-putting or intimidating. In any area of specialization, an insider language emerges in order to allow professionals to be more precise and concise with descriptions and analyses. In the case of cultural studies, I find that most non-professionals can grasp the basic underlying concepts of these technical terms. For instance, undergraduate students in my classes are able to understand a core poststructuralist idea about how discourses can be untrue but still have truth effects. They appreciate how even if a story about the past or present is mere myth (e.g., "global warming is not real," "vaccines cause autism," or "the United States is a meritocracy") it can still affect how people think, feel, and behave.

Fortunately formal training in cultural studies can be fairly easily had at most universities in the humanities, a few professional colleges like those specializing in education, and some of the social sciences, especially certain sub-disciplines such as socio-cultural anthropology, qualitative sociology, cultural geography, gender and queer studies, and critical race studies. In my experience, literary and film studies offer some of the best places to build a cultural studies adeptness. The added advantage of taking courses in these academic fields is that one can build an area or regional studies proficiency as well. For instance, if Germany were to be the interpretive economist's focus of study, then taking a class in German literature or film would not only give the researcher formal training in cultural studies but also help her or him to develop a deeper knowledge of German society.

Area studies (i.e., training in the culture, history, language, and politics of a country or region) are a must.

Without question the best way to acquire area studies knowledge is by living in the country that is the subject of development study. This allows one to socialize with various people, forge friendships, absorb the different smells, sounds, and rhythms of daily life, and deepen one's knowledge about the culture and language through newspapers, TV, and popular music. The more one can submerge oneself in the culture by, for example, minimizing contact with expatriates, the better. This can be one of the most challenging parts of interpretive economics because, at least initially, it is lonely and alienating attempting to make one's way in a place where the language, expectations, and norms are different. But the payoff is well worth it. After a few months, one usually adjusts and is rewarded with a much deeper understanding of both oneself and the society in question.

This learning process can be greatly enhanced if one is curious, adventurous, and remains open to a wide range of experiences. So, for instance, listen to, question, and learn from as many different kinds of people as possible. Experiment broadly with foods, modes of transportation, sporting events, and subcultures. Visit schools, businesses, hospitals, places of worship, prisons, and any other organization that will allow you access. Read what historians, writers, and social scientists—preferably domestic ones—have to say about a particular place. Explore libraries, bookstores, movie houses, art galleries, museums, concert halls, and relevant online search engines and blogs. And while doing all of this, keep detailed fieldnotes reflecting upon what you are seeing, feeling, and learning. This routine of reflection, which can be very difficult after a long day of exploration and struggling with a foreign language, ensures that the researcher has a record of her or his data and helps immensely in identifying noteworthy patterns and themes.

Finally, some formal training in one's area of research is highly recommended —both before and after conducting ethnographic research if possible. I do not believe that an interpretive economist needs a degree in area studies—although this could be very helpful—but I would definitely encourage her or him to take at least a few classes with experts in their area of study. Comparing my experiences in Brazil and Vietnam, I found it to be a huge advantage to have had courses on Brazilian history, literature, film, political economy, and various aspects of Brazilian society (something I was not able to do vis-à-vis Vietnam).

It has become more challenging to obtain this training in the United States as area studies programs have been defunded in recent decades, thanks in large measure to the rise of rational choice theory. Bruce Cumings notes how utilitarianism has

> [p]ut at risk the sub-fields of economic history, historical sociology, and comparative politics and the entire area studies project. Why do you need to know Japanese or anything about Japan's history and culture, if the methods of rational choice will explain why Japanese politicians and bureaucrats do the things they do? [Utilitarianism] has no use for (and indeed views with deep hostility) anyone who happens to know something about a 'foreign area,' or, for that matter the United States: they are all threats to the universality of this model, which can explain everything from how Japanese Diet members control the Ministry of Finance to why Indian widows throw themselves onto funeral pyres—with every explanation contingent on the listener knowing little or nothing about the subject itself.[5]

Nevertheless, even where area studies programs have been reduced or eliminated, there is often an area specialist or two at most major universities in the world. Seek out their classes and guidance when possible. Ask if you can audit their courses or have a copy of their syllabi. Quiz them about their five favorite books and films in the region. Have them recommend what they see as the top academic journals, listserves, scholars, and academic institutions. Consult, too, with a reference librarian and go through the same exercise. And then follow up on these leads—enroll in a recommended listserve, put together a short reading list of key texts, view or read a few issues from one or two of the area studies journals—and you will soon start to build a solid area studies expertise, especially when combined with the in-country, fieldwork experience.

Acquire an in-depth knowledge of development studies.

Interpretative economics could, of course, be used for different ends but the focus of this book has been specifically on advancing development studies and practice. Assuming that this is one's goal, then a deep knowledge of development studies is indispensable for at least two reasons. First and foremost, this literature will help the interpretive economist to refine and narrow down her or his ethnographic findings. After the initial phase of fieldwork, one can quickly become overwhelmed with information about a particular society. However, in learning what development scholars are saying and discussing about a country, region, or development more generally, allows one to identify where her or his regional knowledge could be helpful and in the process bring focus to one's research and empirical findings. In my case, by reviewing the comparative development literature, I came to recognize how there were weaknesses and gaps around key economic variables like social capital, institutional monocropping, and capacity building. I was then able to use these flaws and puzzles to help me cull through the large amount of ethnographic data that I had been accumulating. I used a comparative approach to further help me with this process, but it is not necessary to compare and contrast two regions or societies. What is necessary, however, is an engagement with development studies.

Another reason for familiarizing oneself with the development studies literature, or at least facets of it, is so that the interpretive economist can affect change within this field. The more one speaks the language, knows the debates, and demonstrates familiarity with respected researchers and texts, the more likely one is to be heard by scholars in any given area of study. And so if interpretive economists wish to mainstream their analytical framework, it is essential that they become well versed with development studies scholarship. To build this expertise, one should at least attempt to minor (if not major) in development studies or some related field like development economics, sociology of development, industrial geography, or political economy.

Avoid ethnocentricism and rigid theoretical attachments.

Ideally an interpretive economist is as inductive as possible—thinking broadly and allowing theories to emerge from research findings rather than using these findings to confirm one's expectations and assumptions. In practice, however, one can never be completely inductive given that people are not impartial, blank slates. But one can try to minimize the impact of his or her theoretical and personal biases. On this issue, Frei Chico offered sage wisdom when he advised that one need muster the courage to abandon beautiful theories. He was referring specifically to his beliefs in certain tenets of socialism and liberation theology as well as notions he held, such as his assumption that he would be a more astute critic of academic texts than his comrade, Lira, because he had a much better formal education than her. In any event, I take his comment not to mean that one *has* to abandon her or his theories but a researcher should try to develop enough self-awareness about theoretical leanings and be prepared to modify or let go of them when they do not fit with one's findings. In the abstract this may sound fairly easy, but it is perhaps the toughest part of this kind of research. In my experience, people have a much harder time giving up material things than letting go of ideas, identities, and worldviews. I recall one set of assumptions that I resisted abandoning when I first starting working in Brazil. I went there with the premise that there was a causal relationship between racial location and consciousness. I had assumed that in a context of anti-black racism with an even deeper history of slavery than the United States, people of African descent would have an anti-racist consciousness. Instead I found colorblindness, whitening, and historical whitewashing prevalent among Afro-Brazilians. It was a rude awakening and initially difficult for me to come to terms with the reality that oppression was not the fountain of sociological wisdom, or as Ta-Nehisi Coates put it, "the boot on your neck is just as likely to make you delusional as it is to ennoble."[6]

Interpretive economics that is focused on economic development almost always entails working across cultures and national contexts. In such cases, ethnocentrism is an ever-present danger and a routine misstep—especially when the development expert comes from a "more developed" country. Despite the best of intentions of development professionals, including wanting the communities that are the focus of improvement projects to be involved in the design and implementation of the changes, it is remarkable how development theories and policy prescriptions often boil down to a simple formula of having the developing country imitate "our" values, identities, institutions, laws, or macroeconomic policies. One of the strategies I use to try to avoid this error is to look for unique, more organic solutions—ones that originated and therefore are apt to be better tailored to the context in question. I also try to be much more self-critical when the implication of my analysis is that a cultural practice, identity, organization, or law should look similar to the nation or community from which I come or believe to be superior. I might still make the case for this intervention, but I scrutinize this theory or prescription much more rigorously.

Finally, in the write-up of one's findings, an interpretive economist should try to be as honest and forthright about her or his background, training, politics, and so on. What this looks like is recognition that bias is inevitable combined with a good faith effort to disclose any relevant information—so that the reader can better evaluate how one's biography, social location, and academic training may have affected the research findings and conclusions. No one expects or wants this to turn into an exercise of narcissistic navel-gazing. All that is required is some relevant background information (e.g., personal history, training, and research motives) and a healthy dose of humility.

Seek out the domestic agents, entities, and social movements that are already practicing or attempting to spread the desired cultural change.

It is rarely a good idea to advance policies based on one study alone, but sometimes we do not have the luxury of multiple studies—especially when so few development scholars address culture. In any event, once one has determined what he or she believes is in need of change, the next step is devising and implementing the appropriate kinds of applied cultural work. In most societies, this labor is likely already being practiced in one form or another by local activists, artists, educators, organizations, and social movements. Thus, before any new policy interventions are planned, an interpretive economist should seek out the individuals and organizations that are already carrying out the chosen cultural work. Simply reframing culture as key to development and identifying which aspects of culture are in need of change to improve an economy will go a long way in rendering visible these local agents. For many it will likely also demand letting go of a latent paternalism that has led countless development professionals to wrongly presume that the stuff required for growth does not exist in a given country but rather has to be introduced and imported from the outside by a development expert. To help temper this impulse, suppose at the outset that much of what is needed is already happening in the community in question. This helps to ensure that the initial emphasis is placed on identifying and legitimating the existing cultural workers, and establishing how best to support and scale up their work.

In devising context-appropriate development projects, do not confuse form with substance, strive to be politically astute without power-evasiveness, and forge collaborative relationships with the targeted communities.

The attempt to identify and work with existing cultural workers will likely not preclude the need for creating and introducing new forms of applied cultural work. We saw, for instance, that Frei Chico did not have this option available. As far as I know, there were no other organizations working to revalorize the identities of the "little people" until he founded the Troubadours of the Valley. Similarly, organizations like Afro-Reggae, mentioned in Chapter 4, do not exist in most *favelas* and so a development practitioner would have to strategize how to create similar institutions and initiatives in other places like Babilonia. Thus on this topic of originating or initiating development cultural work, I have three suggestions:

1. When brainstorming and formulating original development cultural work, try as much as possible to avoid confusing form with substance. With respect to improving racial literacy, for instance, the remedy may not be to create the kinds of racial identities that are associated with anti-racism in the United States, but rather achieve it through distinct, more locally-legible identifications: *quilombola*, *mestizo*, Afro-descent, indigenous, or *favelado*. At minimum, one should keep in mind that there are usually many different ways to do the same thing. One lesson the history of improvement projects has taught is that formal equivalents are often the wrong way to create substantive equivalents. A good example of this is political reform in Jordan. Until recently, Jordanians had five votes per election. In recent years there has been a move toward a "one person, one vote" electoral system. In practice, however, this has made the society less democratic. This is because in Jordan one is socially obligated to vote for uncles and other close relatives. With five votes, one could fulfill these social and familial obligations and then have the other votes available to back the person one found most meritocratic or best able to represent one's community. Limited to just one vote, citizens have not been able to do this and so the election outcomes have become less democratic.[7]
2. Power evasiveness, as we have learned, is a major problem in development studies and so clearly, interpretative economists should be careful to avoid this misstep. However in creating interventions that touch directly on economic, political, or social power, one should, whenever possible, steer clear of being a provocateur. In this way, Frei Chico and Lira offer good role models. They found ways to challenge discourses and symbolic orders that undergirded the social order in a way that were not especially inflammatory or off-putting to the elite or the Catholic Church. Vik Muniz offers another good example of political astuteness. He was able to challenge the conventional images of the poor through his portraits of garbage collectors. His exhibition of this art at the Museum of Modern Art (MAM) in Rio de Janeiro in 2009 drew record numbers of middle- and upper-class attendees. As far as I know, this project was warmly received across much of the political spectrum.[8]
3. When formulating proposals for original kinds of cultural work, try to build collaborative relationships with the communities who are the target of development. Frei Chico cautioned how hard this is when the power imbalances

are so skewed, but found a reciprocal relationship was possible once he was able to recognize and shed some of his biases. He came to see Lira, for instance, not as a poor person with little education whom he was helping but instead as a person who brought invaluable experiences, sensibilities, and talents to their partnership. Attempting to tackle this issue of power and collaboration, Paulo Freire recommended the expert assume the role of the student. The most effective communicators are, of course, the ones who listen well and so this analogy can be incredibly useful in getting the development professional to assume a more listening posture. But ultimately I find this recommendation unsatisfying because, if read too strictly, it instructs that the development expert should be a passive participant. Concomitantly there is the presumption, reminiscent of Paul Farmer, that "the oppressed," as Freire called them, have more sociological wisdom or are not equally delusional. The implied remedy is, then, to create the space for the poor to better voice and articulate their thoughts and perspective. But what happens when part of the problem is the identities, discourses, and norms of the marginalized? Moreover, is the development expert ever the student or does he or she have some expertise, knowledge, and ideas that are of value and should be voiced as well? This is why a better analogy for me is what people in Aracuai call the methodology of *roda* (the wheel)—see Chapter 5. The wheel implies no hierarchies of teachers and students, but rather a conversation in which individuals are primarily students but also, albeit a smaller percentage of the time, teachers. This is not to suggest that there are not a number of logistical and political challenges with this method—such as whom to include or exclude from the circle of collaboration and the disproportionate voice a development agent can have if she or he controls the required resources—but I find it a better metaphor for how to structure the relationship between the development expert and the community with which she or he is working. The development agent is not expected to be a passive student at all times but rather a humble collaborator who shares and contributes her or his thoughts and expertise in a more reciprocal fashion. Moreover, the ability to determine how a given community ought to think and behave is minimized, given that she or he is just one of many experts.

Notes

1 Taussig, *Shamanism, Colonialism, and the Wild Man.*
2 Ball, "The Poor Man's Plutocrat," 22.
3 Bourdieu, *The Logic of Practice*, 66–67.
4 Wittgenstein, *On Certainty*, New York: Harper and Row, 1972. Cited in Taylor, "Two Theories of Modernity," 186.
5 Cumings, "Boundary Displacement," 286.
6 Coates, *Between the World and Me*, 50.
7 National Public Radio (NPR), "For One Parliamentarian, A Stronger Jordan is Key to Fighting ISIS."
8 *Waste Land*, directed by Lucy Walker, 2011.

Bibliography

Ball, Molly. "The Poor Man's Plutocrat." *The Atlantic* (January/February 2016), 21–22.

Becker, Howard S. *Tricks of the Trade: How to Think about Your Research While You're Doing It*. Chicago, IL: University of Chicago Press, 1998.

Bourdieu, Pierre. *The Logic of Practice*. Palo Alto, CA: Stanford University Press, 1990.

Coates, Ta-Nehisi. *Between the World and Me*. New York: Spiegel & Grau, 2015.

Cumings, Bruce "Boundary Displacement: The State, the Foundations, and Area Studies during and after the Cold War." In *Learning Places: The Afterlives of Area Studies*, Masao Miyoshi and H. D. Harootunian (Eds.), 261–302. Durham, NC: Duke University Press, 2002.

Gordon, Avery. *Ghostly Matters: Haunting and the Sociological Imagination*. Minneapolis, MN: University of Minnesota Press, 2008.

Luker, Kristin. *Salsa Dancing into the Social Sciences: Research in an Age of Info-glut*. Cambridge, MA: Harvard University Press, 2010.

Mills, C. Wright. *The Sociological Imagination*. Oxford: Oxford University Press, 2000.

National Public Radio (NPR). "For One Parliamentarian, A Stronger Jordan is Key to Fighting ISIS." www.npr.org/player/v2/mediaPlayer.html?action=1&t=1&islist=false&id=389269550&m=38932167. Accessed February 26, 2015.

Taussig, Michael. *Shamanism, Colonialism, and the Wild Man: A Study in Terror and Healing*. Chicago, IL: University of Chicago Press, 1986.

Taylor, Charles. "Two Theories of Modernity." In *Alternative Modernities*, Dilip Gaonkar (Ed.), 172–196. Durham, NC: Duke University Press, 2001.

Waste Land. Directed by Lucy Walker. New Video Group. United States, 2011.

Appendix A: Interview Schedule in Vietnam

1. Where are you from? Where are your parents from? What do (or did) your parents do professionally?
2. What are some of the biggest problems facing people in Vietnam today?
3. What are some of the principal ways you and your generation differ from that of your parents and their generation?
4. What should be the objective of education? (Examples: train for jobs, teach morals, produce creative and critical thinking citizens—if possible, do not prompt).
5. What is the difference between Westerners and Vietnamese? (If they use the term "modern," have them define it. If they use economic development as an indicator of the "West," ask them if they consider Japan to be Western and have them elaborate why or why not.)
6. Have you ever referred to someone as "too Western" (*tay qua*)? If so, what do you (or others) mean when you use this term? (Try, in this context, to get interviewee to elaborate on such concepts as "traditional" (*truyen thong*) and "backward" (*co hu*)).
7. What sort of occupation would you like to see your children have as adults?
8. Are there differences between people who are "blue collar" workers (*lao dong chan tay*) and "white collar" workers (*lao dong tri oc*)? If so, please elaborate.
9. What is your image of "business people" (*doanh nhan*)?
10. What do you see as the impact of globalization on Vietnam? Do you worry that it could have a negative impact? Explain.
11. What should be the criteria used to determine how people obtain jobs, especially well paying or high status ones in Vietnam (examples: hard work, luck, talent, relationships or personal connections—if possible, do not prompt)? In practice, what tends to be the way in which individuals obtain such jobs in Vietnam?
12. What should the government prioritize in order to facilitate development (*phat trien*) (examples: improve access to quality education, lower taxes, improve the infrastructure, reduce poverty, accelerate the pace of integration into the global economy, give more control to the free market—if possible, do not prompt)? Explain.

13. Are there poor people in Vietnam? If so, who are they and why are they poor?
14. How would you categorize yourself: rich, poor, or middle-class? Explain.
15. During the Southeast Asian Games there seemed to be a lot of national pride in Vietnam. Do you think the Vietnamese are proud of their nation? Why or why not? Are you proud to be Vietnamese? Why or why not?
16. What makes one Vietnamese?
17. Should individuals from other countries such as Cambodia, China, or the United States be able to immigrate to Vietnam and become citizens? Why or why not?

Appendix B: Demographics of Interviewees in Vietnam and Brazil

	Vietnam	Brazil
Sex	Male 27, Female 17	Male 13, Female 14
Residence	Urban 43, Rural 1	Urban 15, Rural 12
Origins	Urban 25, Rural 19	Urban 13, Rural 13
Age	18–25 6 26–35 19 36–45 12 46–55 5 56–65 1 66–75 1 75+ 0	18–25 2 26–35 2 36–45 10 46–55 4 56–65 5 66–75 3 75+ 1
Class	Poor 0 Middle-class 44 Rich 0	Poor 15 Middle-class 11 Rich 0
Education	None 0 Primary 7 Secondary 6 College 18 Post-Grad 13	None 0 Primary 3 Secondary 9 College 5 Post-Grad 10
Occupation	Manufacturing/Construction 2 White Collar/Admin Assistant 5 Education/Teacher 8 Upper Management 1 Government/Civil Sector 4 IT/Finance 3 Small Business Owner 5 Taxi Driver/Nanny/Cook 9 Lawyer/Doctor/Accountant/Journalist 4 Artist/Artisan 3	Manufacturing/Construction 0 White Collar/Admin Assistant 5 Education/Teacher 6 Upper Management 2 Government/Civil Sector 4 IT/Finance 1 Small Business Owner 0 Taxi Driver/Nanny/Cook 2 Lawyer/Doctor/Accountant/Journalist 5 Artist/Artisan 2

	Vietnam	Brazil
Monthly Salary	Unknown 3 <$50 1 $50–99 13 $100–249 13 $250–499 8 $500–749 2 $750–999 0 $1000+ 4	Unknown 0 <$50 0 $50–99 0 $100–249 8 $250–499 6 $500–749 2 $750–999 5 $1000+ 6
Marital Status	Married 28, Single 15	Married 16, Single 10
Transportation	Unknown 2 Bike 1 Motorbike 31 Public Transit 4 Car 5	Unknown 1 Bike 0 Motorbike 0 Public Transit 13 Car 13
Rent or Own Home	Rent 9 Own 22 Parents 11	Rent 4 Own 18 Parents 3
Children	0: 19 1: 7 2: 15 3: 0 4+: 1	0: 11 1: 3 2: 6 3: 6 4+: 0

Index

Made in the USA
Middletown, DE
02 November 2020

23197260R00113